The
Glamorgan
Village Book

THE VILLAGES OF BRITAIN SERIES

Other counties in this series include:

Avon

Bedfordshire

Berkshire

Buckinghamshire

Cambridgeshire

Cheshire

Cleveland

Cornwall

Cumbria

Derbyshire

Devon

Dorset

Durham

Essex

Gloucestershire

Hampshire

Herefordshire

Hertfordshire

Kent

Lancashire

Leicestershire
& Rutland

Lincolnshire

Middlesex

Norfolk

Northamptonshire

Nottinghamshire

Oxfordshire

Powys Montgomeryshire

Shropshire

Somerset

Staffordshire

Suffolk

Surrey

East Sussex

West Sussex

Warwickshire

West Midlands

Wiltshire

Worcestershire

East Yorkshire

North Yorkshire

South & West Yorkshire

Most are published in conjunction with
County Federations of Women's Institutes

The Glamorgan Village Book

Compiled by the Glamorgan
Federation of Women's Institutes from notes
and illustrations sent by Institutes in the County

Published jointly by
Countryside Books, Newbury
and the GFWI, Port Talbot

First Published 1993
© Glamorgan Federation of Women's Institutes 1993

Countryside Books
3 Catherine Road
Newbury, Berkshire

ISBN 1 85306 254 5

Cover photograph of a view over Treorchy and Cwm-parc
in the Rhondda Valley taken by Mrs Maisie Smith

Designed by Mon Mohan

Produced through MRM Associates Ltd., Reading
Typeset by Acorn Bookwork, Salisbury, Wilts
Printed in England

Foreword

The county of Glamorgan, since local government reorganisation, has been divided into three counties – West Glamorgan, Mid Glamorgan and South Glamorgan. Our WI County Federation has retained the old administrative county of Glamorgan.

West Glamorgan extends westward from the large steel town of Port Talbot, through Swansea to Pontarddulais. To the west of Swansea, and still in Glamorgan, lies the enchanting peninsula of Gower, with its limestone cliffs and yellow sands – an astonishing piece of unspoilt country. Bordering Swansea is the industrial and former mining community of the Neath Valley.

Mid Glamorgan extends northwards from the seaside resort of Porthcawl to include the former coal mining areas of the Ogwr (Ogmore), Rhondda, Taff and Cynon Valleys and Caerphilly – a maze of narrow valleys. Coal mining has now ceased in these areas, but the Forestry Commission is busy re-clothing all the hillsides.

South Glamorgan includes the coastal resorts of Penarth and Barry and the mainly agricultural areas of the lovely Vale of Glamorgan with its old market town of Cowbridge. The administrative life of Wales is centred on the capital city, Cardiff, with its many fine buildings such as the Civic Centre and National Museum of Wales.

We are launching this book to celebrate the 70th anniversary of the Glamorgan Federation of Women's Institutes. We hope you enjoy reading it and are encouraged to come and discover for yourself the warm welcome you'll always find in Glamorgan.

Margaret J Powell
County Federation Chairman

Acknowledgements

The Glamorgan Federation of Women's Institutes would like to thank all the Institutes who have so willingly contributed to its compilation and we are especially grateful to Mrs Mair Morgan and Mrs Eve Wiltshire who co-ordinated the project.

GLAMORGAN

DYFED

Afan Lliw

Afon Llan R. Tawe

MYNYDD

R. Ne

LOUGHOR ESTUARY

NEATH

SWANSEA

Cw

GOWER PENINSULA

PORT

SWANSEA BAY

TU R

GLAMORGAN W I FEDERATION

POWYS

N

GWENT

MYNYDD MERTHYR

R. Cynon

R. Taff

D NANT Y BAR

MYNYDD BLAEN RHONDDA

Afon Rhondda Fach

CEFN Y RHONDDA

MYNYDD LLANGEINOR

Afon Rhondda Fawr

MYNYDD BACH

R. Llynfi

R. Garw

R. Ogwr

MYNYDD MAESTEG

R. Rhymney

PONTYPRIDD

CAERPHILLY

MYNYDD Y GAER

OT

g

FIG ROWS

R. Ogmore

BRIDGEND

COWBRIDGE

R. Ely

R. Taff

CARDIFF

OGMORE-BY-SEA

Marcross Brook

VALE OF GLAMORGAN

Col-huw

R. Thaw

PENARTH

Afon

LLANTWIT MAJOR

BARRY

FLAT HOLM

BRISTOL CHANNEL

Lewis Merthyr Colliery, Trehafod

Aberdulais 🌿

Aberdulais is in the Vale of Neath, West Glamorgan, a place which has seen copper smelting in the 16th century, followed by flour and grist mills and in 1830 a tinplate works which operated for some 60 years. The industrial remains are visible today.

Aberdulais Falls cascades over the rocks at a rate of 160,000,000 litres of water every day. The copper, milling and tinplate industries were all dependent on harnessing water from the river to drive waterwheels. The copper refined from 1584 was used for the coinage of Elizabeth I.

In the 19th century many children as well as adults were employed in the various industries. Eight year old David Williams toiled from 6am to 6pm every day as a plate carrier. Amazingly he never got burned but did sometimes cut his toes. He ran home for 15 minutes' break to eat and never went to school. David was found to be the youngest child at work, together with 16 boys and one girl under 13 years of age, when investigated in 1842 by the Children's Employment Commission.

Now the technology of water power is being used for one of the industries of the future, hydro electric power. Owned by the National Trust, Aberdulais Falls came without a legacy and has to generate adequate funds for its future needs.

February 1993 saw the official launch of the largest electricity generating waterwheel in Europe, computer designed at Swansea University College.

The falls are now generating electricity and sell much of it to the National Grid, to the benefit of the National Trust.

Built into the project is a lift for disabled visitors to use to view the top of the falls and a fish pass, which will enable salmon and seatrout to swim upstream to new spawning grounds in the river Dulais.

Near the entrance to the property is the shop and the old works library, a multi-purpose centre shared between the National Trust and the local community.

Aberkenfig 🌿

Aberkenfig derives its name from the point where a tiny stream, Nant Cynffig, flows into a larger river, the Ogmore, which in turn takes its name from the ancient Welsh name for its lower reaches, or estuary, 'Eog-Mor' (Salmon Water). The Ogmore, until the pollution of the

Industrial Revolution, was one of the noted salmon rivers of Wales. Here also, the river Llynfi joins the Ogmore while nearby the streams of the Garw and the Ogwr Fach do the same.

Aberkenfig is essentially a mining settlement and is comparatively recent in relation to its older associates of Tondu, Ynysawdre and Llansantffraid with Wern-Du. Tondu, originally 'Ton Ithel Du' (the fortified settlement of Black Ithel) has found its name corrupted and shortened. Ynysawdre was a separate hamlet and the present farmhouse of Wern-Du was a medieval grange of Margam Abbey, closely involved with the adjacent 13th century church of St Bride (Bridget), Llansant-ffraid. This is the parish church of St Brides Minor, a widespread parish which includes only part of the present-day Aberkenfig. The remainder was formerly in the parish of Newcastle but much is now in the parish of St John's, Tondu, a new parish created only in 1923 and currently served jointly with Penyfai. St John's church was built as a chapel-of-ease to Newcastle in 1868.

While Aberkenfig itself grew mainly as a residential settlement associated with local coal mines, now all defunct, Tondu developed as an industrial centre in itself. Its long departed ironworks were of great importance and the development of railways, especially to serve collieries in the valleys, made Tondu a natural location for a very important railway junction for both passengers and goods traffic. The site of Tondu House, high above the village, was possibly the site of Ithel Du's ancient 'ton' long before the Norman invasion of Glamorgan at the end of the 11th century. In more recent years it was the home of several industrialists, including James Brogden, Cadman and Boyd-Harvey, before becoming in the 1940s a Government Research Establishment of the Ministry of Supply. Also above Tondu is the ancient farmstead of Cwm Risca, one home of the Maddocks family and featuring in the romanticised story of *The Maid of Cefn Ydfa*. The names of the Brogdens, Sir Robert Price and Col. North are particularly associated with Tondu and, by association, with Aberkenfig. Between Aberkenfig and Tondu, now joined, was a small area associated with the establishment of brickworks and named Evanstown. Now the name is all but forgotten. A small woollen mill was established in the late 19th century alongside the river in Aberkenfig and its remains can still be seen below Factory Terrace. Pandy Park and Pandy School take their names from a 'Pandy' or fulling mill which took its power from the river Ogmore.

Sarn, about 1½ miles from Aberkenfig, whose name originally denoted a 'ridgeway', is a large collection of housing estates, best known for the long-gone house of 'Sarn-Fawr', once the residence of Glamorgan's first Chief Constable, Capt. Napier. The earlier housing estate at

Sarn was essentially a settlement of a high percentage of mining and railway employees and began to expand greatly after the Second World War, until now it has as great a population as Aberkenfig and Tondu.

With the closure of the ironworks, then successively the collieries, coke ovens, brickworks and most of the railways, Aberkenfig/Tondu lost all its industrial identity and today is almost wholly residential, depending largely on Bridgend, three miles to the south for trade and employment, with local shops and other establishments competing bravely with an increasing number of large superstores in the area.

Barry 🐚

The development of Barry began with the construction of the docks in the 1880s. Eight miles from Cardiff, it was one of the largest dock areas in the world at that time. It transformed the village with a then population of some 85 people. Millions of tons of coal were exported from the docks and hordes of day trippers used the railways, built to carry coal, and enjoyed the sands of Whitmore Bay, Barry Island and Pebble Beach. Barry Island is now joined to the mainland by a causeway.

David Davies the industrialist created The Barry Docks and Railway Company. He left an estate valued at nearly £405,000 when he died in 1890. A bronze statue of David Davies stands before the Dock Offices at Barry sculpted by Alfred Gilbert, who designed Eros' statue in London.

The Dock Offices at Barry cost £59,000 to build. Constructed of red brick and Portland stone, a clock tower was added at an additional cost of £6,000. It has a 'theme' of the calendar. There are four floors – the seasons of the year; seven lights in the traceried fanlight window – days of the week. The porch has twelve panels – months of the year.

Within the building are 52 marble fireplaces – weeks of the year. The windows number 365 days of the year. Each window has four panes of glass – weeks to a month. In the east and west walls of the entrance hall are two circular windows – Sun and Moon. The staircase, made of Portland stone, has 31 steps (days of the month) from ground to first and second floors and has an ornamental ironwork balustrade with circular foliage and fruit trails. The Dock Offices are now the headquarters of the Associated British Ports.

Major David Davies, the grandson, was Parliamentary Secretary to Lloyd George 1916–17. He was a very generous man and it is said he donated over £2 million to educational, medical and religious charities in the Principality. Barry Memorial Hall was built at a cost of £23,000 with donations by Major Davies and his sisters totalling £10,000. As part of a campaign against TB, Major Davies inaugurated a mobile X-ray Unit at Cardiff and elected to be its first patient; sadly an incurable cancer was discovered and he died four months later at Sully hospital in 1944.

Sometime during the Second World War, American forces used Barry as one of their main cargo ports and 4,000 US troops and equipment were transported from the docks to the beaches of Normandy.

Barry has some very old buildings. Rose Cottage was once a farm built around 1600, named then Greenhouse Farm, in the Old Village Road. Alongside are the remaining terraced cottages used by labourers on the Romilly Estate in 1861. Their thatched roofs were replaced by tiles and in 1960 they were saved from demolition by the efforts of the Barry Preservation Society. On the corner of Old Village Road is Barry's first shop, originally a grocer's shop, built in 1860 in Tudor style. Now it is an off-licence.

Cold Knap Farm is Barry's oldest domestic building, built in 1570 and extended in the 17th century. Richard Garby, a farmer, once occupied the house and was also employed by the Romilly Estate. He collected payment for shipments of limestone from the beach, but he also did his share of smuggling, a profitable trade. The farmhouse was ideally situated for this as it was on the headland. Barry was rife with smugglers and pirates around its coast.

Close by Porthkerry Country Park once stood Cliffwood Cottage. There is a rather sinister story about a notable occupant, Anne Jenkins, who lived there with her sons, Robert and William sometime in the 18th century. Anne was reputed to have been a witch and William a wizard. Anne was visited by a young gentleman and his deformed servant, seeking a love potion. This he was given by Anne and he ran off laughing with his servant without paying. The witch vowed they would never emerge from Barry wood. A tall straight tree and a shorter crooked tree stood close by the edge of this wood. Could it have been the young gentleman and his servant? For the story goes that they never left the wood!

Over the 20th century Barry has changed enormously. By the 1950s tourism was becoming important. The foreshore of Whitmore Bay, Barry Island was landscaped and redevelopment of the Fairground was undertaken. The sweeping headland of Nell's Point, giving extensive views of the channel, was leased to Butlins for a Holiday Camp. Today it is the Majestic Holiday Camp.

The trade through the docks fell steadily as the steam coal was replaced by oil as the major energy source in ships and factories. Today it is very quiet.

Barry has a fine shopping centre, a Leisure Centre, lovely parkland, a lake in the shape of the Welsh harp, a Memorial Hall and many places for outdoor pursuits. The Civic Offices of the Vale of Glamorgan Borough Council enjoy splendid sea views and the Council is very proud of the fact that they won The Keep Britain Tidy Awards for the Environment for two successive years in 1991 and 1992.

Beddau 🌿

The village of Beddau is situated two miles north east of Llantrisant. The word Beddau actually means 'Graves' and according to maps dated 1776 and 1833 four cart tracks are marked at the meeting point named Croes-heol-y-Beddau meaning crossroads of the graves. These four tracks now form Castellau, Penycoedcae, Gwaun Miskin and Llantrisant roads. Where the roads met stood a large beech tree which survived until the early years of the 20th century. The tree was used as a gallows. One of the branches grew at right angles to the main trunk and from this were hanged sheep-stealers, horse thieves, and robbers. Their bodies were then buried at the cross-roads where travellers would walk on the graves.

The oldest building in the village of Beddau is the Ty'n-y-Nant farm. The Williams family have always farmed there through its 400 years of existence. The family sold the farmhouse and land, the land later being purchased in 1952 by the National Coal Board.

Between 1860 and 1865 the village of Beddau expanded from the original few houses. In 1869 a lady was born named Jean Etta Thomas who lived to the ripe old age of 112, dying on the 2nd December 1981. She was in the Guinness Book of Records as the then oldest living female.

Then in the South Wales region mines opened up all around the surrounding districts. The coal pits of Dduhewid, Ystradbarwig and Ty'n-y-Nant yielded 140,000 tons during the period of working in the 1860s. There was a haulier's strike in 1898 leaving many of these pits abandoned. During this period cottages were built on Beddau Square, including the old Beddau Post Office. Two further cottages were built together with the Gelynog Inn and Bethania Baptist Chapel. In 1877 the school was opened and the building was a great advantage to the community with concerts, and all forms of entertainment for the local inhabitants. During this time it was hard for the locals to make a living and in order to increase trade, rabbit coursing, pony racing and pigeon

13

shooting matches were arranged. Many of the races were run along the present Llantrisant Road.

Then 1909 saw the beginning of the rapid development of Beddau, as the first turf was cut on the site of the Cwm colliery by Mrs C. H. James, the wife of the Managing Director of the Great Western Colliery Company. John Hughes, the composer of the hymn tune *Cwm Rhondda* was employed at the colliery. In 1928 the colliery was acquired by the Powell Duffryn Company who worked the mine until it was nationalised in 1947.

Right through the 1960s Beddau flourished with the building of further houses and in the 1970s saw a real difference to the community with the building of well over 1,000 houses in the estate named Gwaun Miskin and the newly developed Yorkdale Garden Village, as it was then called. This soon became a dormitory area for the people who were transferred to the area with the opening of the Royal Mint at Llantrisant.

Sadly, the era of King Coal has diminished, putting many people out of work. The area has a large population of unemployed persons who are now glad to use the Cwm & Llantwit Welfare Hall which was opened on Saturday 21st October 1933. When built, the whole building and furnishings cost just over £5,000.

Many residents remember an infamous building set up by the local council, nicknamed 'Colditz', which laughingly received an award for design. When it was realised that thousands would have to be spent on refurbishing and renewing, it was decided the lesser of the two evils would be to demolish, much to the delight of local residents. This eyesore was razed to the ground in 1987. Like a phoenix rising from the ashes the delightful replacement town houses – built in 1988 and renamed Trem-y-Cwm, stand on the original site. Many of these have been allocated to senior citizens in the area. There is also a warden, and a community hall for the residents.

Bishopston 🐝

The village of Bishopston – in Welsh, Llandeilo Ferwallt – lies six miles west of Swansea at the beginning of South Gower. The Gower Peninsula has been designated an Area of Outstanding Natural Beauty. Bishopston has direct access to two scenic bays: Brandy Cove and Pwlldu.

The village history dates from about 1100 when it belonged to the Bishop of Llandaff, hence its name Bishopstown. Right up to the Second World War it was sparsely populated, most villagers owning or working

St Teilo's Church, Bishopston

on farms or market gardens. Although the population has risen considerably, there are still a number of farms being worked today.

The old village school has given way to a modern comprehensive, which pupils attend from as far west as Rhossili. The lane adjacent to the school which houses the Guides HQ is still known as Providence after the old chapel.

From the head of a valley, a stream runs for over a mile to the sea at Pwlldu Bay. The valley is a well known beauty spot which attracts a number of walkers in Spring when its meadows are carpeted with bluebells and cowslips and the scent of wild garlic fills the air.

St Teilo's church is sited upon one of the earliest Christian settlements, dating from AD 408–409. For many centuries, St Teilo's was in the Diocese of Llandaff, but since the dis-establishment of the Church in Wales in the 1920s it is now in the Diocese of Swansea and Brecon. The church is of Norman architecture of the late 12th–13th centuries.

Within the grounds of the church an enormous yew tree once flourished. Local legend has it that the bowmen of Gower used to make their strongbows from the branches, which they purchased from the incumbent of the Parish. Sadly, this wonderful yew came to a sad end during an horrific storm in 1986. Although the tree was completely uprooted, another phase of its life was about to take place – a miracle of re-incarnation. The tree was taken away after many difficulties by the firm of wood carvers, who processed the wood by 'high tech' drying methods. From this giant of the churchyard, beautiful carvings were created by skilled craftsmen; apples, pears, vases, urns, pots and small items which the villagers were anxious to purchase before the last chip of yew disappeared. The texture of the wood, so rich in colour, beauti-

15

fully marked and grained, so smooth, is almost therapeutic if handled and smoothed. The churchyard looks strange without its massive presence, but on closer scrutiny a shoot has started to sprout where it was uprooted. We wonder if this will grow and flourish on the site of its ancestor of the tree world.

During the Second World War, when Swansea was badly bombed, many people walked to South Gower to get a night's rest, carrying their bedding, and one resident remembers her parents telling her that one night they put up 45 people.

The village also gained some notoriety and publicity in 1965 when the dismembered body of Mamie Stewart who had been missing for 40 years was discovered in an old lead mine at Brandy Cove. The murder is still unsolved.

Blackpill ❧

Blackpill is a semi urban village, situated half way along the curve of Swansea Bay. The village hall and the former school building face the sea and the main road. One of the two remaining buildings on the sea side once housed the power station to provide the Mumbles train with its energy as it ran along the oldest standard gauge railway line in the world. Sadly the line was removed in 1962 and its loss to Swansea's tourist industry is still regretted.

Blackpill is so named as the area was once highly industrialised with an arsenic works and drift coal mines so the creek or pill looked black with the coal dust. Today it is an Area of Outstanding Natural Beauty with a Country Park where formerly the Mid Wales line made its way to Killay. There is varied bird life on the foreshore and the highly praised Clyne Gardens, famous for its collection of azaleas and rhododendrons, planted by the last owner of Clyne Castle, Admiral Walker-Heneage-Vivian, who died in 1952.

Clyne Castle was originally Woodlands House. It was built by Richard Phillips, who came from a landowning family in Carmarthen. Having no occupation, he interested himself in the building of Swansea Docks and became a Trustee. Looking across he realised that every ship had to negotiate the bay and so Mumbles lighthouse was built. There were two subsequent owners, one of whom was Charlotte Hall, whose brother Benjamin Hall gave his name to Big Ben in London.

John Henry Vivian came to Swansea from Cornwall to smelt copper ore imported from Chile. In South Wales coal, limestone and cheap labour were abundant. It was his second son, William Graham Vivian who built the estate in Clyne Valley. He was a reclusive bachelor and died a millionaire, leaving his estate to his unmarried sister Dulcie for her lifetime and then to a nephew, an Admiral of the Fleet.

The story is told that William Graham Vivian once travelled by horse and carriage and took four weeks to reach Portsmouth to visit his nephew. The Admiral looked over the side of his flagship on hearing that his uncle was there and, seeing a very shabby gentleman, declined to see him as he had important duties for King and Country. This impressed William Graham Vivian and he decided to make his will in favour of this nephew.

In 1921 when Dulcie died, the Admiral accepted the addition of the name Vivian, a condition of the will, and lived at Clyne Castle until his death. Many important visitors came, including the Duke and Duchess of Teck with their daughter Princess May (later Queen Mary), Lord Palmerston and the Prince of Wales. The Admiral had six Daimler cars which were named after ships he had served in, including the *Albion* which carried gold from South Africa to help pay for the First World War.

On his death, under the terms of the will, all the contents and the castle had to be sold but the villagers managed to retain the village hall, built by Dulcie Vivian, for their use. Blackpill WI has met there for 43 years and with others has struggled to maintain it. It is now the hub of our one-sided village about which a resident said 'It's a funny place, fishes to the front of us and foxes behind us'.

The castle was bought by the University College of Swansea from the County Borough of Swansea who retained the 27 acre grounds. This is now open as a public park. So the delights of this once private estate are shared by students, visitors and residents and Blackpill has become one of Swansea's leisure areas. Its industrial origins are now largely forgotten.

Bonvilston

Bonvilston is a pretty village situated on the A48 road close to Cowbridge. Its name is derived from the early Norman holders, de Bonville. Members of this family gave much of their lands to the monks of Margam and in time their whole estate passed to the Abbey.

A little distance from Bonvilston stood the house called Cottrell where in the 16th century lived Rice Meyrick who was a lawyer, the town clerk of Cardiff and also Clerk of the Peace for Glamorgan. He was a noted antiquary, the author of *Morganiac Archaiographia – A Book of the Antiquities of Glamorganshire*. Through various marriages the property passed to the Rev Samuel Gwinnett, brother of Button Gwinnett. Button Gwinnett was one of the 17 Welsh signatories to the American Declaration of Independence, eventually becoming the Governor of the State of Georgia.

Boverton

Boverton can be found one mile east of Llantwit Major in the Vale of Glamorgan. It is a very old rural village and can trace its origins back to the Bronze and Iron Ages. It is thought that the Roman fort of Bovium once stood here. The name Boverton is derived from the Latin 'Berton'.

There is no church in the village, but in the Middle Ages it was a very important place, possibly due to its proximity to Llantwit Major and the coast. Roger Seys (died 1599) was Attorney General of Wales and the Seys family built Boverton Castle in 1589. Today these ruins remain in the village. It is thought that a fortified manor house stood near the site. The village grew up around this castle and the Seys family were owners of Boverton from Elizabeth's reign until the mid 18th century. The castle fell into ruin and a new farmhouse known as Boverton Place was built in the 1820s within the grounds.

In 1936 Boverton Place was taken over by the Welsh Land Settlement Association (1936–1961). This Association was established by Captain Crawshay who was the main force behind the scheme. He established in Boverton one of the largest commercial enterprises of its kind in the country at that time, which became a model co-operative farm of 650 acres, worked by men who were unemployed from the mining valleys, mainly due to ill health.

In the mid 19th century, apart from the usual village trades there was also a tannery in Boverton. Today there is no industry, just a few shops, a sub post office/general stores and a public house. There are several houses in the village dating from the 16th and 17th centuries.

At Summerhouse Point on the cliffs a mile from the village is an octagonal summerhouse, built during the 18th century, which stands within the remains of an Iron Age fort.

Bridgend 🌿

It is hard to believe today that until the Industrial Revolution Bridgend was just a tiny agricultural centre straddling the River Ogmore (or Ogwr). On one side of the river the village of Newcastle, standing high on a cliff, was reached first by a ford and, after the 15th century, by a stone bridge.

The Industrial Revolution brought prosperity and a good communication system to Bridgend, for, although itself outside the rich coal seams, the mining valleys of Ogmore and Llynfi sent their coal down by small railways to meet Brunel's main line. The present railway station actually incorporates part of the original building, and around this time busy ironworks were making machinery for the agricultural community. As time went by a new bridge was built to accommodate the increasing traffic over the river, but parts of the original bridge are still to be seen in the small foot-bridge alongside the road bridge. In 1923, the first bus station in Wales was opened in Bridgend – sadly, today there is no operating bus station!

Just before the outbreak of the Second World War, a huge Royal Ordnance Factory was built at Waterton and a massive underground armament store dug into the hill of Brackla, towards the village of Coity. Subsequently this was converted into a complex nuclear bunker, but since the end of the Cold War, the communications pylon stands amongst hundreds of fast-growing broadleaf trees – a peaceful home for many species of wildlife. The Ordnance Factory was demolished after the war, and the first of Bridgend's industrial estates was built. During the war, German prisoners of war were confined in a camp at Island Farm, to the west of the town. From this camp several prisoners escaped, some reaching the east coast of England before being recaptured.

Since the war, the face of Bridgend has changed with the ever-growing industrial complex. Ford and Sony have huge factories, and are the foremost employers, attracting workers from most of the surrounding areas, and most of the well known retail names have built, or are building on trading parks now virtually surrounding Bridgend itself. The Headquarters of the South Wales Police are here, and The Princess of Wales Hospital, together with two older hospitals, provide excellent medical and nursing services for the district. Rugby football is enthusiastically followed at the Brewery Field. There is a first class indoor bowls hall, new swimming pool, and many other sports facilities in the Leisure Centre.

Naturally, homes are needed for all the workers and their families, and, in anticipation of the rapidly growing population of the town, Brackla was chosen as the site for what was to evolve as the largest private housing estate in Europe.

Traditions are being built here for the future, in the Community Centre, the doctors' and dentists' surgeries, the Scouts, Cubs and Brownies, the over-50 Club, and the WI. Friendship is being generated in all these places, in the shopping precinct and at the school gates. When the bricks have mellowed, the trees grown tall, and all those bored teenagers waiting for the school buses are parents themselves, Brackla will have a tale to tell of the foundation and growth of a new 'old village'.

Bryncoch 🌿

The village of Bryncoch lies on the road from Neath to Pontardawe, approximately two miles from Neath town centre. It is essentially a valley village with hills rising on either side and the narrow river Clydach flowing gently down to join the river Neath at Neath Abbey. Farms are to be found on both hillsides. It was originally a very small quiet village well spread out with long gaps between groups of houses. Since the 1950s a great deal of building has taken place and the village has now become a suburb of Neath. It still retains its village character and the older inhabitants keep their mother tongue alive by speaking in Welsh.

Relics of the Bronze Age have been found on Drymma mountain and a large stone, Carreg Bica which is over ten feet tall is to be found here. It is thought to be connected with some religious rite and is said to come down to the river for a drink on Easter morning!

In the second half of the 18th century there was rapid development of heavy industries in the area. Bryncoch had its ironworks with furnaces and forges, and the name Old Furnace is still used for a row of small cottages. Between 1870 and 1920 the village was a mining community. Black tips are still to be found nearby.

The Whitsun tea remains, now held in the Community Centre and members of both local chapels and the church combine for their march through the village.

Whitsun Monday was a big event here in times past.

Preparations for Whitsun always started early. Weeks before there would be the trip to town for new Clark's white buckskin sandals, white 'Brettle' socks, new celanese petticoat and of course the dress!

The Whitsun Tea was always held in the Old School. Everyone sat at long tables set out in the big room. Each table was presided over by members of the Church Guild. The tables were covered with a beautifully starched white tablecloth and laid with bone china cups, saucers and plates, all with a gold band around the edge. The cake always arrived in huge slabs and was cut into pieces. There was cherry, madeira and seed cake. There was a great rivalry to be in charge of a table. There was Mrs Thomas Goshen's table, Mrs Crwys Evans' table, Nurse Garland's table etc and they all had their retinue of helpers. After tea, everybody lined up and marched the few hundred yards down to the 'field'.

Cadoxton (Barry) 🐚

Cadoxton in 1881 was an agricultural village set amid open countryside with its parish church, three chapels, post office/shop, bakery, carpenter, smithy, wheelwright's shop, inns and school. It derives its name from the 6th century St Cattwg to whom many church settlements are dedicated throughout Glamorgan. The 15th century St Cattwg's church is still well attended and, because of its rural charm, is a favourite venue for weddings. It owns an Elizabethan silver chalice hallmarked 1576, now on permanent loan to the National Museum of Wales. In the churchyard is the grave of William Jenkins, deceased 1781, said to be a wizard, the son of Anne Jenkins the 'witch' of Barry. William rose from humble beginnings to become a wealthy farmer and landowner. Other well known local families remembered here are Palmer, Jenkins and Brock. The latter arrived from Somerset, Brock Street being the earliest recorded street name in the village in 1844.

For those who like to journey through time and history, go from the church to a large red brick house built in 1887 named Hebbles, once a private school, passing Yew Tree House where lived Marie Press, a well known local artist. Cross the Coldbrook stream, used until the beginning of the 20th century for baptisms and we find ourselves outside what used to be Evans the blacksmith's shop. We see The Bowers, a 19th century farmhouse, and eventually come to a busy road junction where once there stood a very fine old elm tree. Here, for centuries, villagers congregated to discuss various topics and nonconformist travelling preachers would speak. Sadly in 1899 the dying elm was removed, following gallant efforts to save it.

After crossing Bridge Street we steal up a small lane to Hillside, constructed in 1776 to become in 1778 a public house. Many years later 'Hillside' was used by the Methodists as a meeting place. Opposite the lane is the King William IV inn built in the 1830s. This inn is known by the locals as King Billy and was once the meeting place for the Garden of Wales Lodge of the Friendly Society of Oddfellows.

Across from King Billy are Hillside Cottages, once the village post office and store, where it is said the postman walked everyday from Ely to Wenvoe, Cadoxton, Dinas Powis and returned to Cardiff. If we now travel up Hatch Hill, Bridge Street and pass the 19th century Daisy Cottage, fine views of the countryside and the old village can be seen. It is also possible to see the 19th century Wesley Cottage, once used as the manse for the Wesleyan Methodist church alongside, and opened in October 1862. English speaking Methodists would appear to have attended the Wesleyan church while the Welsh speaking supported the Calvinistic Methodists. In Cadoxton the 19th century chapels became larger and more grand.

In this area are the Cadoxton Board Schools, the finest of which was built in 1879 for an intake of 72 children, rising in 1887 to 241 pupils, indicating the quite rapid population increase. Passing the bowling green we soon enter Victoria Park and take in a superb view of Barry Dock before we exit by the tennis courts. We eventually arrive at Ael-y-Bryn where at one time lived the late Jimmy Wilde, the 'Mighty Atom' World Flyweight Boxing Champion 1916–1922.

We journey onward to Cassy Hill past Church House, a National Church of England school built in 1847 for the poor children of the parishes of Cadoxton and Merthyr Dyfan which closed in 1876 and pass to Hillcrest (the village bakery) built in 1876.

Soon we have passed the Double Cot (two cottages) built between 1790–1840 and used as a summer residence by Cardiff businessmen. Originally they were thatched but this was replaced by slate in 1922. We then head for Church Road where the terraced houses were built for the people employed at the Cadoxton Brickworks. Incorporated into the red brick walls close to the front doors are boot scrapers, needed because the clay for the bricks was dug from red marl pits. We reach what was the Hatch quarry, which provided carboniferous limestone for the Barry roads. Quarrying ceased in 1911 when quarrymen struck a spring which flooded the area.

We are now nearing the end of our journey through history as Oddfellows Cottages come into view, built early in the 19th century for the Friendly Society of Oddfellows, a few steps away from The Three Bells Inn which is over 200 years old. In 1855 nine gallons of beer here was worth ten shillings, less than a penny a pint today!

In the 1880s David Davies, the owner of Ocean Collieries, with Lord Windsor, the eldest son of the Earl of Plymouth, combined to create the port of Barry. Where there had been farms, new houses were built to house the labourers for the excavation of the docks and the stevedores, coal trimmers and other workers who would be employed on these docks. So the small village expanded rapidly, with whole families coming from a variety of areas in South Wales, Somerset, Devon and beyond. In the 1930s the then Barry Borough Council built many houses and in the 1980s, 100 years after the port commenced, many more houses have been built. Today, the area known as Cadoxton is a large part of the town of Barry.

Cadoxton (Neath) ৵৶৫৹

The village extends from Pen-y-wern corner, the nearest point to the town of Neath, to the Iron Bridge at Maes-gwyn, which leads to Aberdulais. Between these two points the village is just over a mile in length. The main road which runs through the centre of the village is the A474. Cadoxton-juxta-Neath is in Welsh Llangatwg Nedd.

The church in Cadoxton is called St Catwg's. It is the only church in Cadoxton and is situated near the main part of the village. Part of the church dates back to the 12th–13th centuries. Early religious teaching in Cadoxton was probably very much influenced by the great Cistercian Monastery nearby (Neath Abbey) which Richard de Granville founded in 1129. The remainder of the church was built in the 16th and 17th centuries. The newer part of the church contains the crypt. An item of interest inside the church is a memorial to Robert Leyson who died on the *Titanic*.

In St Catwg's cemetery is the famous Murder Stone.

1823
To Record
MURDER
This stone was erected over the body of
Margaret Williams
Aged 26

A native of Carmarthenshire living in service in this parish who was found dead with marks of violence upon her person in a ditch, on the marsh below this churchyard on the morning of Sunday July 14th 1822.

Although the savage murderer escape for a season the punishment of man. Yet God hath set his mark upon him either for Time or Eternity and the Cry of Blood will assuredly pursue him to certain and terrible but righteous Judgement.

'Canys nyni a adwaenom y neb a ddywedodd,
Myfi biau dial, myfi a dalaf,
medd yr Arglwydd'   Hebreaid X,30

This inscription, composed by a well-known Quaker businessman Elijah Waring of Neath, father of hymnwriter Anna Laetitia Waring, says it all.

The stone, once a black slab, can be seen near the edge of the path leading from St Catwg's church. Margaret Williams was a milkmaid at Gelliau Farm in Cadoxton. She was found in water on Cadoxton marsh with marks on her neck and no water in her lungs – examination revealed that the girl was pregnant. On the day of her death she had gone to the marsh with the cowman, her lover, who after the murder fled to America.

The stone might have been commissioned by fellow Quaker and Lord of the Manor, John Nathaniel Miers of Cadoxton Lodge. It was the only standing stone in that part of the churchyard at that time and was deliberately positioned to face the road leading to the cowman's home. The stone still attracts many visits from tourists and local school pupils.

Caerphilly Castle

24

Caerphilly

Caerphilly is situated seven miles north of Cardiff in the Rhymney Valley, encircled by the Border Ridges, Mynydd Eglwysilan and Mynydd y Crug. The name suggests Roman connections as the word 'Caer' is derived from the Latin 'Castra', meaning fort. There are certainly a lot of Roman finds in the area and in 1960, a Roman fort was partially excavated about 100 yds south east of the castle. Although Caerphilly and its surrounding area is known to have been inhabited in pre-Roman times it is with the Roman occupation that Caerphilly's recorded history began.

In 1268, Gilbert de Clare, the Norman Lord of Glamorgan, started the building of Caerphilly Castle. Two years later, however, these early structures were razed to the ground by the army of Llewellyn, Prince of Wales. It was only after the intervention of Henry III that further attacks by the Welsh Princes were averted and the building of the castle resumed.

Over the centuries, numerous attacks on the castle by warring factions led to its decay and disrepair and during the Civil War the Parliament-

arians tried unsuccessfully to blow up the towers, which resulted in one tower being blasted nine feet out of perpendicular, so now it leans more than the Tower of Pisa.

Caerphilly Castle is the second largest in Britain and is 30 acres in extent. It has always played an important part in the life of Caerphilly, one of its functions in the 15th century being a local jail. In the 19th century it was used not only for the town's eisteddfodau and religious rallies but for festivals, concerts, military tattoos and horticultural shows.

Every self-respecting castle has its ghost and Caerphilly is no exception. For centuries, legend tells us that the 'Ghost of the Green Lady' has haunted the Castle. It seems the Green Lady was once Princess Alice of Angoulême, a niece of Henry II, and bride of Gilbert de Clare, the 'Red Earl' who rebuilt Caerphilly Castle.

With her husband constantly away at wars, she found 'Kaerfili' a very lonely place and she soon succumbed to the advances of Tew Teg, Griffith the Fair, a prince from the village of Brithdir. However, after the 'Red Earl' found out, he divorced Alice, sending her back to her homeland. Alice later died in France but even death could not stop her from seeking her Welsh lover, who had returned to his valley.

So, if after midnight on a cold, frosty moonlight night, you look up to the towers and see a shadowy form standing there and hear the sound of hoof beats coming down the valley – your skin will tingle and you'll wonder after all, if the legends are true.

Until the 1850s, the main function of Caerphilly was its weekly market and annual fairs. However, in the 1890s, after the sinking of the deep mines and the resultant flourishing railway system, Caerphilly experienced a period of rapid growth. It was soon transformed from a mere Welsh speaking rural village, its 1,500 inhabitants being housed in about 250 small whitewashed cottages hugging the castle wall, to a population today totalling over 30,000.

But it is for its cheese, 'Caws Caerfili' that Caerphilly is known worldwide. The early cheese makers described it as 'a most creamy cheese of a quick ripening kind', ready for sale and consumption 10–14 days after manufacture. Miners in particular, found it an ideal sustaining food and today cheese makers in several countries have made use of its fame to produce and market Caerphilly cheese.

The making of farm cheese dates from medieval times and in 1874 there was a cheese market operating in Caerphilly. This was an open building into which farmers drove their wagons etc to unload their cheese – the weekly sale amounting to approximately 2½ tons. At that time the first Truancy Officer appointed in Caerphilly was also the town's

'Lamplighter' and 'Market Cheese Taster'.

The Caerphilly Cheese Market finally closed in 1910 and today little farm-house Caerphilly cheese is made locally.

Cefn Cribwr 🌿

Cefn Cribwr is a modern village of about 1,800 people, lying four miles north-west of Bridgend, about half way between the cities of Cardiff and Swansea.

It is a long line of buildings along the crest of a conspicuous ridge. There is a splendid view from it. Across the Bristol Channel in the distance, we can see the Quantock Hills in Somerset, Selworthy Beacon, 1,000 ft high and Porlock Bay. Then to the west of Porlock Bay, Devon begins, with Dunkery Beacon, 1,700 ft high, the heights of Exmoor, and Foreland Point with its lighthouse. From the ridge westwards, we see the headlands of Gower and Swansea.

Cefn Cribwr was a mining community, not far from a number of collieries. Fatal accidents often occurred. The most memorable disaster was the Park Slip Colliery Explosion, which happened on Friday, August 26th, 1892 – the day of the Annual St Mary Hill Fair. Of the 151 men who went to work, 112 men lost their lives on that terrible day. The 39 men who survived must have thought it was sheer good luck or the hand of Providence that they had come through that nightmare alive. Dr J. Twist, the local doctor, endeared himself forever to the working-men of Cefn Cribwr for his personal bravery at the Park Slip explosion. A memorial to the victims was erected some years ago at The Fountain, Aberkenfig, an adjoining village to Cefn Cribwr.

There were numerous shops in the village, and these were mostly in ordinary parlours. The first Co-operative Store is now the meeting-place for senior citizens and is called Unity Hall. The second Co-operative Store is now The Happy Shopper grocery store and is run by Mr Patel. Mr and Mrs D. Williams own another general store.

The fish shops of previous years owned by Mr and Mrs T. Shell, Mr and Mrs T. Jenkins, and later by Mrs Howells and Mrs Tovey, are now replaced with a Chinese take away and fish shop.

A butcher's shop was owned by Mr W. Clark and later by Mrs Cattle. There is no butcher's shop in Cefn at present. Mr Bob Bryant was a barber and Mr Garfield Vaughan owned a barber's shop. A ladies' hairdressing shop was run by Mrs Caroline Bradshaw and later by Mrs Stephanie Jones. Mr Tom Browning and Mr Will Jones were cobblers.

Mr John Stenner (and later his son Ieuan) had a newspaper and stationery shop in the front room of his house. The present newsagent's, general store and off-licence is now owned by Mr and Mrs Roger Evans. Sadly, the disappearance of the little shops has continued throughout the years.

The Granville family have been delivering the local post since before the First World War. The older daughters and younger sons used to deliver the post and travelled to many outlying farms and districts on foot. Later, they used bicycles. The post office itself was transferred in 1917 to John and Kate Granville's parlour, the room where it has remained to this day. The present postmistress is Mary Williams, great grand-daughter of Mr and Mrs J. Granville.

There are six places of worship in Cefn Cribwr, namely: Wesleyan Methodist Church, Nebo Welsh Baptist, Siloam Independent, Calvary English Baptist, Bethlehem Pentecostal, and St Colman's Anglican Church.

The Farmers' Arms, Three Horse Shoes and White Lion are the three remaining public houses, whilst The Plough, Star and Bankers have long since gone. We have, however, a British Legion Club and Athletic Club. The village war memorial, the first of the numerous bus-shelters to be built in Cefn, was raised next to the British Legion headquarters in 1953. Like many other towns and villages in the country, Cefn sent out its young men to war, and the names of the 13 who did not return can be read on the plaque at the Memorial Shelter.

Cefn Cribwr Community Centre used to be called the Public Hall and was opened in 1924. It was originally conceived as a Miners' Welfare Hall and supported by colliery owners and colliers. Many meetings were held there – a lot political. Ramsay Macdonald spoke there in the closing weeks of the General Strike. The Wesley Dramatic Society entertained, as did the members of Siloam Chapel who performed many good dramas and concerts. Very popular were the Cefn Cribwr Pantomime Society. They started about 1949, and the pantomime usually ran for a week or so. Many people came in busloads from surrounding places. The Davies' sons – Messrs. Haydn, Royden, Teify and Windsor Davies and their families were for years the leading performers and organisers.

A cinema used to be held in the Public Hall, but with the coming of television it was closed. During the war years it was a very welcome addition to our entertainment. Mr Sid Waters was a projectionist and later Mr Ted Pemberton. At 6.30 pm five evenings of the week, two different programmes were shown, much to the enjoyment of everyone.

The Community Centre is still used a great deal today for different kinds of meetings, functions, entertainments etc. The Women's Institute

28

meetings are held there on the first Tuesday of every month.

Cefn Cribwr Primary School has seen numerous changes in the past half-century. The pattern of secondary schooling has changed considerably in recent years. Cefn Cribwr School was earlier of the type known as 'Elementary', which meant that most pupils stayed at that school until the age of 14, never attending any other. However, now when children become 11 years old they are transferred to the neighbouring Comprehensive School, at Kenfig Hill. During the Second World War the school canteen for the Primary School was held in the Ambulance Hall and a familiar sight was the mid-day procession of chattering children two by two along the pavement to the Ambulance Hall.

Our village green is called the 'Mynydd Bach Common' and belongs to the people of Cefn Cribwr. It has a rugby pitch, with swings etc., for younger children. Sport has played a big part in Cefn and it produced many fine rugby players and athletes. Further along the village we have the Cae Gof Playing Fields opened in 1958, which consist of rugby and soccer pitches, tennis courts, and a very fine bowling green. Men and women play and hold tournaments there regularly, and bowling has become a very popular sport for all ages.

One pastime of a different kind was destined to become very important in the history of Cefn Cribwr. The movement to establish an Ambulance Division sprang from the realization of the sheer poverty of medical facilities in local places of work. Early officials and supporters of Cefn's Ambulance Division were Isaac and David Downs, Bob Bryant, John Watkins and George Myers, while Dr J Twist became the first Divisional Surgeon. In later years Ambulance classes were held, with Mr Rees Davies and Mr George Watkins in charge. There were many brigade triumphs in Cardiff and London, and at the Royal National Eisteddfod of Wales in 1970. In June 1974, too, the St John's Ambulance Brigade opened their third Ambulance Hall. We still have a very fine and active Ambulance Division to this day.

Although there have been many changes in Cefn Cribwr over the years, it still remains a very close-knit and friendly place to live in.

Church Village ❦

Church Village is situated between Llantrisant and Pontypridd. The Community Council of Llantwit Fardre controls the five villages of Newtown Llantwit, Efail Isaf, Tonteg, Church Village and Upper Church Village. At one time these villages were quite separate from each other,

29

but so many houses have been built that now they are almost merged into one large built-up area. A large number of farms have disappeared. Those which no longer exist were known as Fardre Isaf, Fardre Uchaf, Ty Draw, Tynwaun, and Ffrwd Phillip.

The main road through Church Village is the A473, which has such a dense volume of traffic that local residents are now pressing for the building of a bypass to skirt the villages, and perhaps allow them to return to the peaceful days of years gone by. The road was first constructed in 1839 by Francis Crawshay, one of the early ironmasters of Merthyr.

A large general hospital is situated in Church Village, which opened in 1938. During the Second World War it was used by the Royal Air Force, but has since served the local communities together with the areas of Pontypridd and Rhondda. A new hospital is today being built near the town of Llantrisant.

The Cottage Homes, known as Garth Olwg, were built in 1892, founded to care for orphaned children. In later years the children were educated at the local Llantwit Fardre School, together with the village children. A new home for the elderly has been built in the Garth Olwg grounds, and some of the very old buildings are used as a 'Welsh School', where children are taught through the medium of the Welsh language.

The main meeting place in Church Village is known as The Parish Hall, where the two Women's Institutes (Tonteg and Church Village) meet, together with functions arranged by many other organisations such as Cancer Research, Save The Children, and committees of various community interests. The Parish Hall was first known as The Carnegie Free Library. £1,500 was given by Mr Carnegie for the building of a new library. A very fine building was built, and opened to the public on 2nd September 1906. Beautiful oak shelves, tables, and reading racks were installed, and the library was in daily use as a reading room, and for the borrowing of a great variety of books.

In 1965 Mid Glamorgan County Council decided to build a new library in Church Village. The beautiful old library, oak tables, bookcases and reading racks were all dismantled, and the building was transformed into our present Parish Hall. A new modern library was built to the rear of the hall.

There has been a considerable change in the industrial scene in our area. The Cwm Colliery, which was started in 1909 and provided work for a large number of people, has now closed down. The Power Station of the Electricity Board has been demolished, and the once flourishing Treforest Industrial Estate now has fewer working factories.

The parish church is situated in Upper Church Village, and is dedicated to St Illtud, whose memory is associated with the 5th century monastic college at Llantwit Major. The church is on a site which has been used for worship since the 5th century, although the present building dates from 1525. The tower dates from 1636, and the registers from 1632. In the early 1970s the church was restored and now has an attractive and modern interior.

The tradition of the Nonconformist movement was well established in Church Village. The earliest building was Bryntirion Welsh Presbyterian Church which dated from the Methodist foundation of 1740. Sadly this old building was closed in 1961 and later demolished, and in 1985 the sister church of Bethesda Llantwit Fardre was also demolished. The small Wesleyan Methodist Chapel at Church Village also suffered the same fate. Thus by 1993 the Methodist cause in the area had been brought to an end.

In 1874, Salem Welsh Baptist Church was built in Hollybush, Church Village, after early Baptist worshippers had been meeting in various private houses. From 1844–54 they had worshipped in the long room of the Cross Inn at Church Village. It was at the present church of Salem at Hollybush that John Hughes (composer of the famous tune *Cwm Rhondda* and many other songs and hymns) was a precentor, as his father had been before him. A marble tablet to his memory is placed near the pulpit, and his tunes are still sung in many of the services.

Bethel English Baptist Church was established at the time of the 1904–5 revival. After worshipping in various cottages, and in a modest wooden building in The Parade, Church Village, it was decided to purchase the vacant Social Club situated on the main road. This was suitably altered, and consecrated for worship.

Church Village is a centre of activity today as it has been throughout the years – a centre of educational, religious, and sporting activities. Times and styles change, but life goes on, and people still go about their simple daily living with the same care and diligence as in days gone by.

Cimla

The oldest form of this word is 'Cimne'. Through change and time this has become in local dialect 'Cimdda' or 'Cimla'.

At the turn of the century the Cimla was, as suggested in the book *Symposium of Neath* by Elis Jenkins, common land. It consisted of farms, odd detached houses, a Sunday school, a junior school, a public house and some mine workings.

William Davies, gentleman and historian (1756–1823) lived at Cringallt House. He has become known as the forgotten historian. A plaque was unveiled to his memory in the Neath Library, on 22nd March 1923. He wrote a manuscript on the history of Glamorgan which was seen, but never published. This manuscript is quoted as being the 'ultimate in historical research'.

The Glamorgan Reformatory School (Farm School), was first established at Hawdref Ganol Farm in 1858, before being transferred to Ty Segur at Mount Pleasant in 1875. Cimla Hospital was built as a hospital for patients suffering with tuberculosis.

Crynallt Junior School was built in the early 1960s. Crynallt Infants School was opened in 1971. The original infants' school had been behind the Cimla Fire Station. It was constructed of tin sheets and was closed when the pupils were transferred to the new school. The old school became the Neath Teachers' Centre. Cefn Saeson Comprehensive School was established further up Afan Valley Road and was the first purpose-built comprehensive school in the district.

These schools were built to accommodate the expected growth in pupil population with the building of a new housing estate known as the Glannant Estate and further development above the Comprehensive School. The sports field above the comprehensive school was originally laid out for the Metal Box Company in 1936.

Cimla Hotel was built in 1936–37. The lounge, as it stands today, was built in the early 1950s. To get a licence to build Cimla Hotel, Evans Bevan had to relinquish two licences in the area. He gave up the licences of the Vale of Neath, which became part of the Cimla Hotel, and that of the Tyn-yr Heol in Bwlch Road.

St Peter and St Paul's church was consecrated in 1970. It replaced a temporary building (now the church hall). The Cimla Co-operative stores, now vacant, was built between the wars and is now designated a listed building. Cimla now supports two public houses, The Cimla and Tudor Inn, a rugby club, Cimla Court Hotel and the Brynhyfryd Social Club. Sport is well catered for by two rugby teams, two cricket teams, adult and youth soccer teams. There is a hall which houses the local cubs, scouts, brownies and guides. There is also a Young Wives Group. The most recent acquisition is the Community Centre, built to serve the whole of the Cimla area.

Cockett and Fforestfach 🦢

In early days Cockett and Fforestfach were separate communities with the unofficial dividing line being Cockett Bridge. Growing urbanisation has brought them together.

Memories abound – none more vivid than the biennial visit of the gypsy women. They would arrive with baskets full of hand made paper flowers. When all had been sold they would retire to St Peter's Terrace and sit there making dozens of pegs from branches of the trees. Those would be sold as well and most of the money spent at the store owned by Mrs Thomas near Cockett Station. Then they would leave and would not be seen for two years. No one ever discovered where they came from.

The saw mill with its railway lines at the side was always a busy place. The railway station won many a competition for the best kept and picturesque station. The local doctor, who had no car, always walked everywhere carrying his black bag. A Nurse Thomas, the local midwife, was a very caring person. The village blacksmith on Fforestfach Cross was where all the local milkmen used to take their horses to be shod. Bread came from Jack Hudson, sometimes known as the 'midnight baker' because he was always delivering long after other tradesmen had completed their rounds. Perhaps that was because he used a pony and trap for delivery. His bakery was at Fforestfach Cross.

Arthur Jenkins (now Arthur LL Jenkins & Co. House furnishers) relied on his horse for transport as well. He came around weekly, a huge shire horse pulling a wagon full of cans of oil, brushes, pots and pans; in fact everything the housewife needed.

Still remembered with affection is Mr Rowe, the fruit and veg man from Sketty who came twice a week and the fragile old lady (thought to be a Mrs Thomas) who pushed her handcart with churns of milk and a pint measure from her home near Cefn Coed Hospital three miles to Middle Road in Fforestfach.

The area once boasted four chapels, but now only one, Bethlehem chapel remains. Calfaria and Jerusalem have been demolished and Saron is for sale. When a new pipe organ was installed at Bethlehem in 1930, over 700 attended a recital to mark the event. There were big attendances at the annual Good Friday eisteddfod at Calfaria and Jerusalem and Saron were also packed for special events.

So many other once familiar landmarks have also disappeared – like Struttons, the big clothing factory, Culleys in Cwmbach Road where beer was bottled, the brickworks, the first greyhound stadium (now located at Ystrad Road) and the Cottage Homes with its six distinctive houses, where orphaned or neglected children used to be placed.

Colwinston ﷼

Colwinston is situated four miles west of Cowbridge. Once a small village with a few farms, now some 200 houses exist, but it is still in a rural setting.

The 12th century church of St Michael and All Angels was restored in 1879, and once came under the jurisdiction of Ewenny Priory until the dissolution of the priory in 1539. It has a stained glass window in memory of Gordon Fairfax Lougher Prichard and other memorials to the Thomas and Prichard families. Also a mural wall painting 600 years old depicting the enthronement of Thomas a Beckett, and St Vitus who was boiled in oil at the age of twelve. The tower houses a pre-Reformation bell, and an old stone preaching cross can be found in the churchyard. Some people can still remember the barrows, or ancient burial sites, in the village, the relics taken from which can be found in the British Museum.

Near the manor house, Pwllywrach, just on the outskirts of the village are said to be the ruins of kennels. The huntsman in charge of a pack of hounds left them for a few days without food, to enjoy the pleasures of drink. On his return the hounds, being so hungry, tore him apart. The cries of this huntsman and the baying of the hounds are said still to be heard in the vicinity today!

Cowbridge ﷼

The Welsh name for Cowbridge is Bont Faen. It is steeped in history and possesses much old world charm with stretches of its medieval town walls, and its south gate. It lies some twelve miles west of Cardiff. There are many traditions associated with the name Cowbridge, one of which is related to a bridge and a cow. The cow, being driven by dogs, took shelter under one of the arches. Her horns became so much entangled that she could not be taken out alive. The arms of the town still show the figure of a cow on a bridge.

Evidence has been found that there was a settlement at Cowbridge during Roman times. It received its first town charter in 1254 from Richard de Clare, Earl of Gloucester and Lord of Glamorgan. By 1307 there were 276 dwellings but by 1349 the Black Death had almost halved them.

The House of Correction once stood in the centre of the main street but when the county jail was moved to Swansea in 1829, it became the new Town Hall. The cells still remain and now house the local museum.

At the west end of the town is Gibbetts Hill where felons were hanged and the old tree could still be seen in the 1920s. The old Toll Houses were near this hill, but they were demolished after the Second World War.

The first printing press in Glamorgan was established in Cowbridge in 1770 by Rhys Thomas.

Farmers used to bring their wool to the Old Wool Barn for it to be picked up and graded and then bought by the dealers. This building now houses some very interesting crafts. Cowbridge played an important part in the economy of South Wales in the 19th century. In 1835 there were six maltsters, three stonemasons, four tailors, nine schools, mills of varying types and possibly a tallow factory. We could also boast about having two or three saddlers who would make harness, also a cooper who made such things as cheese vats. He was a most interesting old man to watch at work.

Flourishing agricultural markets are still held every Tuesday. They were held on a Monday until recent times. In the 1920s one market was held in the old station yard. Stock could be bought in Hereford and Gloucester and delivered by train to the goods station, usually in the early hours of the morning, and then walked to their destination. Hence probably the reason for so many inns. Once the business side was concluded, all would retire to them for liquid refreshment and merrymaking.

There are some 70 or more buildings listed as of special historic and architectural interest.

The church, The Holy Cross, is near the centre of the town just behind the Duke of Wellington public house. It is a large building in Early English and Perpendicular styles. The 13th century central tower has a defensive look about it and is crowned by an eight-sided parapet. Both the nave and the chancel have single aisles but the aisles are curiously arranged on opposite sides to each other, giving the interior an un-balanced appearance. The church was restored in 1848.

The Duke of Wellington was a coaching inn and dates from the 17th century. Originally it was called the Black Horse, but when the Iron Duke stayed overnight in the building on a journey to visit General Picton in Carmarthen, the name was changed. In its lounge is a well which is said to have been used in Roman times. It is reputed that there is a ghost called the 'Grey Lady' who used to walk along the narrow

35

passage way on the ground floor of the pub, from the front to the back of the building.

In the early 1920s a cinema was built and above it was a ballroom, reputed to be the finest in South Wales. Many important functions were held there, but unfortunately it was burnt down and now little more than the outer walls remain.

We had many characters in Cowbridge, one of whom was a doctor who, it was said, did not send bills to his poorer patients. He could be seen driving his pony and trap wearing his top hat and tail coat. Johnny John was a well known follower of the hounds. With his terrier and cloth leggings he was known as 'Johnny Grassy'.

To the east of Cowbridge was fought one of the bloodiest battles of Glamorgan in 1405 between the English and the Welsh of the Vale and Owen Glyndwr and his army. Following many hours of fierce fighting Owen drove his enemies away.

The site of the battle is now called Stalling Down, also known for many years as 'Bryn Owen' (Owens Hill).

Edward Williams (1747–1826) kept a bookshop at 14 High Street, Cowbridge. He was better known by his bardic name of Iolo Morganwg. He was born at Llancarfan in the Vale of Glamorgan, and worked as a stone mason for most of his life but is remembered as a poet, writing in Welsh and English, and as a controversial antiquary. He was responsible for introducing the Gorsedd ceremony into the form of the eisteddfod. He died in Flemingston a few miles from Cowbridge.

The Glamorgan Agricultural Society was formed by a number of prominent gentlemen meeting at the Bear Inn in August 1772. This was the beginning of the Cowbridge Show, which has become The Vale of Glamorgan Show and held at Penllyn, near Cowbridge since 1953.

Much housing development has taken place since the Second World War but such growth has not altered the old charm of Cowbridge.

Coychurch ✤

Coychurch is an attractive village near Bridgend and just a few miles from the coast. It is situated on the edge of the Vale of Glamorgan. The village has grown since the 1960s from a few hundred inhabitants to over 2,000. This is in part due to the availability of employment on the Bridgend Industrial Estate only half a mile away and its easy access to the M4 motorway about a mile distant.

History records that there was a Celtic settlement in Coychurch in the

6th century, on the site of the present church. It was on the safety of rising ground, above floods, yet with springs and on ancient routes. The oldest monuments are the Stone of Ebissar of the 9th century and the Celtic Cross. The preaching cross marks the central meeting point of the settlement. Later St Crallo from Brittany founded the church in the 10th century and the theological college adjoining it. The existing church is a 13th century building.

Much history is associated with the village. The great yew tree is a reminder of the days when the trees were grown to make weapons for the bowmen. The neighbourhood greeted Nonconformity with enthusiasm and John Wesley preached at St Crallo's in 1771.

The village blacksmith, local historian and a father figure in the community, was regarded with great affection by young and old. He was First World War veteran soldier, Edward Lewis. He died at the age of 93 and left behind personal papers painting a vivid picture of life in his beloved Coychurch from Victorian times until after the Second World War.

The village school was opened in 1896 and 10 year old Edward Lewis took his place there. As an old man he returned on a number of occasions to talk to the pupils. 'I started my school life at the old National School which at the time belonged to the church and is a very old building. Things at that school were very much different in those early days before the School Board Act came into force. We had to pay twopence per week for our schooling and discipline was very strict and punishment very severe if you did not behave yourself.

'There were three special days in the year to which we all looked forward. First, the summer outing to the seaside. We always went to Ogmore-by-Sea or Southerndown and we went in farm wagons or carts. What a grand sight it was to see the horses gaily bedecked with bells and ribbons and harness polished up and everything spick and span. Later on, brakes and wagonettes came along, which made the trip more enjoyable. Second was the tea party for the schoolchildren at 'Plas Coed-y-Mwstwr' (a large mansion house outside the village, which has since been a Remand Home for girls and is now a high class hotel and restaurant), kindly given by Mr Arthur Williams, Liberal MP for South Glamorgan, and Mrs Williams. Third was the Christmas tree, also given by the Coed-y-Mwstwr family. These events were outstanding in our lives. The Williams family were great benefactors to the school – baskets of fruit etc. always arrived for us in their season.

'Every village was more or less a self-contained community then and lived mostly dependent on each other, by selling or bartering their goods to one another. In Coychurch at this time there were two tailors who came to our homes to make our clothes. They generally came for a week and lived with the family. The same applied to the dressmakers who made the women's and girls' clothes. There were two shoemakers in the village. We had to go there to have our feet measured for our boots to be made – and those boots were expected to last at least a year.

'There were three flour mills. They ground the wheat, barley and oats as flour for bread, oatmeal and porridge and meal for feeding the animals. The miller worked by the system of tolls. A measure of corn was taken out of every sack brought by the farmer for grinding. This was sold by the miller to the cottager or worker for his benefit. This will give you some idea of how the system of barter worked. The farmer had his corn ground and the miller had his means of livelihood. Some of the mills had kilns for roasting the oat grains to make oatmeal for porridge. On Saturday we had to go to Tycandy Mill for a shilling's worth of the meal for our breakfasts.

'About this time coal mining was booming in the valleys and the trek of men and boys from the village began, attracted by the big money they could earn there. The Welsh language was predominant in the home and about 90 per cent of the children in the village were bilingual – they would speak and read in both languages.'

Mr Lewis would have been the first to admit that they were not always 'the good old days'. If you became destitute you had to go to the workhouse which was degrading to say the least. There was tragedy too. An epidemic of typhoid fever in 1894–5 caused a number of deaths in the village. Some years later whooping cough swept through the village and the number of children who died was heavy. Two of his own family, a brother and sister, died in the same week.

One distinguished Welshman Mr Lewis would have much admired is also buried in the village churchyard, the Rev. Thomas Richards, author of the first comprehensive Welsh-English dictionary which was published in 1753. A handsome plaque was unveiled at St. Crallo's church in 1990 by Lord Tonypandy, former Speaker of the House of Commons, to mark the bicentenary of the death of the Rev. Richards.

Creigiau 🦋

Creigiau is about seven miles north west of Cardiff on the main Llantrisant to Cardiff road. The village at one time had a railway station and was on the main Barry-Cardiff-Pontypridd line. This has long closed and there is no longer any trace of this railway line. The village is within the parish of Pentyrch and is bounded by four farms: Creigiau to the north, Castell-y-Mynach to the south, Pant-y-Gored to the east and Llwynmilwas to the west. Although these farms and some houses had existed in Creigiau for many years, the village was not separately recorded in the national census until 1871 when a population of 300 was recorded.

Records show that Castell-y-Mynach farm existed in the 17th century providing food for Miskin Manor. Its name suggests an earlier monastic association. Plans of the building show details of priest-holes and an escape tunnel, running west towards Groesfaen and directly in line with Miskin Manor.

Before the late 1960s there was no public house in Creigiau. What is now the Creigiau Inn was originally a Temperance Hotel and then after being granted a licence became a non-political club attracting members from far and wide, due to the fact that it opened on Sundays.

The railway arrived in Creigiau in the late 1890s when the village consisted of scattered farms, farm workers' cottages and a few houses for the railway and quarry employees. The surrounding countryside was made up of woodland, lush fields and grassy banks which provided an abundance of primroses and, in their season, plump juicy blackberries. It was this that led to a custom probably unique to the village. Large groups of people would travel to Creigiau on the trains from the valley towns and villages to pick the primroses and later, the blackberries. They would spend several hours in the village bringing with them baskets of food and drink and then returning home with these baskets filled with the results of the day's harvesting.

These trips continued for many years but with the demise of the railways and possibly the need for more sophisticated activities, they have now ceased.

In the 1970s and 1980s several well designed housing estates sprang up in the village greatly increasing the population. Creigiau is a very pleasant place as it is still surrounded by green fields and delightful walks. This, together with its easy access to Cardiff and the M4 motorway, makes it an attractive place to live.

Crynant 🐾

Crynant is an old village in the Dulais valley in West Glamorgan. There was a chapel-of-ease on the site where the old church stands and the monks from Neath Abbey, on their way to Chester, would spend a night there as it was a day's journey from Neath to Crynant.

Before the Second World War when our village was half the size it is today, Station Road was the commercial centre of the village. Across the top end of the street was the railway station, the only station in the valley that had a downline, an upline, a watershed where the steam engines filled their boilers and a signal box. Next to the station was the doctor's surgery, held twice a day on weekdays and once on Sunday mornings and opposite that was the small chemist shop. Besides houses, and although only about 50 yards long, the street had a shoe shop, a paper shop, a gentlemen's barber and sweet shop, a bank held twice a week, a cake shop and bakery, a memorial hall (that was also the village cinema, concert hall and dance hall) and attached to the hall was the reading room and billiard hall. The front room of one of the houses was used as a dentist's surgery two evenings a week and next to that house was a draper and toy shop. The Home Guard headquarters was in what had been an exclusive milliner's shop. At the end of the street was the village grocery shop and the post office. Across the main road, opposite the post office, there were two ironmongers, two petrol pumps and a police station.

Today, Crynant has no station, no shoe shop, no bank, no bakery, no ironmonger, no cinema, no reading room, no billiard hall, no police station, no petrol pump and the surgery, which is on another site, is held once a day from Monday to Friday.

The same family kept the post office from 1900 until 1988. In the early days, the mail was sorted in the post office and franked with the Crynant date stamp and placed in sealed mail bags ready to be taken to the station to catch the 7 pm train to Neath. The first morning train from Neath brought the mail to Crynant. From the mid 1930s, mail vans brought the sacks of mail to the village and the mail was sorted in the post office until the 1970s.

The busiest time of the year was Christmas, especially Christmas Day, as all the local people expected to receive their cards from their village friends on Christmas Day. It was all hands on deck in order to help the postmen sort and deliver the cards before Christmas dinner. Often a Christmas card was addressed to, for example, Mr and Mrs Jones, Neath Road, Crynant, and as there were many Joneses in Neath Road, the postmen would open the unsealed card to find out who was the sender and then they would know to whom to deliver it, because they knew all the family connections in the village.

One postman delivered to the majority of the village for the first and second delivery, while the other postman did the lower part of the village and the farms. There were about fifteen inhabited farms surrounding the village in the 1940s, many about a mile from their nearest neighbour and as there were no vans for the postmen then, only Shanks's pony or a bicycle, the postmen were very healthy. Many of the houses had no numbers, only names, and because there were so many similar christian and surnames, the name of the house or farm was tagged on behind, for example, John the Gould, Will Ton Mân, Dai Llwynfelish, Annie Ynis fadog, Beti Brynawel. Of course, Welsh was the language of the village then.

The village grocery shop was next to the post office. Many older residents still remember the sugar in a blue bag, dried fruit in another coloured bag and the large cheeses. There was the household area with the long bars of yellow and green soap, boxes of soda and cubes of blue to whiten clothes, tins of Brasso and blacklead; the tobacco drawers, filled with various cigarettes in packets of fives, tens and twenties, pipe tobacco and tobacco twist that was coiled like a rope and chewed by the colliers when they were underground. The dairy produce area was where the bacon machine lived, with its sharp circular knife. Near the cheese and the butter barrel there was always a hessian bag filled with yeast.

Evacuees from Gillingham arrived in Crynant in the early 1940s and one of them was billeted with a theatrical family. She organised the children of Station Road into a concert party and they used to perform in the shop's garage behind Station Road. The village children were invited to these concerts and they had to pay a halfpenny for the privilege of seeing them dancing and doing handstands. When these children, with their English accents told village children about television, a box in the home that showed pictures transmitted from a distance, they wouldn't believe them, because at that time the wireless was a new thing in the village and some families didn't even have a wireless. But childhood seems to have been much freer than the village children experience today, as they were allowed to explore the village and the surrounding country-side, but of course at that time there was very little traffic going through the village and everybody knew everybody in the village.

Culverhouse Cross 🐦

Culverhouse Cross is on the outskirts of the city of Cardiff and derives its name from a farm on Cowbridge Road, just opposite the present Culver House public house. Many farms and manor houses at one time had a dovecote, as the birds were a valuable source of meat when there was not much else available. The old word for a dove is a 'culver', and so a dovecote was a culver house. The dovecote itself stood opposite the Culver House pub, on the land between the Woodlands Surgery and the Western Cemetery.

In the 1960s much development took place on private estates in the

St Fagan's Court and Culverhouse farm areas. To make way for progress, the lovely old lane leading to St Fagan's from Culverhouse Cross disappeared as it was totally inadequate to take the volume of traffic generated.

In recent years Culverhouse Cross has developed, with out of town stores of Marks and Spencer and Tesco, the Copthorne Hotel and HTV television studios, increasing even more the volume of traffic. On leaving the stores and travelling up the hill known as the Tumble, one has a marvellous panoramic view of the city of Cardiff, including Castell Coch and the Garth Mountain. The parish church of St George-super-Ely, restored in 1886, has a weathervane of St George and the Dragon on its four-gabled, saddleback tower.

Cwmbach 🐦

Cwmbach is a small village situated about two miles from Aberdare, and is in the Cynon Valley. The chief industries in this area were farming and coalmining. The first colliery in the village was Abernant-y-Groes, sunk in 1837. The coal from the pit was transported down an incline (locally known in these days as the 'Lambeth Walk') and taken by horse-drawn barges on the canal to Cardiff docks. Incidentally, the first lump of coal extracted from the mine can still be seen in a local garden. There are no mines left today.

An adjacent housing estate is named Tre-Telynog. Telynog is the bardic name of the poet Thomas Evans who lived in the village and worked in the local mines. He died in 1865 at the very early age of 25 years.

The Co-operative Society had its foundations in Cwmbach. The introduction into the co-operative arose from a meeting at a local hostelry. Each shareholder was given a membership number, shop-book with which to trade and a pass-book. All debts had to be cleared by what was known as pen-quarter (quarter-end). The dividends were duly entered into the pass-book and later withdrawn either to purchase further goods, or to pay off the debt incurred during the preceding quarter. Alas, all good things come to an end, and the only reminder of the once flourishing venture is a commemorative plaque mounted at the site of the old co-op shop.

Goods for the co-op shop were unloaded from barges at the dock of the nearby canal. Along the canal – and in the small hamlet – there were twelve public houses, three very aptly named: Lifeboat, Ship and Scales.

Besides the large number of inns in the village, there was quite a preponderance of chapels and churches of different denominations.

The village boasted two lamplighters, one at the top end and one at the bottom end, a steep hill determining the areas. The hill was so steep that when coal was delivered by horse and cart, it took two teams of horses to pull the load.

The Church school was the first school in the village, built in 1856. Later came the Board school in Bridge Road. This road was the high street of the village where the narrow double-doored post office, strictly ruled over by the Misses Jones, stood opposite the surgery of the local and well loved Doctor Murphy where patients sat on wooden benches, dreading that voice calling 'next'.

Cwmbach is renowned for its Male Voice Choir. The first choir was formed in 1921 by a group of miners in an open air meeting at the local park and has gone from strength to strength over the years. The venue for their many concerts was the Workman's Hall, where village children religiously attended the Saturday matinee to see the latest films. During the Second World War, local talent was supported in the 'go-as-you-please' shows, the proceeds of which went towards the war effort.

The events at the Hall were announced by our Village Crier with his tinny bell and such a raucous voice for a man of such small stature.

Dinas Powys 🪺

Over the centuries the name of the village has varied in its spelling from the early Denispowys to the modern Dinas Powys, and once was spelled Dinas Powis. Perched on a stony outcrop, the Norman castle has watched over the comings and goings of the inhabitants and witnessed the transition from a small but important settlement to the lively, bustling village of today.

In the small old hamlet life was firmly based on agriculture and its attendant pursuits such as hunting and fishing. The early form of transport was the horse which helped maintain the links for trade via the old turnpike road to Cardiff. At the bottom of Pen-y-turnpike Hill a spare horse was kept to help pull up heavy loads and a windlass was used.

The Common still reminds us of the system of land usage of the Middle Ages. Our place and field names might be Welsh, English, or Norman French.

Progress came to Dinas Powys in the 1880s with the revolution

The Twyn, Dinas Powys

brought by coal which led to the building of the docks at Barry and Penarth and a railway line being built through the area, with a station at the centre of the village. The first passenger train ran on Sunday, 20th December 1888 and from that day the increase in population commenced. In the census of 1881 the population was 576, in 1921 it was 529 and in 1992 about 10,000.

Once a familiar part of the waking day, the rattle of the milkcart with its churns and measuring ladles no longer disturbs the present occupants of the old cottages once known as Darlings Arcade.

Gone are the church school and schoolhouse from the Square. Time was when the headmaster, himself a former pupil, would emerge from the house each weekday morning only to disappear into the adjoining school where the insistent clanging of the bell called pupils to their lessons. The sound of the children's voices raised in unison assured the passer-by that, for the next three hours at least, the business of the village could proceed without let or hindrance.

Heurtley Newnham Rees, affectionately known as Nutt Rees, was headmaster for 25 years and a stained glass window to his memory is to be found in St Peter's church.

Just across the Square, time has dealt kindly with the Three Horseshoes, once the home of the White Bard, Dewi Wyn o Essyllt, whose monument stands in the parish churchyard of St Andrew's. Parts of the church date back to Norman times and the base and steps of the old preaching cross are of medieval origin. The village boasts two other ancient hostelries – The Star and The Cross Keys, both serving the needs of villager and visitor alike. The Twyn, once the scene of wild junketing and merrymaking, nowadays presents a more sober image with its memorial to the dead of two world wars.

Long gone is the private school of St Winifred's and the Trust School founded in 1899. It was later an approved school by name Bryn-y-Don to be closed in 1979. It is owned now by the Hebron Trust, a Christian organisation, and the site has been developed. There is also a National Children's Home, Ardwyn, to be found on the Pen-y-Turnpike Road.

General Herbert Lee was the last Lord of the Manor, who assumed the title in 1876. He exercised much influence over village affairs for almost 50 years. He was appointed Chairman of the first Parish Council and his death in 1920 brought to a close a long era in the history of the village. Under local government reorganisation in 1974, the Parish Council disappeared and gave way to the now enlarged Dinas Powys Community Council. There is a Parish Hall next to which stands the Lee Hall where much village activity takes place. Young and old alike are well provided with educational activities, clubs, scouts, guides, Sunday School, aerobics, W. I., and sports.

Our Common no longer plays host to Whitsun treats but summer brings the sound of willow striking leather while winter heralds the rugby season with its scrums and tries and the inevitable cuts and bruises. But the women's baseball team, so active in the 1930s, is no more.

Farmer Meredith, complete with long flowing beard, was once a familiar figure as he walked along Murch Road with his herd of cows. Perhaps his ghost still walks over the bridge seeking the pastures that are forever buried beneath supermarket and take-away.

The spirit of the village can be summed up in the Annual Dickensian Evening on the first Friday in December when nearly all the local clubs and organisations are represented at an open air fayre. It is truly well supported by local residents at the various stalls and activities with music by the Ecumenical Seven, and the monies are given to charities.

Dunvant 🦢

A village of Gower, four miles from Swansea, Dunvant is not a picture postcard village, but what it has got is character, and lots of it! The first thing newcomers notice is the great sense of identity and community spirit. What other smallish village can boast a male voice choir of over 100 voices, famous both in Wales and further afield? Or a team doing well in the Second Division of the Welsh Rugby Union? The large Community Centre was built and paid for by the local people, and hosts a variety of activities – including a very lively and flourishing WI.

The fact that this is such a close-knit community stems from the time, many years ago, when this was a mining village, with almost all families having someone working down the pit. The hardships and disasters these folk suffered drew them closer together. People still talk of the awful day in 1924 when Killan Colliery flooded, with the loss of five lives.

There was another unusual industry here too, in those days. There was a laverbread factory, where the seaweed brought from Cumberland was processed, ready for sale in Swansea Market.

One of Dunvant's most famous sons was the internationally known painter Ceri Richards. He was born in 1903 and left Dunvant at the age of 21 to study at the Royal College of Art in London. He became a teacher, but spent his spare time producing art which in the 1960s began to attract world-wide attention. His themes grew out of his love for music, nature and what he saw of life around him. He was influenced by the work of Matisse but in 1936 became a member of the British Surrealist Group. Richards' international reputation owes much to his series of paintings based on the poetry of Dylan Thomas. He lived in London for most of his later life but he frequently returned to Swansea and often incorporated Gower features in his paintings. He died on 9th November 1971. A Ceri Richards Festival is held here biennially. This is a week of cultural and recreational activities and everyone in the village pulls together to make it a resounding success.

Dunvant is a very pleasant village in which to live, and has the added advantage of being near Swansea and all the delights of the Gower Peninsula.

Ewenny 🦋

Ewenny is a village one can seek when journeying from Cowbridge to Bridgend. At the very mention of its name, Ewenny Priory and Ewenny Potteries immediately spring to one's mind.

The river Ewenny, a tributary of the river Ogwr, glides by the village and priory. Maurice de Londres, son of William de Londres, is credited with the founding of the abbey in the 12th century, William building the neighbouring castle of Ogmore.

It can be said that the monks knew how to build their monasteries in pleasant and convenient places. The Benedictine priory was built near a stream where fish were to be caught in the clean waters and all around were fruitful orchards, thick wooded areas and green meadows.

The priory was considered a fine example of a fortified monastic building and remained in existence from its foundation to the dissolution of the monasteries under Henry VIII. The nave of the priory church is today Ewenny parish church, the remaining buildings, ruins and crenellated walls are in the care of Cadw.

The Ewenny Potteries were in existence in the early 17th century and the family of 'potters' working at the Potteries today are the seventh generation. Visitors are welcome and can see the potter's wheel in action.

Ferndale 🦋

The town of Ferndale lies at the top of the Rhondda Fach valley, some ten miles from Pontypridd, and has a population of about 5,000. When it was a very small village its original name was Glynrhedyn, but it was changed to Ferndale by a coal owner after 1850 when four pits were sunk there. Today all the pits have closed.

In 1867 the worse pit disaster in Rhondda's history occurred when 178 miners were killed in No 1 Pit, and again in 1869 in the same pit 68 miners lost their lives. In memorial to these men, in 1988 a garden of remembrance was established on the site of the old colliery.

A massive shale tip near where some of the colleries stood, was known locally as the Banana tip because of its shape. This area has been reclaimed for industry and recreation and is known as Oakland Park. The other light industries in Ferndale are on the Highfield Estate.

Garden Village 🌿

Halfway between Swansea and Llanelli, Garden Village was built by a syndicate of Gorseinon businessmen and shares were bought at £10. The first house foundation was built on 23rd October 1913 at No. 1 Garden Crescent. The foundation stone was laid by Mr John Glasbrook (a Gorseinon coal magnate).

The Bryngwyn steel and sheet mills were built in 1908 and around 1911 the Mardy tinworks followed. Local businessmen knew that houses were needed for people working at these mines and Garden Village was built for this purpose.

The Mardy tinworks lies parallel with the railway (used to transport coal, tin and steel to Swansea Docks). Houses were built running parallel to this railway, namely Clos-y-Mardy and Clos Melyn Mynach, the latter named after Monks Mill which was situated behind today's Gateway superstore.

Monks Mill was owned by William Lewis (who hailed from Llandeilo) who was married to Catherine Glasbrook, a member of the wealthy local family. His son, John Lewis, lived in Bryngwyn Hall (a stately mansion) down the lane from Bryngwyn Ave and Ffordd Bryngwyn, which again runs parallel with Clos-y-Mardy and Clos Melyn Mynach. The Monks Mill provided water for the tin plate works. At the rear of the mansion was Bryngwyn Farm, a large farm worked by two brothers, Tom and John Bayswater, in around 1915.

The original plan for Garden Village was for 264 houses to be built in a triangular fashion with two circles. The outer circle would have been Garngoch Terrace and the inner Garden Crescent. The word Garngoch is derived from the common-land nearby where Prince Einon fought his big battle in 1166 and where he was killed. The story was that the common was flowing with blood – hence the 'coch' for blood and 'Garn' would be the hooves of the horses as they were covered in blood.

The church and church hall were intended to be built on a triangular piece of land where the houses are built at Garngoch Terrace, with their backs facing St Paul's Terrace, which would have meant the church would have been situated right in the middle of the village.

John Lewis of Bryngwyn Hall had three daughters and one married a local Dr Thompson – hence Thompson's Court at the top of the village. There are also two fairly new houses adjacent to this court: Llys-Aneurin (Aneurin's Court) and Ffordd Talfan (Talfan's Way) named after a very eloquent family who moved from Alexandra Road, Gorseinon to live in Brynaman between the two wars.

These houses were recognised as the best built in South Wales at that time, as they had cavity walls, were built of brick and enjoyed the luxury of hot and cold water and a bath!

Garw Valley ॐ

The smallest of the three valleys of Ogwr, it lies between the Llynfi and Ogmore Valley, and unlike the other two it is a cul-de-sac valley extending for some five or six miles. It is, for much of its length, just wide enough to accommodate the river and railway line. The road was built into the side of the mountain. Like most of the other valleys of Glamorgan, coal has been its main industry with the major population concentrated around the head of the valley at Pantygog, Pontycymmer and Blaengarw, the sites of several coalmines. Coal production in the valley has now ceased and the ugly black scars of the industry are being removed and grassed over, and the valley restored to its former beauty.

The sides of the upper regions of the valley are very steep and have, during the early part of the century, been planted with coniferous trees. Lower down the valley lies the pretty parish of Llangeinor, the birthplace of Dr Richard Price, one of Wales' most distinguished philosophers. Born at Tynton Farm, Llangeinor, on 23rd February 1723, he was the son of a dissenting minister Rice Price, successor to the Rev Samuel Jones at his Nonconformist Academy at Brynllywarch Farm, Llangynwyd, where young men were prepared for the Ministry. Richard Price was educated at Pentwyn Academy under the care of Samuel Jones. Dr Price was a passionate defender of human rights and deeply committed to Civil Liberty and Parliamentary Reform. Dr Price's *Review of the Principal Questions of Morals* is now widely regarded as a classic of British Moral Philosophy.

Richard Price was the pioneer of Life Assurance and his writings in the field of public finance brought him fame on both sides of the Atlantic. He received the Freedom of the City of London on 14th March 1776 and in October 1778 Congress invited him to become a citizen of the United States of America. Dr Price died in London on 19th April 1791 and lies buried in Bunhill Fields. As a tribute to one of Wales' greatest sons the Richard Price Centre was built in the village of Llangeinor by the local authority in 1976 and is used for leisure and recreational purposes.

At the foot of the valley tucked away beside the river Garw, is a secluded and self contained world of woods, grassland and formal gardens, where you can walk, picnic alongside the river or simply relax in tranquil surroundings at Bryngarw Country Park, Brynmenyn. On approaching the park, one has the feel of grandeur with the Lodge at the entrance gates, formerly the home of the game-keeper, an ornamental lake with several species of wildfowl, and immaculate gardens adorning the driveway leading to a handsome country house dating back to the 18th century. The house was the country residence of the Traherne family, a local landowning family of some importance, who accumulated great wealth from leasing out land for collieries, ironworks and mills during the Industrial Revolution. It is to the last of the Traherne family, Captain Onslow Powell Traherne, that we owe thanks for the Bryngarw that we admire today. It was he who was largely responsible for the beautiful landscaping of the grounds and the planting of the park's exceptional variety of exotic trees, rhododendrons, azaleas and magnolias. Bryngarw is a country park full of scenic contrast throughout the seasons. Within its 113 acres, the park offers a wide choice of walks or rambles through woodlands or wetlands, meadows or formal gardens.

The Traherne family had close connections with the church where several members of the family are buried in the crypt. The church in the centre of the village of Bettws, a little more than a mile from the park possibly dates back to 1104. A stone dated 1189 still remains in the church. Bettws church has many interesting features, including 'leper windows' or squints in the wall on the northern side. Leprosy was quite a common disease in the Britain of those far off days, and the unfortunate sufferers had to watch the services from these small windows away from the main body of the congregation. The church also has a piscina on the south side of the sanctuary, and a very interesting weather vane, shaped as a fish, which was one of the earliest symbols of Christianity. There are only four or five such weather vanes left in the country. The tower is a vantage point from where one can see seven other church towers.

In 1944 Captain Onslow Powell Traherne retired to a small cottage on the outskirts of the estate and Bryngarw was then purchased and occupied by Mr R S Hayes and his family.

In 1961 the house and grounds of Bryngarw were sold and passed into public ownership. By 1980 the local borough council realised Bryngarw's great potential for countryside recreation, and it was designated a Country Park and opened to the public in 1986.

Glais ✒

At the beginning of the 20th century Glais was a small village, but a village of great geological and geographical significance. It is a village on the track of a moving glacier, built upon the resulting moraine known as 'Y Garth' meaning hillock.

According to learned opinion this moraine is one of the finest examples of its kind in the country, some even claim it is the finest in Europe. Today on this moraine are the ruins of a drift mine, a couple of farms and an old cottage, the home of a Welsh Dissenters' chapel named Pentwyn dating back to 1834. The namestone was later placed in a new chapel called Seion which is still the present place of worship. So Glais can boast a Congregational chapel which is now 155 years old, an Anglican church of 110 years, a Baptist chapel of 100 years and not forgetting the village school aged 110 years. It is very worth noting that when the centenary of Seion Chapel was celebrated in 1934 a congregation of 2,000 gathered for the evening service. This necessitated holding this service not in the chapel but on the 'Mond' field.

In addition to its geological importance, Glais was a lively culturally rich community. It boasted an active chapel life, eisteddfodau, choral singing by Glais United Choir, Seion Juvenile Choir, ambulance classes, evening classes for girls etc.

One of the important events was the Whitsun Teas. The three churches united in a service, followed by a parade of witness around the village. Each contingent was led by the older boys carrying their respective banners. This was followed by a special tea and then sports on the school field. For many years some churches from Swansea chose to come to Glais for their annual tea outing.

In the early years, farmers travelled on horseback to their Sunday services or to conduct their business in other areas. Cattle was often driven from areas such as Llandeilo which was across the mountain to Graig Cefn Parc and then to Glais to be kept in cattle pens, located near the centre of the village, from there to be collected and driven to the new owner's farm.

Milk was transported by horse drawn floats and measured from the churn into your jug on your own doorstep. The farmer himself would always have time for a little chat and would pass on any news he had gleaned on his 'round'. Among others who delivered their wares by horse and cart was the 'oil and hardware' man. When he had completed his tour of the village he would tether the animal outside the pub where an iron ring was built into the wall of the building for the purpose of tying up the horse whilst the boss refreshed himself.

Glais also boasted a racecourse. Horseracing was very popular and attracted crowds from quite widespread areas. After the horseracing era there was a period of greyhound racing.

Tragedies too are remembered. Two village men were victims of the sinking of the *Titanic*. There were also losses of young men during the Second World War. But of significant importance was the capture by a local farmer of four prisoners of war who had escaped from a camp at Bridgend. They had made their way across country and ended their journey on a mountain above the village. They were escorted into the village and then to the post office where they were glad to be handed over to the police.

Glyn Neath

Glyn Neath is situated at the head of the Neath Valley, very near to the point where the boundaries of the counties of West Glamorgan, Mid Glamorgan and Powys meet. The Neath Valley has long been deemed one of the most beautiful valleys in South Wales. In 1797 William Weston Young settled in the area and in 1835 published his greatly valued book *A Guide to the Scenery etc of Glyn Neath*, Glyn Neath in this context meaning the Vale of Neath. The book, illustrated by William Weston Young, extols the beauty of the rivers, waterfalls and countryside of the area of what is now Glyn Neath.

In 1791 the Neath Canal Act began a process of change in the valley and an acceleration in its industrial development. A canal, ten and a half miles long, was constructed and, because it was then easier to transport coal down to the coast for export, many coal-bearing areas were leased out to prospectors. Cottage industries disappeared and large scale deep mining began. Although there were other works e.g. brick works and powder works (the latter making gun powder, not cosmetics!) mining was the principal occupation in Glyn Neath for many years. Deep mining is now, however, an industry of the past, although there are still a few small private mines.

At one time Glyn Neath supported many small shops – a jeweller, furniture store, several butchers and grocers, shoe shops etc but sadly these have almost all disappeared.

The largest local estate was that of Aberpergwm, where the Williams family lived for four centuries. Very little of the house remains. It has suffered the depredations of 20th century vandals, after being empty for several years. When Cromwell marched through this area on his way to Ireland he spared the Royalist house of Aberpergwm because he himself was a Williams and a kinsman, or so the story goes. Aberpergwm was the home of the last domestic bard in Wales.

He was David Nicholas, a scholar and poet who translated the *Iliad* into Welsh. He lived with the Williams family for 40 years and is buried in the church on the estate. The church itself is very interesting and the West Glamorgan environment director has recommended that St Cadoc's at Aberpergwm deserves listing by Cadw, Welsh Historic Monuments. The most well known member of the Williams family was Jane Williams, the musician. She assiduously collected the folk songs of the area and the collection *Ancient Airs of Gwent and Morgannwg* published in 1838, remains a treasure for present day musicians.

There is some uncertainty as to what the future will hold for Glyn Neath and its valley. On the one hand British Coal plans to open-cast mine each side of the valley which will inevitably result in destruction of the beauty enjoyed by previous generations. On the other hand the area is also being designated for the further development of tourism. We can only hope for the one which will have the least harmful effect on what is truly a beautiful part of Wales.

Gwaelod-y-Garth 🌿

Gwaelod-y-Garth is a conservation village situated across the river Taff from Taffs Well, six miles from both Cardiff and Pontypridd. It lies at the foot of the Garth Mountain as is indicated by its name and is part of the community of Pentyrch. The Garth provided livelihood for local people through its many coal levels, in use since the 1700s. Three were still being worked until the beginning of the 20th century.

Gwaelod-y-Garth was made a conservation village mainly because of the row of miners' stone cottages, many of them being more than 150 years old. The old schoolhouse can still be seen in School Lane with its circular window but the school was replaced by the present primary school (originally a Board school) in the early 19th century. The Garth Inn was also built in the early 19th century and has known some interesting characters as landlords. One of these was Dai Peters, a past Welsh Light Heavyweight champion who gave boxing lessons from the pub.

There were three places of worship in the village, a tin-roofed chapel by the side of the stream under Ty Newydd, Salem the Welsh Baptist chapel and Bethlehem. The small tin-roofed chapel has now been demolished, Salem has closed due to poor attendance and lack of funds and is now a listed building and a private house. Sadly, only Bethlehem remains as an integral part of the village. There is no longer a choir although in the past the choir was well known and sang in the Cory Hall and the Dramatic Society no longer exists either, but Bethlehem still thrives and the singing at Gymanfa Canu can be heard from afar.

There have been many well known characters in the village but in more recent years the best known were John Thomas, the harp maker and Arthur Miles, the water colourist who painted beautiful pictures of local scenes.

The Heath

The Heath is approximately one mile from Cardiff and probably derives its name from a tract of waste land – common land known as Little and Great Heaths. The land was partly woods and farmlands comprising Heath Park wood, Heath wood and Prosser wood. During the Second World War an army camp was sited at The Heath, which was taken over by Cardiff City Council and used as a Teacher Training College.

A site at Heath Park was chosen for the University Hospital of Wales, known locally as The Heath Hospital. Opened in 1971, the hospital comprised 800 beds with a clinical medical school, plus a dental hospital and dental school. A combined Training Institute was built to provide centralized training facilities for nurses and all other paramedical disciplines. It is still a centre of excellence.

Getting to school was quite an adventure in the 1930s. The train puffed and whistled through town and country. It was ninepence return for a twelve mile journey. The carriages smelled of smoke and above the seats there were pictures of places unheard of. On market days schoolchildren were sometimes accompanied by chickens in boxes carried by buxom country women. Each small station was a blaze of colour in summer with roses.

Back in the 1920s people came from as far away as the Rhondda Valley to spend a day at Roath Park. There were facilities for boating, swimming, tennis and bowls and a large area known locally as 'the rec' where children of all ages could play.

There were very few cars on the roads in those days, so many children stood on the pavement and wrote down car numbers. Imagine trying to do that today!

Kenfig

The name Kenfig is thought to be derived from the Welsh 'Cefn Y Figen' a ridge or land rising above marshy ground. Kenfig, a small village between Pyle and Porthcawl wasn't always so. In the 12th century it was a medieval borough with a castle and a guildhall and held two fairs a year. The guildhall was a very busy place with its tradesmen, tanners, smiths, bakers, armourers, chandlers, butchers, brewers and many others. The first parish church of Kenfig was built in 1147–1154 and was known as the church of St James.

By 1316 the encroachment of sand was gradually overwhelming the town. The castle was probably destroyed in the 15th century by the forces of Owen Glyndwr. In 1607 further inroads of sand severely affected the coast and by 1634 only four families were recorded living near the site of the castle.

Kenfig today is a very beautiful place. The dunes and Kenfig pool are managed as a local Nature Reserve and have hundreds of visitors a year. The pool itself covers about 70 acres and attracts a variety of wildfowl in large numbers, including teal, coot, moorhen, tufted duck, great crested grebe, whooper and Bewick swans. The dunes in spring and summer are full of colour with wild flowers and grasses. Also many varieties of orchid are to be found from May onwards. Dewberries and blackberries are there for the picking in August and September and people from all over the world come to study the rare dragonflies to be found here.

The ancient borough of Kenfig, which had been in existence for over

Kenfig Castle

seven centuries, virtually came to an end when its corporation was dissolved in 1886 as a result of The Municipal Corporations Act of 1883. The Kenfig Trust was then set up with twelve men forming a committee to administer the borough's property. The Trust is still in existence today.

One of the properties of the Trust is the Prince of Wales inn which houses the guildhall on the first floor and is regularly used for meetings by the trustees. The Borough Mace and a set of weights and a copper measure are now held in the Welsh Folk Museum at St Fagans. A replica of the Borough Mace can be seen at the Prince of Wales inn.

Kenfig Hill 🐑

Mynydd Cynffig is the Welsh name for Kenfig Hill. This is a fairly large village situated about four miles north of Porthcawl and about eight miles east of Port Talbot. The B4281 road passes through the village to join the A48 road at Pyle.

As with other villages in the area, its main industry was coal mining. There were quite a few farms and smallholdings, which also provided some employment, but coal mining was the main source of income for most families. One of these mines was called Park Slip which was sited about two miles from the village. On the morning of Friday, 26th August 1892, a terrible explosion at this mine brought a sudden end to the lives of many of its workmen. Those who had been seriously injured were to join the ranks of the dead within a matter of days, bringing the total number of fatalities to 112. Apart from the indescribable grief borne by the bereaved, one can only imagine the hardship and poverty endured by so many families after the loss of the beloved breadwinner, be it husband or sons and in some instances, both. The full account of this major mining disaster has been very well documented by Mr Neville Granville, his book is entitled *The Park Slip Explosion*. Exactly one hundred years to the day a new memorial was unveiled to the memory of those who died. We are told this is now sited on what was the entrance to the mine.

Gradually, since the mid 1960s, all the mines within and around the area have been closed. The last three were Aberbaiden, Newlands and Pentre.

In days gone by local bakers allowed customers to bake their Christmas yeast cakes in the bakery ovens one week before the special day. Most homes in the village had a Christmas goose, which was cooked before the fire, suspended from a brass 'jack' which would slowly rotate. Usually it was the children who took turns basting the bird.

Like villages everywhere we had our share of 'characters'. One such was an undertaker, who, after giving his price for a good oak coffin to a prospective buyer, was told that the district's other undertaker was £5 cheaper. 'Oh yes,' came the reply, 'well I can tell you now, I'll give you three months in that cheap old coffin, by then your behind will be through it!'

A chapel minister who was not quite as long winded as his fellow ministers, particularly at funerals, was appreciatively referred to as being 'very much more dispatchable'.

Our village of Mynydd Cynffig is still a friendly place to live. As one resident stated: 'Where else can you go out to buy half a pound of butter and be out enjoying yourself for two hours!'

Pyle, which is the next village to the south (just one mile away) has for many years had a through main road from London to West Wales. Pyle Inn was a well used stop and hostelry for passengers and Royal Mail Coaches. One of the inn's most famous guests was Admiral Lord Nelson. He is reputed to have stayed there when he visited Milford Haven. Pyle Inn was demolished about 1970.

Laleston

Laleston is between Porthcawl and Bridgend. The first two buildings in Laleston were the church and Great House Farm. This farm had the cow shed actually attached to the living quarters or kitchen of the house. During the winter months there were twelve cows in day and night, a most unusual but effective form of central heating when the body temperature of the animals penetrated the four foot thick walls.

The Blandy Hall, as it is called today, was left to the village as a Community Centre. It was the changing rooms for the football and cricket teams. The Rifle Club met there and it was the monthly meeting place of the old Parish Council, which is now the Community Council.

The most important feature of the village before 1928 was the well, the only means of water supply for the village. There are 14 steps going down to the bottom and the water has been down to the number 13 during some of the very dry summers. Water was rationed to two gallons per house. This was distributed between ten and eleven o'clock in the morning, then the well would be locked until the next day. Water for washing clothes etc was obtained from two ponds at Broadlands. It was the task for children after school to go with five gallon earthenware pitchers in home-made hand trucks to collect this.

Then in the late 1920s and early 1930s piped water was brought to the village, followed very soon by mains electricity.

The school up until 1927 was in what is now known as the church hall. The annexe at the back was the infants and the main hall the juniors. The average number of infants was 26 and the average number of juniors was 64. It was, up until 1927, a Church of England school and the sole Governor was the Rector, later Canon of Newcastle, Bridgend.

There were no partitions in the junior section and the only divisions were made by sitting back to back. Then in June 1927 the new school was opened and this came under the Glamorgan County Council.

Lavernock

Lavernock is a very small village on the outskirts of Penarth, and near to Sully, overlooking the Bristol Channel. There is a pleasant coastal walk from Penarth cliff top to Lavernock Point. It was on the 18th May 1897 that Guglielmo Marconi, assisted by a Cardiff Post Office engineer George Kemp, transmitted the very first message by wireless telegraphy across the water between the Flat Holm Island and Lavernock Point, a distance of 3½ miles.

Close by is the new housing development named Lavernock Park, opposite which is the superb Cosmeston Country Park which includes a reconstructed medieval village and a lake formed by flooding the quarries of the now closed cement works. The lake attracts water birds and enhances a very attractive park adjacent to the Glamorganshire Golf Club.

Leckwith

Leckwith is a small village which possibly derives its name from Llech-wedd, meaning a hillside. It is on the B4267 road leading towards Cardiff and is two miles from the city.

Pretty cottages once bordered the road by The Gower but they made way for road widening schemes. Attractive houses were built further back, overlooking what is now Leckwith Green. Here it is very pleasant walking country and on leaving Leckwith village, hidden away off the main road, is Ynyston Farm, standing empty and forlorn. Presumably its fate will be the same as so many other farms today and become a site for housing development. Ynyston Farm served Llandough and Leckwith people daily with their milk, which was put into milk churns, placed on a horse-drawn cart and delivered by Mr Coles and later by his family. On hearing the sound of the horses' hooves, the villagers would appear with their milk jugs and the milk was measured accordingly into them.

The Woodlands Nursing Home is also set back from the road. It was once the Shirley's family home and later used by the University of Wales for residential and study purposes.

Go to the summit of Leckwith Hill to enjoy the views across the Bristol Channel and Penarth Head. Travel down Leckwith Hill to see and enjoy the marvellous panoramic view of Cardiff, the Capital of Wales, and its surroundings. Midway on the hill and partly hidden under the bank is Factory House, purported to be a woollen factory in days gone by. Leckwith Hill leads to Leckwith Common. Sadly the common, where horses used to roam, has gone and all one sees now is a sports stadium, warehouses and offices.

Lisvane

The village of Lisvane is situated to the north east of Cardiff in the shadow of the Graig Mountain. It has an agricultural background and although it now serves as a commuter suburb for Cardiff, there are still farms in the area.

The church of St Denys is an ancient building in the Early English style.

Opposite the church is the Griffin Inn where Oliver Cromwell, who had relatives in Lisvane, is reputed to have stayed overnight.

Although in the past 50 years the population has increased from 1,000 to 4,000, Lisvane still retains a feeling of ocmmunity, with various flourishing societies and a well-established festival held in June. Lisvane was an agricultural area. One resident remembers life on the farm there.

'We learned at a very early age to turn the handle of the churn to make butter once a week and wash and dry the vats to make cheese. The whey and buttermilk was fed to the pigs.

We learned the importance and value of herbs: the right way and time of the year to gather them. We made our own bread (once a week). The flour was bought in large quantities that came in large flour bags. When the bags were empty, they were washed and dried and they were used to gather elderflowers in – that was in May or June. The flowers we then laid out on paper to dry. Later on, in July and August, we gathered centaury, agrimony and yarrow, three valuable herbs.'

Llanblethian 🌿

Llanblethian is said to have derived its name from St Bleddian, a Bishop from France. A most attractive and ancient village, it is a fine community in the heart of the Vale of Glamorgan, with the M4 and Cardiff-Wales Airport easily accessible.

There are lovely countryside walks around Llanblethian which take in the 18th century Great House, the wool factory (now a large dwelling house), terraced cottages, the remains of St Quentin's Castle, the kissing gate near the old village pump, the church cottages and the church of St John the Baptist.

Wander off into the country lanes to find Llanfrynach, and the ancient church of St Brynach which stands alone in the fields. Its village, it is said, was destroyed in the rebellions of Owen Glyndwr. Search in the hedgerows for the coffin stiles, two in number, so called because they are double stiles with a central resting place of stone on which the coffin was rested whilst the bearers climbed over the stiles. The church has a south porch with very low entrance, no east window, and a stone bench on either side of the nave where the old and infirm would have rested during the service.

There are seven listed buildings of special historic or architectural interest scattered within the intricate maze of narrow lanes that climb the hillside, which adds to the charm of the village, offering unexpected vistas as one rounds a corner. Llanblethian pre-dates the Romans. There was a large Iron Age settlement at Caer Dynnaf on Llanblethian Hill. A hill fort was also built there by a local Celtic tribe, known as Silures.

The parish church is St John the Baptist. Standing high above the village, the main part of the church was built between the 13th and 15th centuries, with its very fine tower dated 1477, a gift of Anne, the Lady of Glamorgan and wife of Richard III. The font and some of the masonry are of Sutton stone. It also houses a pewter chalice, thought to date back to Elizabethan times.

The church overlooks a small green upon which is sited the remains of a medieval roadside cross.

The old village is dominated by the massive ruins of the 13th century

Llanblethian Castle and the river Thaw can be seen wandering through rich pasture land. The river is fed by fresh springs from Bowman's Well and Factory Brook, once used by the woollen mill, hence its name. The workers' cottages are still lived in to this day.

Llancarfan 🐚

Llancarfan is set amidst a steeply wooded valley some two miles or so from Bonvilston and is in the Vale of Glamorgan. One assumes its name derives from the 'Llan' – land around the church, the river Nant Garman and the brook Nant Carfan.

Llancarfan was one of three principal monastic communities existing in Glamorgan. The monastery was headed by St Cattwg, a saint of great reputation. The present church at Llancarfan, dating from the 14th and 15th century, is dedicated to St. Cattwg and was once the largest parish church in Glamorgan.

Llancarfan came into the possession of Blondel de Mapes and it was he who married the daughter of its Welsh Lord. Walter de Mapes, their son, became Archdeacon of Oxford and Chaplain to Henry I. In his youth he translated *The Chronicle of the Kings* from Welsh into Latin and in his latter days he re-translated the Latin version into Welsh with additions of his own.

Caradoc, a learned monk who was born at Llancarfan and lived at the same time as Walter de Mapes, was believed to have written parts of '*The Chronicle of Princes*', a history of Wales from 686–1157.

Iolo Morganwg was the bardic name of Edward Williams (1747–1826). He was born at Penon' Llancarfan and earned a great reputation for his transcriptions of Welsh manuscripts.

The pretty brook which runs through the village was once the scene of much local industry, powering four mills at one time. One was used for the locally grown corn and another for its wool, woven into cloth. In monastic times Llancarfan was famous for its cloth and breeches.

Strolling through this picturesque village one finds the church hall, once the old poor house, the 19th century Bethlehem Chapel, now converted to a dwelling house. The building which was once the old blacksmith's and the 18th century Fox and Hounds are situated within walking distance of the ripple of the brook. Close to the village is the old Corn Mill, renovated now to a house incorporating the old mill wheel. Leaving Llancarfan behind and climbing the steep hill to Pancross one can enjoy a very fine view of the village.

Llandarcy

Llandarcy village is unique having been built in 1921 by the Anglo Persian Oil Co. (now BP). Its name commemorates not a Celtic saint, but an oil concessionaire. Although we were truly rural, in those early days we were surrounded by various industries, oil refinery, copper and tin works, coal mines etc.

In the very early days the population of the village was 99% Scots, but as time went by they were joined by Welsh, Irish and English families and so we became a British international community, absorbing each other's culture, songs, dances, literature and customs.

We have a village green and sported a bandstand complete with silver band. We also had a maypole.

Homes and the two roads which make up the village were lit by gas until 1937. Our milk was delivered daily by local farmers and arrived by horse and float, the delicious creamy milk being ladled from churns into jugs. Llandarcy also boasted policemen, including an Inspector. A very orderly village!

Most activities centred round the Institute: dances, whist drives, concerts, fruit, vegetable and flower shows, and WI, scouts, cubs, guides and brownies.

We also had a shop which sold practically everything. Local tradesmen from Skewen called regularly bringing fish, meat, fruit and vegetables, paraffin oil and seed for people who kept poultry. Then there was the man who sharpened knives, scissors and axes and the 'onion johnnies' with their bicycles festooned with strings of onions.

Church services were held every Sunday in the Institute and conducted by a member of TOC H. In later years either the vicar or the curate fron St John's church in Skewen would attend for those wishing to take communion.

There are happy memories of Sunday school outings to seaside and pantomime, Whitsun teas and sports, Nativity plays with every child playing their part. Long lazy summer days were for listening to sounds of haymaking and picnicking in one of the many surrounding fields.

Then as autumn and winter came there was the Halloween party and ducking for apples. This was held by the W I for the children and, as Christmas drew near, a grand party with a Christmas tree, and gifts for every child presented by Santa Claus. If we had a heavy snowfall out would come the sledges, or failing them, large tin trays.

In 1945 King George VI visited the refinery and Queen Elizabeth toured the village speaking to many of the residents. She was most impressed with the Institute and very interested to hear of all the activities taking place there.

From the early 1950s onwards more people became car owners and so gradually our lovely summer Sunday coach trips to Gower, Porthcawl or Barry ceased. No more piling children, food and extra clothing onto the coach. And of course there was the obligatory stop on the homeward journey for chips.

Now Llandarcy has been designated a conservation area. Sounds well, but although we still have our red Edward VII post box and red telephone kiosk, we are minus shop and church, and sadly our close sense of belonging is a thing of the past.

Llanddewi with Knelston

Llanddewi and Knelston are two small neighbouring villages situated about 15 miles south west of Swansea on the Gower peninsula – an area of outstanding natural beauty.

Llanddewi is a farming community with a small caravan site and farm museum for tourists. Some farms offer bed and breakfast accommodation.

The church of St David stands on the brow of the hill amongst farm buildings. It has a low corbelled west tower with a transverse saddleback roof and was built in the 13th century; however there is a small Norman window on the north wall and it has a Norman tub font. Llanddewi means David's church, or church of David.

Knelston has no industry apart from farming with a small permanent caravan site for holidaymakers. It has a chapel – English Baptist built in the mid 1880s.

Ploughing has for centuries been part of the rural scene, the traditional image is one of a gently plodding pair of shire horses beneath a blue sky on a fine autumn day with screeching white gulls overhead following the plough. Today those gulls are more likely to accompany a gleaming monster tractor.

The original idea underlying ploughing competitions was to provide an interest for those directly involved with farming, but today townspeople are encouraged to attend and appear especially attracted to the horse ploughing. The West Gower Ploughing Society was founded in 1941 and their first match involved both horse and tractor ploughing. However, during the next two decades the numbers of tractors increased while the horse teams became fewer until in 1958 at a ploughing match held at

Harding's Down, Llangennith, the last horse class was won by Mr David Davies of Betlands Farm, Llanddewi. Unfortunately, the horses were becoming too old to compete, rather than the ploughmen. It was to be nearly a quarter of a century later in 1982 that horse teams again competed in West Gower.

Llandough (Cowbridge) 🐏

Llandough by Cowbridge (pronounced Llandoff) is a pretty village situated on the slope of a wooded hill overlooking the valley of the Thaw. Inside the church of St Dochau, situated within the fragmented walls of the once medieval Llandough Castle, is a rather sad memorial to the three children of the Bassett family who died within one month of one another. There was William, 18 years old, who died 3rd March, John, 23 years old, who died 17th March and Friswith, 26 years old, who died 16th April – all in the year 1713.

The Rev John Walters, rector of the parish in the 18th century was the famous lexicographer, who published an English-Welsh dictionary, the first part of which was printed at Cowbridge in 1770.

Llandough (Penarth) 🐏

The name Llandough (in Welsh Llandochau) is derived from 'Llan', area around a church and 'dough' from St Dochau.

Llandough, a village two miles distance from Penarth, was in the last century a quiet Welsh speaking rural farming and fishing village.

During the early Christian period there were three principal monastic communities existing in Glamorgan, one of which was Llandough, the others Llantwit Major and Llancarfan. At Llandough churchyard is the highly decorated Irbic Cross – the Celtic pillar cross dating from the early 9th century. A replica can be seen at the National Museum of Wales.

St Dochdwy's church dates from 1866, built at a cost of some £3,000. The previous church on this site was taken down and rebuilt at Leckwith – St James. Inside St Dochdwy's is a Father Willis organ.

Alongside the church once stood Great House Farm, the site of a Celtic monastery and a missionary centre. In 1974, 1,700 people signed a petition for the preservation of this farm where a wealth of history lay hidden. It was the home of Mr John Williams' family for generations and was opened on occasions for local people, schoolchildren and visitors to view. Work was undertaken to replace the stone floor with timber. Underneath the floor in the elegant dining room were found the remains of a soldier and his horse. This suggested there may have been a battle on the site and the soldier was buried where he lay in his armour. The remains were re-buried in the churchyard and his visor and lance given to the National Museum of Wales. Visitors to the farm saw how people lived in the past, how they made their butter, cheese and beer and dried pork, and sent their sheep's wool to the woollen mill on Leckwith Hill for spinning into yarn. They saw the cheese drying room hollowed out of a solid wall and the bedroom where in earlier centuries monks took rest on their travels. Marconi too slept here in a four poster bed whilst working with his experiments in wireless telegraphy between the Flat Holm and Lavernock Point. Great House Farm was demolished during the night of 6th December 1988 by British Petroleum Pension Funds following a 33 year dispute over its ownership. Today the site is overgrown, awaiting housing development.

In 1960 Llandough was expanding rapidly. Houses were built on fields where cattle and sheep once grazed. An action group was formed for a school, urgently needed. Numerous letters to the House of Commons resulted in Mr Anthony Crosland, the then Secretary of State for Education and Science granting permission for a school which was officially opened by the Rt Hon James Callaghan, MP for Cardiff, on 16th October 1970, quite different from the first National school which served both Llandough and Penarth, known as the Old School House and now a listed building and private house.

The Marchioness of Bute performed the opening ceremony of Llandough and Leckwith War Memorial Institute on the 11th November 1924. It was built from contributions given by families living in the two villages. Fifty years later the institute was replaced by a new hall formally opened by Sir Cennydd Traherne. Both the old and the new institute have been used for almost every village function, with the exception of the Second World War years when the building was used by the Royal Air Force. During the war an anti-aircraft battery and a balloon barrage unit were situated in the village. Often smoke screen motors came out to throw smoke screens over Cardiff.

The Llandough Scout and Guide Association used the institute until 1975 when they moved to their newly built centre at Lewis Road. Behind the institute stands the Llandough and Leckwith British Legion Club.

Her Royal Highness Mary Viscountess Lascelles laid the foundation stone for Llandough hospital in 1928. The land was purchased by the Cardiff Board of Governors in 1912, but building was postponed because of the First World War. Alderman Donovan officially opened the hospital in 1933 with 340 beds, capable of future extension to 916 beds.

In 1946 the Medical Research Council commissioned a ward for investigation into pneumoconiosis, of great concern to the mining industry. Mabon, the miners' ward, remained open until 1986. The hospital is generously supported by its League of Friends. Close by is St Mary's Day Hospital, opened in 1905 as an isolation hospital.

In 1543 King Henry VIII granted the Mansion of Llandough to Lord Clynton. In 1793 it was purchased by the Earl of Bute and Cogan Pill House was occupied in 1851 by Mr and Mrs John Stuart Corbett and their four children.

The harvest festival was always a great event, followed by a large gathering at Cogan Pill House where there was a supper with beer, whisky and cigars. On New Year's Day the local children used to visit Cogan Pill to sing carols. This custom was carried on until the late 1940s, the number decreasing from about 200 to a handful of small children. Finally no one thought it was worth singing anymore for buns or pennies. The house remained in the Corbett family until the late 1960s when it became the Elizabethan Restaurant and is known today as the Baron's Court Restaurant and public house. There are memorial windows and plaques to the Corbett family at St Dochdwy's church.

In 1979 the site of a Roman villa was uncovered in the centre of the village when a Housing Association commenced work for blocks of flats. The Glamorgan and Gwent Archaeological Trust Ltd started excavations, assisted by many interested individuals. It was to be a very exciting find when indications were that the villa stood on the site between the second half of the 2nd century AD and the middle of the 4th century AD. A skeleton, skull and bones were found. The Romano-British family, possibly farmers, must have enjoyed excellent living conditions. The buildings were built of mortar, the roofs consisted of red pottery tiles and pennant sandstone.

The walls were rendered with plaster and decorated. The floors consisted of red mortar made of crushed tiles and bricks. The main living quarters were found and also a well preserved sunken bath. The site was of national importance. A last minute bid to save this unique villa proved unsuccessful and the blocks of flats were built.

Llangan 🌿

Llangan, situated four miles from Cowbridge, has been populated since the Bronze Age. The Romans were attracted here because of the presence of lead ore, and mining continued for centuries. Lead mine stack and underground shafts remain to this day. A Roman burial ground has been found near Llangan School.

Prominent is the parish church, St Canna, dedicated to a female saint of that name. It dates from the 12th century, but its pre Norman cross shows it was founded earlier. It stands in a peaceful, secluded, shady setting. Its western bellcote contains two bells dated 1450. A stained glass window depicts the Ascension of our Lord and portraits of St Canna and Reverend David Jones. Rev Jones was a strong supporter of the Methodist movement, wrote many hymns and provided funds to build the first Methodist chapel in Glamorgan – Salem, Pencoed. He was described by his followers as a communicative and sensible man with cheerfulness and good humour. Children plucked at his coat to share the good man's smile. Some of his writings are among the best examples of 18th century Welsh prose. Llangan became a famous part of Methodist history.

The churchyard has two crosses, the oldest being a 9th century Celtic wheel cross on which is carved a representation of the Crucifixion, and on the reverse side is a plain Greek cross, illustrating its antiquity. There is only one other such cross in Wales and that is at Meifod. The other cross is a 15th century churchyard cross with elaborate carvings of sacred persons and incidents. Crosses like this, with the heads complete, occur only at Llangan, St Mary Hill and St Donat's. Other interesting features of our little church are an Elizabethan chalice, two fonts of Sutton stone, a silver bread dish, the original brass lamps on pulleys overhanging the altar rail and a statue of the Virgin Mary above the south door.

John Pritchard (1817–86) was born at Llangan where his father was rector of the church. John Pritchard trained to be an architect and in 1847 he became diocesan architect of Llandaff and was responsible for the design of many churches and schools throughout the county as well as a number of houses and public buildings. He was also responsible for the restoration of Llandaff Cathedral between 1844 and 1857 and added the tower and spire at the south-west corner. He was in partnership with J. P. Seddon, a well known Victorian architect, for approximately ten years. Pritchard was buried in the graveyard of Llandaff Cathedral.

The village today looks unchanged to those passing through but more houses, mostly of executive type have been built. A public telephone kiosk and electricity have been installed but no gas to date.

Llangennith 🎵

You will find Llangennith village if you travel 16 miles west of Swansea. Throughout its long history, Llangennith must have had many characters amongst its population, from the crippled child washed up on its shore about the year AD 800 who became Saint Cennydd and gave the village its name, to Phil Tanner, a folk-singer of renown who found fame through the BBC in the last years of a long life.

Born in 1862, he was the youngest of the seven children of Isaac and Jennet Tanner, who were local weavers. As a youth he worked for his father, but broke away to become a farm worker, and for most of his working life he was a 'hedger and ditcher'. Although he was generally available to help out with seasonal jobs on the farms, he always preferred singing to working.

About the age of 22, Phil married Ruth Nicholas, a middle-aged widow with a daughter, who was licensee of the Welcome to Town public house at Llangennith. As husband of the landlady of a village pub he had ample opportunity of learning the old folk-songs and tunes for which he later became famous. When the daughter married a local butcher named Charles Rees, the licence was transferred to him and Phil and Ruth moved to Lower Mill where for a time he operated the mill, grinding barley meal etc. This did not last long, for 1899 saw the introduction of the oil engine to Gower enabling farmers to grind their corn at home, making the old water mills obsolete. Phil returned to farm work and his lovely tenor voice could be heard round the area as he worked in the fields. He was the last of the 'Bidders' in Gower. Dressed neatly with a flower in his coat and a ribbon-decorated walking stick, he would call at the houses and, with a suitable rhyme, bid the villagers to a 'Bidding Wedding'. He would invite them to give or 'heave' a contribution towards setting up the young couple as man and wife. Records of gifts were kept and returned in equal value when a member of the donor's family married.

When Ruth died in 1921, Phil moved to Stormy Castle, a small cottage on the side of Rhossili Down, and continued to collect songs and to perfect a distinctive form of mouth music which became his trade mark. He was a familiar sight as he sat inside or out of the Kings Head, glass in hand, singing the old songs of Gower and beyond to any who would listen.

His memory was phenomenal, and little of his vast repertoire was ever written down. His recitals were always circumspect, certain songs being 'for the boys only'. The *Gower Toast* Phil reserved for 'no ladies in sight'.

He sang to tell a tale not to display his talent.

In the 1940s he was featured in an article in *Picture Post*, and appeared on an *In Town Tonight* broadcast on the BBC where he refused to be hurried, and sang his songs as he had done for over half a century. He eventually recorded 13 of them and achieved fame in his last years.

He died in 1950 aged 88 and is buried in Llangennith churchyard.

Llangyfelach 🦋

Look to the north of Swansea, 5 miles distant and there is the village of Llangyfelach. For centuries Llangyfelach was renowned for its fair, the origin of which was purely religious. On the first and second days of March, a religious festival was held in the church to celebrate the anniversary of the dedication of the church – Gwyl Mabsaint – and to view the relics, namely Cloak, Staff and Bell – deposited there by St David on his return from a pilgrimage to the Holy Land. People from far and wide crowded to Llangyfelach to participate in this festival.

Our village has one church and one chapel. The former is the famous Llangyfelach church on the site of which was once a monastery and it was a seat of learning many centuries ago. The latter, Bethel chapel, was built in 1808 but the original chapel was there many years before that date. Prior to the present day village school being built the children in this area attended school in Bethel chapel vestry.

During the two days when the famous Llangyfelach fair was in progress, parents kept their children at home because it was too danger-ous for them amongst the huge crowds of people who came here. It is estimated that as many as 30,000 people attended. In its heyday the village had as many as five public houses but only a tiny community of houses and outlying farms.

The Llangyfelach Community Council revived the fair in 1988 (it had not been held for many years during this century) but changed the date to 1st May. Every organization in the village has a stall to sell their wares and many dress in old fashioned or traditional Welsh costume. This is now an annual event and has proved successful and most enjoyable.

How customs and life styles have changed during the 20th century! Older members of our community remember going to a 7 am service on Christmas morning, an afternoon tea party for children and grown-ups followed by a concert in the evening. On Boxing Day evening a drama was performed in the vestry of Bethel chapel playing to a full house. The New Year's Eve party was followed by Watch Night service at 11.45 pm.

Our oldest inhabitant, Mrs Sophia Thomas, was post mistress many years ago. She recalls how telegrams had to be delivered on foot or by bicycle throughout the district, sometimes to outlying farms. On one occasion, after travelling a few miles with a telegram the charge of one shilling was not forthcoming. So it was returned to the post office unopened!

Some ladies who are at present between 80 to 95 years of age recall serving apprenticeships in millinery or tailoring in Morriston about two miles from this village. They had to walk back and forth each day to lessons which were from 9 am to 7 pm with a half day on Thursdays and from 9 am to 9 pm on Saturdays. Buses only started running about 1927 and the fare was threepence to Morriston.

Just four generations ago a farmer's daughter from Tir Doncyn Farm and other farmers would travel around by pony and trap selling eggs, butter, vegetables and other farm produce house to house. In the spring-time wild daffodils were picked from the hedgerows and sold to provide pocket money.

The neighbours in Llangyfelach village collected fresh milk from Pen Pant Farm. Mr Garland of Penwain Farm (situated behind the Velindre Tinplate Works) delivered milk to the doorstep until the 1950s.

Mrs Goss travelled each week from Penclawdd to Llangyfelach (no mean achievement many years ago) to sell cockles outside the village post office. She later became the subject of a painting by Evan Walters, Llangyfelach's famous artist. This particular picture now hangs in the Glynn Vivian Art Gallery in Swansea. Evan Walters (1893–1951) bequeathed many of his finest works to the National Museum of Wales, Cardiff where, unfortunately, they seldom see the light of day.

An interesting account appeared in the 1990 Llangyfelach Community Council Christmas Newsletter. It relates how around the year 1875 the method of securing tenancy of a house was by squatters rights. This entailed spending a day and a night in the house and lighting a fire in the hearth. One young couple and their four little daughters needed to move to a healthier location because the husband had contracted tuberculosis. As a result of their exercising squatters rights in Llangyfelach we now have the fifth generation of this family living in that property.

Llangynwyd 🎵

The village of Llangynwyd sits high on a hill near the head of the Llynfi Valley. The church of St Cynwyd was founded in the 6th century and the two olde world inns attract thousands of visitors each year from all over the world. The focal point of the village is undoubtedly the church with its connections with the Rev Samuel Jones, former vicar of the parish who in the 17th century, deprived of his living in the church, set up the first Nonconformist Academy at nearby Brynllywarch Farm, from where Nonconformity spread throughout the valley. Yet, despite the attractions of the quaint village, with its historical and cultural connections with the church, it has become a tourist attraction because it is the setting of one of the best known romances in Welsh history – 'The Maid of Cefn Ydfa' – an 18th century love story.

Ann Thomas, the Maid of Cefn Ydfa, was the daughter of a wealthy farming family. Being an only child and heir to the estate, Ann was expected to marry someone of her own social status. However, Will Hopkin, a local thatcher and poet, was occasionally employed at Cefn Ydfa to repair the roof of the farmhouse and buildings on the estate. Will had a sweet musical voice and the hills of the neighbourhood would echo his songs as he went about his work. It was at Cefn Ydfa one day while singing one of his favourite love songs that Ann, standing nearby, heard him and was delighted with his singing. She immediately fell in love with him, and invited him to stay for supper.

The two lovers saw much of each other in the ensuing weeks, but soon it became apparent to Mrs Thomas, Ann's mother, that the humble thatcher had a deeper place in Ann's affections than she had anticipated. Unfortunately for Will, Ann's mother had promised Anthony Maddocks, a lawyer and son of an adjoining farm that he should have Ann's hand in marriage, and she forbade her daughter to see Will ever again, locking her up in her bedroom. Ann was heartbroken. She wrote love letters to Will and gave them secretly to one of the housemaids to place in the hollow of the sycamore tree from where Will would collect them after dark. It was at this time that Will composed *Bugeilio'r Gwenith Gwyn* (watching the white wheat) which is still part of every Welsh choir's repertoire.

Ann, despite her pleas, was forced to marry Anthony Maddocks, who in the marriage settlement would receive a large portion of the estate of Cefn Ydfa. Ann did not love her new husband and continued to pine for her true love, Will Hopkin. Within two years Ann became ill. The joy and cheerfulness formally characterised in her eyes had been replaced by pale and furrowed cheeks. Her secret sorrow had pierced her heart like a sword, and she could think of no-one but Will, and could stay with her husband no longer.

Ann returned home to Cefn Ydfa, ill and still grieving for Will, who had, the day after the marriage of his beloved Ann, vowed to leave his native homeland for ever, and with tears in his eyes had bade farewell to the place which held so many precious memories for him.

By now Ann's mother had began to regret her cruel treatment of her only child and sought to find Will that his presence would lessen the torment of her dying daughter. Will, it is said, who was now working in Bristol, had a dream that Anthony Maddocks had died and that Ann was now free to marry him. He immediately returned home to Llangynwyd only to find Ann on her deathbed. On his entering the bedroom, the Maid of Cefn Ydfa recognised him and, lifting her body towards him, cried out, 'My dear Will I love you, you are the only object of my affections although I have been forced to marry another. Will, my first and only love, it is sweet to spend the last moments of my life with you'. Will could say nothing, his breast was ready to burst with grief, his eyes full of tears. There was a renewed tenderness in Ann's eyes and voice. The tears rolled freely down Will's cheeks as he bent over the bed and held her in his arms. She rested her head on his arm and gazed up into his face. A heavenly smile came over her face, and the soul that had suffered was freed.

The graves of both Ann and Will Hopkin are to be found at Llangynwyd church. The grave of Ann, the Maid of Cefn Ydfa, is in the chancel of the church, the old memorial stone having been replaced in 1893 by a tablet of marble and brass. Will's grave is under the yew tree at the side of the path in the graveyard. Wheat and sycamore leaves are woven into the design of the gravestones.

Llanharry

Until the closing of the iron ore mine in 1975 it could be truthfully said that the history of the small village of Llanharry had been inextricably linked with iron since the time of the Romans or even earlier.

The first known people to be attracted to these parts were not miners however. A chance archaeological discovery of 1929 proves that the first visitors were a semi nomadic tribe of Bronze Age people known as Beaker Folk. At Naboth's Vineyard, a skeleton of a young man, aged about 35 years, 5ft-9ins tall and broad headed was unearthed, together with the customary beaker pot.

When the Romans came, centuries later, it was the rich iron ore deposits that brought them from their Vale villas and the settlement of Cowbridge. It is possible that the first Christian settlement grew up around a tiny wooden church in the Age of Saints, although whether St Illtud or one of his followers founded the church or whether it is of 12th century date is uncertain.

The Normans made a visible and more lasting impact on the landscape, providing a stone church with a finely decorated font, a fortified manor house at Trecastle and two manors, one of which was partly run along the lines of a typical English manor. The lords of Llanharry lived in the distant comforts of Coity Castle but the lords of Trecastle at least rubbed shoulders with their Welsh peasants in church and in the fields.

By the time of Elizabeth I some of the lords lived further away in Kent, but iron mining was back on the agenda as the Sidneys of Penshurst, foiled by an Act forbidding the felling of timber because of the Spanish threat, exploited the abundance of woodland and high grade ore at Llanharry to great profit and even dug up coal on Llanharry Meadow.

For several centuries life in a rural village changed only slowly, apart from a rude awakening during the Civil War period when Rector Edmund Gamage was unceremoniously ejected from his house and glebe land by the Puritans, who even had the audacity to steal from his tithe barns. Llanharry was to remain a quiet, self sufficient little community of a hundred or so souls, employed in a wide range of rural crafts with two public houses, a mill, a pound, a shop, a washing pool, and by Victoria's reign, a dame school run by the church.

Bigger changes occurred with the rise of Nonconformity that was sweeping over the whole of Wales, but where else was a chapel built as a direct result of a game of football? In Llanharry in the 1820s Penuel was built when local lads were discovered playing 'ungodly games' on the Sabbath and was to remain the spiritual home of the majority of citizens for a century or more.

From the mid 19th century even greater changes were at hand. A mini industrial revolution occurred at Gwaun Llanhari and 'The Patch' with the establishment of a colliery, brick works, coke oven, distillery and iron mines, thanks to the pioneering work of a local farmer William Hopkins and relatively small scale entrepreneurs such as John Bethell and Reuben Plant of Staffordshire. Yet when a well known antiquarian visited the parish in the 1880s he could still describe Llanharry as the place where the cuckoo first sang his song in Glamorgan.

The 20th century saw iron mining come into its own when large scale production was started in 1901. The mine was to last 75 years, becoming eventually the only such mine in Wales. The mine employed the majority of men in a greatly expanding village. It was a happy place to work and has been described as a 'mine without malice' in a local history book. At this time a host of village characters came to the fore, men such as Billo Rosser, Tom Witto, Jack Dawley and Fred Hunt enriched the lives of ordinary mortals with their antics! The mine closed in 1975 and the shock waves extended into nearly every household. It can be truly said that despite being near the M4 motorway and the prosperous Vale of Glamorgan, the ancient mining village is still finding that life without iron in the bloodstream is still far from easy in a harsh economic climate.

Throughout its heyday as an industrial village, farming still continued. One resident remembers life on the farm before the Second World War.

'In those days the work force on the farm consisted of three men, a girl in the house and the family. All lived in and fed mostly off the farm produce. The same farm today is farmed by the farmer and a boy.

'Monday was the day I most disliked as a young worker on the 200 acre farm. It was the day I was sent to work in the farm house. It was the day for washing, baking and butter making.

'My first task on the Monday morning was to fill the boiler with water pumped by hand out of the cistern, then light the fire to heat it. Next the same with the bread oven, after a strict supervision from my grandmother that only ash sticks were used for the baking oven.

'After a hasty breakfast, preparations for churning the cream into butter. The 40 gallon churn fitted in a frame with a handle each side. It took two men to turn it. It could be a monotonous job. In favourable weather conditions one could hear the welcome sound of the butter beginning to flop in the churn, then you knew you were coming to the end of the churning. If there were thundery conditions it could take four to five hours. The buttermilk was then drained and used to feed the pigs. The butter was rolled and patted. Some customers liked salt added, others preferred it plain. It was then weighed into pounds. This butter was taken on Wednesday by train from Llanharry station to Pontypridd and sold in the market.'

Another villager from a farming family recalls that farming was still hard work up to the 1950s. 'One important job on the farm was threshing. It was also a social occasion, for neighbouring farmers would join up and do the work in gangs, helping one another. As many as a dozen men were needed for this operation. You usually had three or four days warning before the threshing machine arrived, giving one time to prepare the food and farm work. The uncertainty of the weather made it a very frustrating operation. Many farmers had up to eight days threshing. Work started about 8.30 am with a tea break mid-morning, a cooked dinner at one o'clock, masses of potatoes and swede or any other vegetable and a small helping of meat, followed by rice pudding. It was hard work, but a happy social occasion.'

Llanmadoc ❧

Once our village green was big enough to play cricket and other games on, now six good strides and you are over it. Our lanes, where one had to run ahead of animal herds to find a niche to step out of the way for them to pass, are now roads where two vehicles can travel abreast.

The dunes on our beaches were once so high it was a joy to slide down them, with sand cascading in all directions. These are now worn flat with the increasing visitors. Small fields have been made bigger by demolishing the hedges. In the old threshing days the excitement started early with the preparation of food, the traction engine rolled up the lane and the house would be full of borrowed labour. Animals were driven to mart by drovers and good dogs. Milk was sent in churns to town by bus. Sunday school treats were taken in loskies to a field where we ate food prepared in advance. There were the monthly visits from the tallyman with a huge pack on his back. The lady of the manor had rules which tenant farmers had to obey without question and her agent would see these orders were carried out.

Post was delivered by the postman and sometimes if he didn't think it was important he would keep it for a few days until it was worth calling.

Milking was done by hand, with all the cows having their special names, and the milk was put in huge bowls for the cream to settle for the butter.

Sunday best outfits were worn for chapel and taken off as soon as you got home. Winter clothes and summer clothes were only changed on 1st June or 1st October. 'Ne'er cast a clout until May is out' always meant the whole month.

There were many old customs peculiar to Llanmadoc and Gower.

One was the Pillory Hole, an opening in the church where the rood stood (rood being crucifix), and was used as a punishment for offenders against the church. As a penance the offender had to stand in this hole dressed in a white sheet during the service (probably in Latin and very long). It was still used as a punishment up to the 19th century, although by then the person deserving punishment was made to stand in the church (not the hole) throughout the service.

Holming took place on every St Stephen's day, December 26th. Boys with bunches of holly chased any woman walking in the village and beat her about the legs. They would also call at the house to catch the women and girls. Sometimes people beat themselves with holly as a penance on this day.

There was a Christmas time custom where the young men had an actual horse's skull and draped themselves with rough cloth and went from house to house shouting and ringing hand bells and supposedly frightening the occupants. They would then sing carols and probably be invited to have a drink and a bite to eat. The jaws of the skull were made to move and the boy inside would make as much noise as possible. They would be joined by someone from each house as they went along, swelling their numbers as the night went by. After the fun was over, they would bury the head until the following year. This custom was observed until the early 20th century.

A Christmas play was acted in the church and identical with the drama of St George practised in Cornwall. The characters were St George, Father Christmas, A Turkish Knight and a doctor, dressed as weirdly as possible. It started with a combat and ended with a Christmas Carol. On New Year's Eve the wassailing song *Rise Up on a New Year's Morning* was sung.

Llanmaes 🦐

Llanmaes is situated four miles south of Cowbridge. The old village of Llanmaes was very small, consisting of a manor house, farms and cottages. The only water supply was from a village pump, and a small well. The well never ran dry even in the hottest weather, but ceased to function when a housing estate was built and the village was put on mains sewerage. Until electricity was brought to the village, the only lighting available was from oil lamps and candles.

There were two public houses, the Blacksmith's Arms, still open today, and the Brown Lion. During the early 1900s, a meeting known locally as the Court Leet was held annually at the Brown Lion. The Marquis of Bute, the lord of the manor, would be in attendance together with the village 'bobby' and a dozen or so villagers who were invited to attend. The reason for the meeting each year was the encroachment of public land. Anyone found guilty of this was fined. Traditionally the landlady prepared a goose dinner at each of these functions.

Cattle markets were held weekly at Llantwit Major, a mile and a half away. Farm animals from Llanmaes were walked to the markets by farm labourers. During harvest time local children would help in the corn fields, stooking up sheaves of corn ready for loading onto the horse drawn carts. During the early 1900s a local man ran a regular pony and trap service into Cardiff – the only one available in the area. Because of the distance, the horse would have to be changed half way. Ponies and traps were also available for hire for shopping trips into Cowbridge.

The Church Hall was widely used in those days. During the week a school was held for all village children, all ages in one room, with one school mistress. During the evenings whist drives and dances were regularly held.

The village post office opened during the 1920s and soon grew into a shop, invaluable to the local community. Sadly today there is neither.

There have been numerous village characters. The village blacksmith also doubled up as a wheelwright, a carpenter and an undertaker. The old forge still stands today but is no longer in use.

A very popular character was known as 'Auntie Gertie'. She made her own butter and cheese and sold it locally. Her house was always open and if she wasn't in you would take the cheese and leave the money.

St Cattwg's church dates back to the 13th century and has always been a focal point in the village. During the Second World War it survived several incendiary bomb attacks. During those frequent raids the village people would make for safety to the rectory where there were large cellars underground.

The village remained largely unchanged until the early 1970s when farm land was sold for housing. Over recent years the village has almost trebled in size.

Llanmihangel

Llanmihangel is a dell one comes upon when travelling from Cowbridge via Llanblethian. The village is just a couple of miles from Cowbridge in the Vale of Glamorgan. Here is the attractive 16th century (or possibly earlier) fortified stone manor house named Llanmihangel Place, majestically overlooking the small church of St Michael and All Angels. Look up to the church tower to find the easily distinguishable old dovecote.

The manor house has a wealth of history hidden in its walls, six feet thick in places, in its huge open fireplaces with the bread oven and its oak panelled rooms. The fireplace in the dining room still has on its mantelpiece coats of arms carved in stone. A stained glass window of St

Michael the Archangel has been placed where many years ago was a doorway. Behind the house are some magnificent old yew trees, remnants of a formal garden laid out in the 17th century.

The manor house was built by a James Thomas. In 1684 Sir Humphrey Edwin bought the mansion, together with other properties in Glamorgan. Born at Hereford, he was an officer of the Artillery Company, later to become a Colonel of Horse. He was knighted in 1687 and became Lord Mayor of London in the year 1698.

The whole manor house is in the process of being carefully restored by its present owners Sue and David Beer.

The church is a picturesque setting for weddings and sometimes used by S4C Channel Television for the filming of weddings for viewing on their Pobol-y-Cwm programmes. There is no electricity or gas in the church and all the services are held by candlelight. This is particularly lovely at Christmas. After the carol service parishioners follow the church path to the manor house for mince pies and mulled wine.

In the grounds surrounding the church is the remains of a holy well, said to have healing powers and used by the local people in bygone days. Carved into the wall of the well sits a 'lady'. Likewise in the grounds of the manor house is a similar well with healing powers where sits a 'lady of stone', built and used too in bygone days by the manor gentry. (It is said the persons of the manor did not wish to use the same well as the commoners.)

There is a large pool close to the church, now silted up, which hopefully one day will be restored. But, there is a ghostly story to relate, that of Eleanor Dhu. She was said to have possessed magical powers and is thought to have been a 15th century heiress who was branded a witch. She wore an iron ring upon her wrist. In moments of frenzy she was tethered by the iron ring. She drowned in this pool and the story goes that the phantom of a female figure clad in white was often seen in twilight hours, rising with the mists above the water – 'the Ladye of the Ringe' perhaps!

Llanmorlais

Llanmorlais is a village situated on the shores of the Burry Estuary on the northern side of the Gower peninsula, ten miles west of Swansea. Originally it was called Glanmorlais meaning 'on the bank of the river Morlais', the stream which flows through the village.

Records of the village go back to Tudor times when it was the centre of one of the earliest coal mining operations in Wales, which no longer exist. The village has always been closely connected with the North Gower cockle-gathering industry and today local inhabitants still gather cockles – though no longer in carts. The only industry here is the cockle factory where the cockles are processed for sale locally, eg at Swansea Market, or sent to various parts of the British Isles.

Llanrhidian 🌿

Two carnivals were held in the village before the Second World War. One was organised by the Church members and held in a Penrhallt field behind Mr Lyndon Tucker's garage, owned at that time by the late Mr Llewelyn Gordon. The other was organised by the Chapel members. It was held in a farmer's fields at Freedown.

A few days before the big day, the mowing machine, drawn by the two horses, would cut all the long grass, thistles etc. At that time, the fields were kept for grazing sheep, and were not ploughed until wartime. All the stalls and big tea tent were put up in the second field, the Long Field. The tea tent had long tables covered by white cloths and the usual home-made goodies which had been made by members beforehand. The water was boiled in a large boiler over a fire, kept going by a man who lived in the Greyhound pub. The tent was in the corner of the field, the water carried through a gap in the hedge. There were various stalls: sweets, Ratti's icecream and the hoopla stall, which no one was allowed to pass, with a born comedian, Mr Parkyn of Three Crosses, in charge.

The bottom half of the field held the sheep dog trials under the charge of Mr Llewelyn Gordon. It was a very popular event and people came from long distances to compete. The sheep were kept by the farm buildings and let out three at a time for the competing dog to fetch through what was known as The Meadow, through the gateway into the Long Field between two hurdles and then penned. There were similar rules to present day events. Once the sheep had been penned, they were sent through a gap in the hedge into the field along side owned by Miss Flora Jeffreys. Sadly it all ended when the war started.

Sunday School was held in Chapel in Old Walls as there was no vestry built until later. There was an annual concert held with singers invited from as far away as London. On these occasions because people would come from all over Gower, benches were borrowed from the Greyhound pub and placed in the aisles in order to seat everyone. Also Good Friday teas were held in Chapel.

The water mill in the village can still be seen today. Corn was ground there for bread for the surrounding district.

Llansannor 🐚

Llansannor is a parish to the south west of Llanharry and is about 1,800 acres in area. It comprises the ancient church of St Senewyr, a fine Tudor mansion called Llansannor Court, the two outlying hamlets of Breigan and City, a sprinkling of modern housing, some very old but derelict houses and a few scattered farmsteads. It has retained its pastoral tranquillity and scenic beauty and it is hard to realise that a busy motorway runs alongside its northern boundary.

In the 12th century the church was known as 'capella St Senwarae de la Thawe' and later as the 'ecclesia de La Thawe' and it is a modest building in the Early English style. Its chief features are a fine 16th century porch, a sundial, some early fragments of wall painting found under the plaster of the church, the Truman grave and a remarkable chancel effigy dating back to the time of the Battle of Agincourt. Of the Truman family it can be said that the most famous member was Thomas Truman, the antiquary, 1713–86, who married the heiress of Pantylliwydd, Llansannor. Mr Truman was descended from Trooper Thomas Truman of Northampton, a Cromwellian soldier. His great grandson, the antiquary, is said to have fired Iolo Morganwg's interest in the history of Glamorgan and given him the chance of studying old books and manuscripts at Pantylliwydd.

Llansannor Court may well be earlier than the 16th century. Its most famous owner was Francis Gwyn, 1648–1734, who held many important political offices, including Clerk of the Council and Secretary of War in the time of the later Stuarts and has been described as one of the founder members of the Tory party. He later lived at Forde Abbey and had immense patronage in the West Country.

In the 19th century Llansannor was a fairly self sufficient little farming community with a water mill, a smithy, a bakehouse, estate and farm workers' cottages and two inns; The Carpenter Arms at Breigan and the City Inn. Little is known of the former inn but the City Inn has intrigued local historians because of its strange name. It may be a corruption of 'saith Ty', but it could be a classic example of a joke name.

Breigan Castle was built by Stephen Bauzan, Sheriff of Glamorgan to

Richard de Clare on three occasions between 1243 and 1247. Our article cannot be concluded without a mention of the little Church School built about 1870 by the National Society to enable children of working class parents to receive a Christian education and still flourishing today with a wider catchment area than at any time in its history.

Llantrisant 🪺

Llantrisant's ancient name was Llangawdraf. It was founded in honour of Cawdraf who founded a seminary there. Llantrisant when translated means 'the church of the three saints': St Illtud, St Tyfodwg and St Gwynno.

It was established as a walled town by the Normans under Gilbert de Clare (1262–1295). Records show that the castle at Llantrisant was occupied and in regular use by the Normans in 1184. In 1346 the town was granted its first charter by Edward III. Llantrisant Castle was demolished in 1404 when Owen Glyndwr raided the country and today there is very little of the Castle remaining apart from one tower and a small portion of the wall.

The only approach to Llantrisant is up winding steep roads. The town still retains much of its earlier character with small houses and cottages built on either side of narrow steep cobbled roads and lanes. From the Bull Ring, a central point in the town, these stone paved lanes and footpaths lead to different parts of the old borough. Llantrisant was formerly a borough in its own right but the corporation was dissolved in 1883.

Facing onto the Bull Ring is the Model Design and Craft Centre which is housed in what was a three storey 19th century workhouse, but has now been completely transformed to provide a dozen light and airy craft studios. There is also a display of coins minted at the Royal Mint at Llantrisant Business Park. In 1968 a Royal Mint was built at this Business Park just to the north. By 1976 all production from Tower Hill London had been transferred, and all coinage was being produced here.

The church dedicated to the three saints – St Illtud, St Tyfodwg and St Gwynno, is stoutly built and dominates the skyline of the hilltop when seen from a distance. The church dates back to Norman times but the tower and western part were rebuilt in the early 16th century. The church was restored in 1873. At this time the *Crucifixion* by Burne-Jones was incorporated in the east window. An early grave slab in the south aisle has three incised crosses and is believed to date from between the 7th and 9th centuries.

Llantrisant still has the ancient Court Leet which started in the early 13th century. Today this Court is a charitable trust and since 1889 has been managed by the Llantrisant Town Trust. The Court Leet of today has very little power. It is held at the small Town Hall (rebuilt 1773), once a year on a Friday in May.

Today the Llantrisant Town Trust has 13 Trustees and they are responsible for the upkeep of Llantrisant Common (known as Cymdda), Graig Common, the Town Hall and the Castle Green. The Town Hall was at one time a market hall and a corn market was held there.

There were many highlights during the year in Llantrisant. One of them was the May fair. The main event was the cattle market, which was held in the Bull Ring. Cattle would be brought from as far afield as Ireland to be sold at this market. They would arrive the night before and be held in Thomas John's field above Swan Street. On the morning of the fair the women of the village would arrive at the field whilst the cows were being milked and have their jugs filled up with free milk. Horses were also sold at the fair and were to be found between the old post office and Newbridge Road. In George Street stalls would be laid out for the sale of tiesen lap, bara brith and Welsh cakes etc.

In contrast to the hustle and bustle of the May Fair, Whitsun Monday would find Llantrisant deserted. Each family would make their way down to the river, cross what was then called the Shaky bridge, past Ynysmardy Farm and up the mountain for a picnic. The men would be carrying heavy ropes and boards, with which they would make swings amongst the trees. This was a day when all the residents came together regardless of their religious persuasions.

Beating The Bounds is a ceremony still held at Llantrisant. It is held every seven years and is usually carried out before Ascension Day. The earliest recorded date when the ceremony took place in Llantrisant was in 1555, although its origins are much older. This enjoyable occasion is now arranged by the Llantrisant Town Trust.

Dr William Price (1800–93) is a well known 'character' in 19th century Wales, associated with Llantrisant. He was born at Ty'n-y-coedcae, near Rudry in the Rhymney valley. He practised as a doctor at Pontypridd and became well known as both a physician and surgeon. He also claimed to be an archdruid and performed druidical rites at the Rocking Stone on Pontypridd Common. He was a very eccentric man and was noted for his unusual clothes which he described as 'the dress of the ancient Court of Glamorgan'. He wore green cloth trousers, scarlet waistcoat and a fox skin hat.

He had a flowing beard and very long hair which had not been cut for many years. He became notorious for his advocacy of free love and at the age of 83 he took Gwenllian Llewelyn as his common-law wife and fathered two children. He became involved in the Chartist movement in his early days, and supported the miners in the great strike of 1871. He enjoyed many skirmishes with the law but he was never convicted and always won his case.

He pioneered cremation when he illegally tried to cremate the body of his five month old son, Jesus Christ Price, Son of God, on the hill above Llantrisant. The body was wrapped in cloth, placed on a barrel which contained paraffin oil and set alight. People were furious and it was only the arrival of the police which saved him. Dr Price was tried at Cardiff Assizes, but was acquitted as he had not broken any laws, and so the acceptability of cremation was established.

Dr Price died at the age of 92 and he left specific instructions for his body to be cremated on the same spot where his baby child's cremation had taken place at Caerlan Fields. The ceremony was conducted by clergymen with, it is said, 5–6,000 people present. It was claimed to be the very first public cremation in the country. A statue of Dr Price can be found at the Bull Ring at Llantrisant. There is also a plaque on the wall of Zoar chapel in the main Street of Llantrisant – this bronze plaque commemorates 'that act of Dr William Price who cremated the body of his enfant [sic] son in Caerlan Fields, Llantrisant'.

Several years ago Llantrisant was made a 'conservation area' to prevent vast new housing development from spoiling its character.

Llantrithyd 🌿

Three miles east of Cowbridge is Llantrithyd, where once tradesmen called every day. Groceries ordered on Wednesday were delivered on Friday and paid for on Monday. Coal was delivered weekly and milk delivered daily with churn and measure. Every household had a garden with apple trees and fruit bushes. Apples were stored in straw, while gooseberries and blackcurrants were made into jam. Other vegetables and fruit were made into chutney and pickles.

Farming was completely different in those days. When a major job like haymaking or threshing needed doing, neighbouring farmers helped each other. Hay making was a three day event. Only farmyard manure was used on the land. It was put in heaps then spread on the fields by hand. Then a farmer was well off if he had ten cows. Farming families ate well, though. A farmer's breakfast was two slices of fat bacon, two eggs and fried bread. Always a cooked lunch and bread and cheese for tea and extras. Supper was toasted bread with milk. Poultry was only killed at Christmas. Geese were very popular. When water was short during a dry spell, farmers drove their cows through the warren to the lake for drinking.

Villagers used to swim in the lake at Pyscodlyn. There were leeches in the water though! The lake was taken over for a reservoir for Tair Onen and bathing prohibited. Swans once nested on the island, now covered with reeds. The lake is now stocked with fish. The beautiful dragonflies, big powder blue and others, are no longer seen.

Outings used be simple, like catching a train at Maendy to go to the March Fair held in Bear Field, Cowbridge or visiting Cottrell Mansion. The Mackintosh family gave the reading room to Bonvilston district for boys only. Girls used it for dancing, concerts and parties but otherwise it was strictly kept for boys. The church was not well attended through the year but come Harvest festival it would be full. Sunday school outings were to Barry or Porthcawl, with a party at Christmas time.

Gipsies were then quite common to see. They stayed by the roadside and would always want something, perhaps candles or tea. They made pegs and sold them. The women would try to sell laces and tell fortunes and they always had a lot of horses and lurcher dogs. They would turn their horses into the fields late at night. The last gipsy with a caravan and horse passed here about 1964. She travelled on her own, stopping overnight on her way to a fair at Merthyr Tydfil.

Before the Second World War work was scarce. The building of St Athan and Llandow Aerodrome was a major development and employed local labour. Everyone cycled to work and enjoyed their improved living, for £5 a week was a luxury wage. The war changed everyone's direction. Farmers ploughed land to grow crops, to keep Britain going. There were Land Army girls at Sycamore and prisoners of war at Llantrithyd Park. There was an American Army camp at Cowbridge downs, while St Athan camp was full of airmen who did flying training, transport and driving.

Today the village is still a pleasant place to live, and the wild mushrooms and cowslips, ploughed up in the war, are growing again in the fields nearby.

Llantwit Major ❧

Llantwit Major lies five miles south of Cowbridge on the B4268 road in the beautiful Vale of Glamorgan. Llantwit Major has a long history dating back to pre-Roman times. The Romans invaded the area in AD

50–78 and Llantwit Major became part of the Roman province for about 300 years. A large Roman villa was excavated in a field known as Cae Mead in 1888 and again in 1938. Fifteen rooms were revealed, one with a beautiful mosaic floor. Roman coins, pottery and skeletons were also found on the site.

The pre-Norman period is of great importance in the history of Llantwit Major. An important monastic school was set up in the 5th century AD, the founder and first abbot of which was Iltutus. The name Llanilltud Fawr, meaning the great church of Illtud, is known in English as Llantwit Major.

The monastery is thought to have been built on the site of the present St Illtud's church and some of the surrounding land. It is said that Illtud had 2,000 students, among them seven kings or princes, and some famous saints – St Samson, who became Archbishop of Dol, St Gildas and St Paulinus who became Bishop of St Pol de Léon.

Farming continued during the Norman period when Robert Fitz-hamon established himself in the Vale and introduced the English manorial system. The gatehouse, the tithe barn (now demolished) and the columbarium date from this period. Much of the land, church treasures, tithes and revenues were transferred to Tewkesbury Abbey. The Normans also rebuilt the old Celtic church, but little remains of their work today.

The present church dates from the 13th–14th centuries and there is a remarkable collection of memorial stones in the west of the church. There is also an elaborately carved Jesse niche near the pulpit. This is a recess on a pillar near the pulpit to the right of the altar. It is about 40 inches high and 18 inches wide. On the stone base of this recess is carved a tree and the branches and leaves intertwine on the three sides. There is a theory that this is supposed to depict the 'Tree of Life'. The wall painting has recently been restored in the beautiful church and it is well worth a visit.

The Town Hall in the centre of the old town is of medieval origin and was used as a guildhall or court of justice for the Lordships of Glamorgan, and cells can be seen below the floors of the present lower rooms. In the reign of Henry VIII, the lower part (to the east) was used as shops. In about 1853 it fell into a bad state of repair and the Oddfellows Society was granted use of it in return for the repairs they carried out.

One story about the Town Hall is that a witch called 'Mollen' used to fly over it on a broomstick, and weary parents used the name 'Mollen' to frighten their children to go to bed early.

Near the Town Hall is the Old Swan Inn, thought to have been a Banking House of the Welsh Princes and later a manorial mint. It then became a residence of the Circuit Judge when an assize court was held at the Town Hall. The old White Hart Inn is said to be of 14th century origin and was once the home of the justices of the peace. It is thought a 'coostring court' was held in the White Hart Inn, to try scolding wives.

There are other historic buildings in Llantwit Major, such as Plymouth House, said to have been built in the 12th century and to have housed some of the monks from the monastery. One of the finest examples of medieval architecture in Glamorgan is Great House. Legend has it that it contained an underground passage used by smugglers. The building fell into decay in the 1930s but was restored in 1945 and has been occupied as a private residence since then.

Llantwit Major Castle or the 'Old Place' as it is sometimes known, was built in the 15th century and, although now a ruin, it is reputed to be haunted by the ghost of the 'White Lady'. She was the wife of one of the owners, who was allegedly starved to death by her husband.

Mr Daniel Jones, one of the first lawyers in the town, rebuilt Woodford House. He amassed a great fortune and gave liberally to the poor and needy. He bequeathed £20 a year to be distributed to the poor of the parish forever. He also bequeathed a large amount of money for the erection of Cardiff Royal Infirmary and liberally endowed it.

For centuries Llantwit Major was a farming community. The 1851 and 1861 censuses show that the main occupation was that of agricultural labourer. Other occupations were connected with farming, such as shepherds, drovers, thatchers and carriers. Today people commute to Cardiff and Bridgend to work. The RAF station at St Athan and the Aberthaw Power Station, both a few miles distant, also employ many who live in Llantwit Major.

Today Llantwit Major is a busy place and because of the easy access to its beach, which is about a mile from the town, attracts a number of visitors in the summer months. It is very pleasant on a fine day just to sit and watch the tide in peaceful surroundings.

Llanwynno 🪶

Two miles from Ferndale and about six miles from Pontypridd is the isolated old parish of Llanwynno, sheltered by the Cefn Gwyngul mountain and the majestic St Gwynno forest. It lies between the Rhondda Fach and the Cynon Valleys. The hamlet of Llanwynno consists of the Brynffynon Hotel and the church of St Gwynno, founded it is said in about AD 547 by St Gwynno himself.

In Llanwynno churchyard lies Guto Nyth Bran. He was a very famous Welsh runner. His correct name was Gruffudd Morgan and he lived on a farm called Nyth Bran (Crow's Nest) which was situated between Llanwynno church and Porth in the Rhondda Fach.

One day, Guto's mother sent him to get yeast so that she could make bread and the nearest place where he could get the yeast was Aberdare. His mother put the kettle on to boil before he left – a big cast iron kettle which hung on a chain. Guto sped across the Gwyngul Mountain and arrived back with the yeast at Nyth Bran Farm (a distance of about seven miles each way), before the kettle boiled.

Guto also went to Cardigan and raced with a horse. Of course, Guto won the race. To loosen up his joints and limbs on the night before an important race, Guto would always sleep on a manure heap.

On one occasion, Guto's father asked him to round up the sheep on the mountain-side, He did so and later told his father that he'd had trouble in catching one sheep, a small brown one. 'That wasn't a sheep my boy!' exclaimed his father, 'that was a hare!'

Guto had a very good friend whose name was Sian and she kept a shop. In every race she bet money on Guto's legs and she became quite wealthy because Guto always won. One day he was challenged by an Englishman named Prince. The race was from Newport town to Bedwas church, a distance of twelve miles and Sian the shop, his friend, bet an apron full of gold sovereigns that Guto would win.

He and Prince set off with the crowds cheering them on their way. Guto was so confident that he would win that he stopped to chat with people on the way. Then he remembered Sian and her sovereigns and off he went like the wind. Some of Prince's supporters threw glass on the road but Guto jumped over it and easily won the race in 53 minutes.

Sian the shop was overjoyed and slapped him hard on the back saying, 'Well done Guto.' As he'd been running so hard the blow must have affected his heart and he fell down at her feet – dead. He was only 37 years of age. Guto was buried in Llanwynno churchyard in the year 1737. People still come to see his grave and the inscription on the gravestone and to pay tribute to such a wonderful runner.

Llysworney 🦢

Llysworney is a very small pretty village some two miles from Cowbridge. It is said to have been the site of an ancient settlement. In the village is an old well enclosed by four walls, now covered by grass but with an outlet into the village pond. The well is overlooked by picturesque cottages and houses, the manor house, and the church of St Tydvil.

The church of St Tydvil is somewhat different from other churches as its nave, central tower and chancel are 'echelon' in plan, thus somewhat restricting the view of the communion table from the nave. In the churchyard, there was a gravestone on which was engraved '7 ber' in place of the name of the month.

Why not sit on the seat by the village well and ponder awhile and enjoy the view of the surrounding countryside!

Lon Las 🐚

Lon Las is a small village three miles west of Neath, two miles from Morriston and five miles east of Swansea. Since the building of the M4 motorway the village has been cut in half and a subway links each side. Today there are no shops in the village.

The forgotten hamlet of Pentre Llwynbrwydrau used to adjoin the village of Lon Las, but today it no longer exists. It was known to the local inhabitants as 'The Pentre' and was a cluster of houses against a sward of green. These houses stood behind where the Welsh school is in Lon Las today. The houses were demolished because there was no main sewerage there and consequently the families had to move – some went to live in Lon Las. Today this area is partly used for allotments.

The focal point of the village was the Welsh Methodist Ebenezer chapel at Lon Las. Many families attended three times every Sunday and many times in the week. Music was very important to the chapel members. Whitsun was an event the children looked forward to. A tea party with homemade food was held in the chapel vestry and afterwards games on the field opposite, together with races for which there were money prizes.

The primary school was built in Lon Las in 1909 and up until 1950 the teaching was in English. In 1950 this school became a Welsh primary school and the pupils were taught through the medium of Welsh. Sadly this school is now closed and the pupils moved to a Welsh school at Llansamlet a couple of miles away.

Welsh and English are both spoken in Lon Las today. At the beginning of the 20th century Welsh was spoken in the chapel and in the homes, but as more English speaking people have moved into the village, naturally Welsh has declined.

Maerdy 🦩

Maery, with a population of 3,500 lies at the extremity of the Rhondda Fach Valley, about two miles from Ferndale. It is a town which possesses a strong community spirit. Maerdy is connected with the Aberdare valley by a mountain road.

The community grew up around the Maerdy Colliery which at one time was the main source of work for the men. Long rows of terraced houses sprung up on the valley sides. This colliery closed in December 1990 and was the last coal mine in the Rhondda Valley, so today there are no mines in Rhondda. There is no trace that a colliery ever existed here. On Christmas Eve 1885, 81 miners were killed in the Maerdy Colliery disaster and in 1985 a memorial garden was opened in memory of these men, at All Saints church (built in 1885). Two of the pit props from the accident were carved into candlesticks and presented to the church and are in use every Sunday.

In December, 1969, there was a near tragedy in the Rhondda Fach in Mid Glamorgan.

One wet and wintry day about two days before Christmas, a young farm hand named Lyn Jones was riding on his horse, *Sally*, near the Lluest Wen Dam which is about two miles from Maerdy. He had been searching for sheep that had gone astray on the mountainside above the dam. Lyn was glad when they were on their way back to the farm as he was cold and wet, but as the mare galloped across the dam wall, suddenly the ground subsided and *Sally* and Lyn sank down five feet nine inches into a hole. The frightened Lyn managed to scramble to the side of the hole and raced to Maerdy colliery, a distance of about two miles, to raise the alarm and to summon help.

Very quickly the fire brigade rushed to the scene and managed, after a struggle, to free *Sally*, the black mare. It was soon realised that the situation was serious and that the dam wall could fracture at any time. The water would then cascade down the valley, sweeping everything before it. This was an emergency indeed! People living in the lower streets of the Rhondda Fach were quickly evacuated from their homes. Engineers were soon on the spot, carrying out emergency repairs on the dam wall but months went by before it was fully repaired.

The residents of the Rhondda Fach owe a great debt of gratitude to *Sally*, the black horse who saved the valley from being drowned.

Maesteg 🎐

Maesteg lies in the largest of the three valleys of Ogwr. The valley of the Llynfi is wide and flanked on both sides by rich farmland with forestation covering the steeper slopes. The population of the valley increased enormously during the 19th and early 20th centuries when rich iron and coal deposits were found in the area. The ironworks at Spelters were opened in 1825 and coal mines and pits were sunk throughout the upper regions of the valley.

Maesteg rapidly became a prosperous place and was soon connected to the holiday town of Porthcawl when in 1825 work began on the construction of a tramroad to transport the coal and iron ore from Maesteg to the docks at Porthcawl, from where it was exported abroad. The trams were horse-drawn and travelled a distance of some 17 miles via Aberkenfig and Stormy, and formed the principal link between Maesteg and the outside world. The line remained in operation until 1855. In 1969 and 1971 respectively, commemorative plaques were unveiled at the Slipway, Porthcawl and Llynfi Road, Maesteg to remind us of our industrial past.

Mining had by now become the major industry in the Llynfi Valley, the quality of the coal ranking with the best produced in the Welsh coalfield. In 1853 Messrs. John Brogden & Co. of Sale, Manchester purchased the controlling interest in the Llynfi Ironworks and opened up several mines in the Valley. They were the principal promoters of a new railway line operated by steam locomotives, officially opened in 1861. This line was available to passengers in 1864. Porthcawl docks had by now become inadequate to handle the large volume of coal from the valley and by the end of the century new railway lines were laid connecting the valley with two large modern docks at Port Talbot and Barry. In July 1873 the Great Western Railway took over the management of the new flourishing Llynfi Railway line.

Colonel John T. North was probably the best known pioneer of industry in the Llynfi Valley. In 1889 a syndicate was formed and became known as the North's Navigation Collieries Ltd, who bought out the ailing Llynfi Iron and Coal Companies and concentrated exclusively on coal. In the late 1920s the Norths controlled seven collieries in the valley and were the biggest producers of the best house coal in the South Wales coalfield, exporting to French, Mediterranean and North American markets. Colonel North gave generous financial gifts for the welfare of the miners of the valley which were used towards the provision of a local library. He died in 1896 and the foundation stone of the Colonel North

Memorial Hall was laid by his widow and son on the 3rd May 1897. The company continued to financially support the valley. A new pavilion was presented to the cricket club in 1920.

During the second half of this century the pits began to close, one by one. Some light industries took their place when large areas of former coal tips were cleared and developed to make way for houses, factories, and leisure pursuits.

The town has an excellent shopping centre with its imposing Town Hall in the middle. This magnificent building with its indoor market underneath has recently undergone extensive redecoration both externally and internally, and is now a popular centre for concerts, male voice choirs, dances and the local Operatic Society performances.

Sport in the valley is very much in evidence with several rugby, soccer and cricket teams to its credit. Nant-y-Crynwydd, a building more recently used to store corn for the pit ponies, a former blast engine house for the iron works and originally a farmhouse, is the last reminder of the iron industry. It has been acquired by the local council, restored and tastefully converted into the new Maesteg Leisure Centre. It is said to be the last blast engine house of its kind in Wales. Maesteg has a wealth of talent, both musical and intellectual.

However, the valley has now become primarily a 'travel to work' zone with most of the workforce finding employment outside.

Margam ✍

Margam is one of four parishes which during Norman times was known as 'Tir Iarll' (The Earl's Land). The other three parishes being Llangynwyd, Bettws and Kenfig. The Earl in question was the Norman, Robert Fitzhamon, Earl of Gloucester and Lord of Glamorgan, in the 11th century. Tir Iarll in all contained 41,854 acres, and in 1349 there were 585 Welsh tenants in Tir Iarll.

There is much evidence of a Roman camp at Rhyd Blaen y Cwm on the Margam Mountain. The Margam milestone, dating from the reign of the Roman Emperor Postumus (AD 258–268), is kept in the National Museum of Wales in Cardiff. A number of tumuli, entrenchments and encampments were found on the hilltops near Llangynwyd, and it was a centre of Celtic culture and Christianity. The famous mound on Margam mountain called Twmpath Diwlith was once classed as one of the seven wonders of Glamorgan, because it was popularly believed that dew never fell upon it. Although one belief is that it was so called because a priest stood once a year on the boundary between Margam and Llangynwyd parishes and from the mound read a lesson from the Book of Homilies while the local inhabitants 'beat the parish bounds'.

The Bodvoc stone, set on Margam mountain, dates back to AD 550. The Bodvoc is thought to have been a British chieftain killed in battle against the Danish or Norse sea rovers. In 1930 it was proposed to remove the Bodvoc Stone from its original location on Margam mountain between Maesteg and Port Talbot, to Margam Abbey. A plaster cast of the original stone was taken to the National Museum of Wales.

On the Dissolution of the Monasteries by Henry VIII, the Margam estate was sold in two lots to the Mansel family. The orangery, a feature of the Abbey, was built in the 18th century by Thomas Mansel Talbot to house an already famous collection of citrus trees. The origin of the trees has given rise to several legends. One recounts that the orange and lemon trees left Spain en route for England as a gift to the reigning monarch. The ship, it would seem mistakenly, sailed into the Bristol Channel instead of the English Channel and unfortunately was wrecked near Margam. However, the trees were saved and kept at Margam Abbey and presented to the Mansel family by Queen Anne.

After extensive restoration in 1976/77 the orangery is now used for exhibitions, musical evenings and summer balls. Today many deer can be seen roaming in these lovely grounds.

C. R. M. Talbot JP, the Squire of Margam, Liberal Member of Parliament for Mid Glamorgan 1830–1890, and Father of the House of Commons had sufficient estate derived from his ancestors to enable him to bequeath several million pounds, in property and stocks, to his three daughters Emily Charlotte Talbot, Olive Talbot and Mrs Bertha Isabella Fletcher. Andrew Fletcher, his grandson, then aged nine was originally due to succeed to the estate, but the entail had been severed earlier and powers given to Emily Charlotte, the eldest daughter. The Fletcher family lived at Margam Castle. Olive Talbot, an invalid daughter, was a major benefactor of the Anglican Church in Wales. The church benefited greatly from the munificence of the Talbot family of Margam. It was the Talbots who paid the greater part of the cost of building several churches in Port Talbot, Abergwynfi, Kenfig Hill and the Llynfi Valley, the enlargement of Bettws parish church and the restoration of Llangeinor parish church. Three quarters of the cost of building St Michael and All Angels church, Maesteg, a truly magnificent building, was borne by Miss Olive Talbot of Margam. The foundation stone was laid on 7th October 1895 and the church opened and consecrated on 19th January 1897. It is doubtful whether a church building on such a scale would have been erected had it not been for the beneficence of Miss Olive Talbot.

Margam Castle was acquired by Glamorgan County Council in 1973 and is now administered by West Glamorgan County Council as Margam County Park.

Merthyr Mawr 🌿

A very picturesque small village about two miles from Bridgend, Merthyr Mawr is an idyllic place, nestling in its tranquil greenery. The church timeless and comforting, the river placidly meandering through, where every cottage is thatched. But it has not always been so innocent.

At the time when Europe was embroiled in the wars that followed the French Revolution, there lived in Merthyr Mawr an evil character nicknamed 'Cap Goch' after the red hat that he wore to emulate the French revolutionaries, whom he admired. He was the landlord of the New Inn, set on the river bank nearest to that point where travellers and pedlars had to cross the Ogmore river. Here they took their rest and sustenance overnight as they made their way to London or to West Wales by coach or on horseback.

Rest was far from what many of them got. The wily Cap Goch would wine and dine his unsuspecting guests and if they were carrying gold or goods of value, they would mysteriously disappear overnight. Cap Goch and his treacherous band of local villains would dispose of the travellers and the stolen goods were easily sold in Bridgend nearby.

At first they threw the bodies of their victims into the Ogmore river but many were washed ashore at the mouth of the river. Suspicion grew, so the murderers then buried the bodies instead in the surrounding fields and woods. Many years later when the inn had fallen into decay and folk were digging in the vicinity the gory remains were revealed.

The fate of the murderous landlord remains in doubt. Some say he was tried and sentenced to death on the gallows at Stalling Down (just off the A48 road to Cardiff) while others say he lived to a ripe old age.

Nothing remains of the fearful New Inn which stood near the present day Dipping Bridge, and Merthyr Mawr retains an ethereal beauty, a peaceful refuge from the stressful pace of life today.

Sir John Nicholl built Merthyr Mawr House between 1806 and 1809, near the site of an earlier mansion. Educated at Cowbridge Grammar School and St John's College Oxford, he became a member of Parliament in 1802. In 1787 Sir John had married Judy Birt of Wenvoe Castle. Between 1834–1838 he was Vicar-General to the Archbishop of Canterbury and a recognised authority on church law. Also in 1834 he became Judge of the Admiralty Court, an office he retained until he died in 1838. His eldest son, the Right Honorable John Nicholl, was a Member of Parliament for Cardiff for 30 years from 1832–1852.

Miskin

Miskin means 'lovely plain'. The village of Miskin grew up around the ancient house of Miskin Manor south of Llantrisant. A settlement was established here by Hywel Dda in the 10th century. The original manor house had a medieval origin. There is also mention of this house in 1540. The house and manor were acquired by the Herbert family, Earls of Pembroke and Montgomery. They later passed to the Marquis of Bute, who was also Lord of the Borough of Llantrisant. The manor has been occupied by several families, among them the Bassett family who were very benevolent in the area. Miskin lay within the parish of Llantrisant, hence the gifts to Llantrisant church by the Bassett family.

Miskin Manor, which today is an hotel, was built on part of the foundation of the older structure. The property was purchased during the mid 19th century by David Williams, a coal owner. He was a well-known Welsh Bard. His Bardic title was 'Alaw Goch' and he was very generous in his donations to the National Eisteddfod. In the late 19th century his son, Judge Gwilym Williams (1839–1906), resided there and it is reported that Edward, Prince of Wales used to visit the manor. The manor house and grounds were developed considerably and by 1900 it was a most charming residence, with beautiful views of the surrounding countryside. The grounds and gardens had shrubs and tropical plants and were considered to be some of the finest in the county.

Judge Gwilym Williams died in 1906 and his son Sir Rhys Rhys-Williams who married Juliet, daughter of Elinor Glyn, the well known romantic novelist, then took up residence. Sir Rhys and Lady Juliet were well known for their public work.

During the Second World War the house was used as a convalescent home by the Red Cross and was visited at this time by Princess Marina, Duchess of Kent.

In the 1960s part of the building was rented as luxury flats, but it still remained the home of Sir Brandon Rhys-Williams MP, who used it occasionally as a family home. Today the Manor is a very attractive hotel which opened in 1985. It now overlooks the M4 motorway so makes it an ideal place for conferences and craft fairs, because of its easy access. A health club has been built in the grounds which is very popular.

In the 19th century Miskin was known as New Mill after the water mill near the manor, which was still working during the early years of this century. However, there is reference to the village of Miskin in records dating 1871, when the following businesses were recorded: the Miskin Arms, blacksmith, mill, butcher, grocer, joiner, boot and shoe maker and New Mill school.

Ebenezer Welsh Methodist chapel was founded in 1860 and closed in 1992. The village school was built in 1875, but closed in December 1962 because of a decrease in the number of children attending it. The children now attend Pontyclun Primary School about a mile distant.

The water mill closed in the early part of this century and for many years part of this building has been used by the local scout troop. Jamborees are regularly held in the grounds surrounding the mill.

Miskin had an iron church which had been built in 1878, but a more permanent building was erected and opened in 1907. The church is dedicated to St David and was built in the Decorated style and is cruciform in plan. Many of the stained glass windows in the church bear inscriptions in the Welsh language.

The present day village of Miskin is a pleasant place to live. In the small square stands the War Memorial and around it are the church, the old public house, the Miskin Arms, old and new houses and old cottages standing side by side. Small housing developments have sprung up on either side of the road through the village during the past 25 to 30 years – but are quite attractively laid out.

Mountain Ash 🔖

Mountain Ash is in the Cynon Valley. The Welsh version is Aberpennar.

Mountain Ash is surrounded by mountains. On one side is Caegarw and the other is Darranlas. On the Caegarw side we have lovely sweeping mountains which are called Cwmpennar. There you will find beautiful gardens which are privately owned and once a year the owners open them to the public for a small charge and the money is donated to charity. These gardens have many unusual and colourful plants and trees.

Darranlas is very different. The bus climbs the hills with houses on both sides as the main road winds up to reach Perthcelyn at the top then drops down to Llanwynno on the other side. Llanwynno is a small village with one house, one public house and a church. In the churchyard is buried a famous young man, Gruffudd Morgan, more commonly known as 'Guto Nyth Bran', who ran twelve miles in 53 minutes. The legend has it, that when he finished his race, he was slapped on the back and he fell dead at the feet of his sweetheart. There is a statue of Guto in the middle of Mountain Ash. Each New Year's Eve races are held in the town in his honour – these are called Nos Galon Races. At midnight there is a mystery runner (usually a celebrity) who lights a torch and runs from Guto's grave at Llanwynno down the mountain side and through the streets to the town hall at Mountain Ash. Many famous runners have taken part. The races are held in the streets all day and hundreds of people come from all over the country to run. It is a very big occasion enjoyed by everyone.

Princess Elizabeth came to Mountain Ash in 1946 to attend the National Eisteddfod and was admitted into the Bardic Order, The Gorsedd Circle of stones was erected in Duffryn Woods and remains there to this day.

The first male voice choir, 30 strong, was formed in Mountain Ash and they were so famous that they sang at Buckingham Palace for Queen Victoria and later sailed to America to sing at the White House in Washington for President and Mrs Roosevelt.

The National Eisteddfod of Wales was held here twice, in the Pavilion, which was a very large building. Choirs came from all over Wales to compete and the many celebrities who came to the Pavilion to participate included Gracie Fields, Paul Robeson and Sir Malcolm Sargeant.

The hymn *Calon Lan* was written by a local young man who collected small coal. Whilst waiting for the bags to be filled, he wrote the words and later his friend put it to music and it was sung in Bethania chapel for the first time.

Mountain Ash developed as a mining town in the mid 19th century, at the lower end of the Cynon Valley, after Deep Duffryn colliery had been sunk in 1842. Today there are no collieries in the Cynon Valley. They have closed and been demolished. Dyffryn House (no longer a private dwelling) was the home of Lord Aberdare, the first Vice-Chancellor of the University of Wales.

One resident gives a glimpse of life in 1926 – during the Miner's Strike. 'The sheep dog trials were held in one of the fields at "Pen Caradog Farm", near Llanwynno. It was the event of the year. There was so little money about, but this was an August Monday Bank Holiday outing that was going to cost very little, but which gave so much happiness to so many. It was a long stiff climb to the field, but hundreds of people, men, women and children set off, some walking, some on horse-back, and others in carts pulled by old shire horses. The field had stalls everywhere, selling toffee apples, toffee in trays, all homemade, and broken pieces of toffee in newspaper, for a penny. There were ice-cream carts pushed along by one man, usually an Italian, called a "Brachi". How gaily their carts were painted: blue, white and yellow. A wafer cost a penny and a cornet a half-penny.

Then came a hush around the field – the first dog and his master were on trial – the six sheep far away, waiting to be herded into the competition pens.

No posh whistles – just their fingers to their lips, and how those dogs responded! The winner was announced and everyone started the long track home. As the sunset, the beauty of this old valley came alive, and those going home over the Rhondda mountain said their farewells, in song. *Calon Lan* never sounded better, in such a setting.'

Mumbles 🐚

Mumbles is called the gateway to Gower, and is a village situated five miles west of Swansea. Visitors have their first glimpse of it at West Cross, when the beautiful Swansea Bay appears through the trees, with the light-house and pier in the background.

The light-house used to house families, and the rescue by 'The Women of Mumbles Head' has been recorded in history books. One reads of the bravery of the two women, daughters of a lighthouse keeper called Ace, who saved the life of a shipwrecked seaman by knotting their shawls together to pull him ashore and were later known as the 'Grace Darlings of Wales.' The light is worked automatically now. The pier has the lifeboat house adjoining it and the present lifeboat is named *Ethel Anne Measures*. Mumbles has had a life-boat service since 1863, and has suffered three disasters; The *Wolverhampton* in 1883, The *James Stevens* in 1903 and *Edward Prince of Wales* in 1947, when all hands were lost.

The village can also boast a Norman castle, named Oystermouth Castle. It stands on a hill where it can survey its domain with dignity. The parish church is All Saints and is over 850 years old. It has magnificent stained glass windows, two depicting the life-boat accidents. There is also a window in remembrance of the Mumbles Train. This passenger railway was the first in the world – starting with horses, then steam and later electric. It was terminated in 1960. In the porch of the church the bells of Santiago stand. These huge bells were made at Swansea and taken to Santiago in South America. Sadly the church there caught fire, killing most of the congregation. The bells were returned to Swansea and have remained in our parish church. There are seven denominations in Mumbles, but in case you think we are a pious race,

97

there are also eleven public houses.

There is a legend that two wealthy sisters lived in the village of Mumbles many years ago, whose surname was Angel. They owned vast property, including farms on Grove Island, which was situated half-way between Mumbles Head and Port Talbot in Swansea Bay. They were dominant ladies and exercised great power over the villagers. One rule they made was to prevent the locals using a thoroughfare through All Saints churchyard, a path they had used for years.

The people were overwhelmed with anger and in their rage put a curse on the Misses Angel. Shortly after this a tidal wave swept over Swansea Bay, destroying Grove Island with its farms. Cattle were drowned, but one wild boar made it ashore at a district called Norton. It was chased and killed by a wooden spear called a spit. Boarspit Lane was named and remained until 1940.

One may not believe in the Angels' curse, but there was once an island in Swansea Bay. When there is a big spring tide, tree trunks are visible as the water recedes. This area is now known to fishermen as 'The Green Grounds'. Boarspit Lane had gone, but the Boarspit Estate still exists.

Mwyndy 🐌

Mwyndy is a small hamlet with a few old houses, a public house with a restaurant, two garages, farmhouses and just a few modern houses. There is also a small business which makes smokeless fuel, a funeral director and a few factories well hidden from the main road. There is a quarry where limestone is still quarried.

The public house called The Barn at Mwyndy has become very popular since it opened on the 20th August 1988. Previously The Barn was thought to be part of an original farmhouse called 'Mwyndy Bach' (Small Ironhouse) dating back to 1570 and owned by Jenneta, daughter of William Morgan and occupied by Lewis ap Jevan. The farm consisted of 13 acres of cleared woodland and in the 17th century was occupied by minor gentry. Evan ap Rees was related through marriage to the Bassetts of Lanelay which is about 2½ miles away.

In 1861 the farmhouse was occupied by Rosser Evans, a widower of 75 years, with his son Edward, aged 33 years, as farm labourer and Jane David, 14 years, as servant. The original house can be identified from the remains, and was probably a long Welsh house with cow sheds attached, covered in thatch. Later the walls were raised to make first floor bedrooms with a stone tile roof. Prior to the old farmhouse being converted into this public house it had been a ruin for many years.

Agriculture remained the principal occupation of the locality up to 1855 when the Bute iron ore (open cast) mine was sunk on the land. It is claimed, but not substantiated, that iron has been mined and smelted at Mwyndy since Roman times.

However, cinders found confirm that iron ore was abstracted at various times prior to 1855. The Bute Works, between opening and 1884, produced 1½ million tons of ore. The works were subsequently operated at various times, but due to the high quality of Spanish ore, it eventually closed and filled with water. Now called Mwyndy Pool, it is opposite the Barn, surrounded by trees and the water is blue in colour because of the incidence of iron.

On the outskirts of Mwyndy are the ruins of a monastery dedicated to St Cawrdaf. There used to be a wheelwright in the village for many years but this closed a few years ago and now a funeral director uses the premises.

Mwyndy House has been described as a gentleman's residence with a small estate. According to records the house dates from medieval times. However, the first recorded date is 1740 when the centre of the house was built. In 1875 a Mr Price purchased the house from the Marquis of Bute and lived there for many years. He was an industrialist and managed iron ore mines in the area. There is a legend that whilst Mr Price was living at Mwyndy House, he hid Dr William Price (the pioneer of cremation) in the house. It is thought that Dr Price was related in some way.

In 1906 Mr Price died and left the house to his two sons. They sold it to a Mr Thomas who was a Recorder in Glamorgan and he restored the house and built another extension, inserted central heating, a bathroom and a gas plant. After Mr Thomas came Colonel and Mrs R. Horley. Colonel Horley was the Registrar to the Church in Wales' Diocese of Llandaff. The house has a large garden of 2½ acres which is very well kept. The gardens were originally designed in the Georgian era, designed again in Victorian times and then Colonel Horley redesigned them in the1940s–1950s. The house is a Grade II listed building.

Nantgarw ꧁

Nantgarw is a small village about eight miles north of Cardiff and four miles from Pontypridd in the Taff Valley. The A470 motorway from Cardiff to Merthyr bypasses the village. Nantgarw became famous when fine porcelain was made there for a very short period of about six years. Today this porcelain fetches very high prices in auction rooms and was some of the finest porcelain produced in Great Britain.

William Billingsley established the Nantgarw Pottery in 1813 with his son-in-law, Samuel Walker. Billingsley was born in Derby and trained as a painter of porcelain with William Duesbury. However, his interest was in the manufacture of a soft paste porcelain. At that time the finest soft paste porcelain produced came from the French factory at Sevres. Until Billingsley started his porcelain manufacture, no English soft paste porcelain had reached the Sevres standard.

In 1813 Billingsley and his son-in-law Samuel Walker came to Nantgarw and established a pottery. It may be wondered why he chose Nantgarw. He had been to South Wales on a previous occasion and might have passed through it. It was a very quiet backwater and a small village so it meant that he could closely guard the skills of his porcelain manufacture from prying competitors. Also at this time Nantgarw was situated on the route of the Glamorganshire Canal, which had been built in 1794; it passed through the village from Cardiff to Merthyr Tydfil. This canal could bring the china clay to the pottery from Cardiff and then take the costly porcelain to Cardiff for shipment to London where most of the porcelain was sold at quite high prices.

A nearby mill was able to grind the china clay and the coal required for the kilns could be obtained from the coalmines within a few miles. So in 1813 William Billingsley built two small kilns and necessary buildings. In 1814 he had to suspend work at Nantgarw as he was short of money. He and his son-in-law then went to work for Lewis Weston Dillwyn at his Cambrian Works in Swansea.

In 1817 William Billingsley and Samuel Walker returned to Nantgarw to begin production again, but cash flow and technical problems caused them to depart in 1819. They had problems firing the very fine porcelain and the amount of wastage was excessive.

After their departure from Nantgarw, William Weston Young took over the pottery. He was, among other things, a farmer, miller, writer and artist. He too had to admit defeat and left in 1822. The pottery was closed for the next ten years. By 1835 William Henry Pardoe took over the works and turned the unprofitable undertaking into a successful venture. He produced Rockingham pottery ware, a glazed rich brown earthenware and clay tobacco pipes. The pottery passed to his sons, but had to close in 1921 as they were unable to compete with cigarette smoking, and the cheaper hardware being produced elsewhere. William Pardoe rebuilt the pottery house and it is today Nantgarw House.

Nantgarw is once again being brought to the attention of the public.

100

In July 1991 an archaeological investigation commenced at the former Nantgarw China Works. This also included reconsolidation of the existing work buildings around Nantgarw House. This is a project worked in conjunction with Taff-Ely Borough Council and Glamorgan-Gwent Archaeological Trust and has received funding from the Welsh Office through the Urban Programme and the European Commission, through the European Regional Development Fund. Since 22nd May 1992 this site has been open to the public for a very small admission fee.

For many years during the 20th century the village was dominated by the large Nantgarw colliery and coking plant, belching out smoke and steam from its many chimneys over the village. Since 1986 when the works closed and was dismantled the village has become a much cleaner place to live. Today one could not tell that a colliery ever existed there, for the land has been completely cleared.

Neath Abbey 🦢

The village of Neath Abbey was, and still is, famous for three very important buildings which are very much part of the life and history of the village.

The first is the abbey, founded in 1129, which now comes under the control and maintenance of Cadw, but village children used to play amongst the ruins, which then were covered in ivy and brambles, and many a family dinner was followed by blackberry tart made with fruit picked from those particular grounds.

Today, of course, the ruins have been restored and renovated and the grounds cultivated. Various festivals, such as flower shows, concerts etc., are held at the site during the summer months and the whole area is floodlit at night.

The abbey is bounded on one side by a small river which enters the river Neath at this point and the Neath and Tennant Canal runs alongside the abbey at right-angles to the river.

Most of the local children learned to swim in this canal and river, but the highlight of the year was the annual Sunday School outing to the nearby seaside at Jersey Marine.

Nearby are the remains of the furnaces of the Neath Abbey Ironworks which provided machinery for ships, locomotives, gas works and steam engines in the 19th century. The works had been developed by Quaker families, many with Cornish origins.

Our other claim to fame was the Neath Abbey Woollen Mill which was sited in a small deep valley called the Cwm. The power for the mill came from the same small river which ran past the abbey. The mill was in its day the main source of employment for local girls. It produced flannel for shirts, shawls etc, and its machinery can now be seen still in good working order at the Folk Museum at Swansea Maritime Quarter.

If one cares to take a stroll on a summer evening, the mill can still be seen, although not now in working order, and for many the memories of friendships formed amongst their workmates in days gone by are very carefully treasured.

Nelson 🐿

Nelson, with a population approaching 6,000, is situated in the north-east of the county, on the path of the A472.

The surrounding area has a range of landscape features of considerable quality which together contribute to a pleasant environment. It includes a prominent central plateau of agricultural land with Berthlwyd Farm, a typical Welsh longhouse, at its western edge, with the higher ground of Cefn-fforest and Craig-yr-efail on either side of the river Taff as an impressive back cloth. The south and east sections rise gradually through farm, wood and open land to Mynydd Eglwysilan and Cefn Gelligaer respectively, while the heavily wooded valley sides of the Nant Mafon run alongside the A472 to flow into the river Taff. In the middle of a natural bowl is the Nelson Bog – a designated Site of Special Scientific Interest (SSSI). It is one of the few remaining wetlands in South Wales with many interesting features relating to its early geographic development, glaciation and more recent events. It has a wide range of habitats from open water to woodland.

From high up on Mynydd Eglwysilan you can appreciate the panoramic view of the whole Nelson Valley and watch a grazing herd of traditional Welsh Black cattle. Even the atmospheric effects of less than clear weather conspire to change horizons in endless variety.

The highest ground on the fringes of the area holds evidence of occupation dating back to the Stone Age but the first people known to have used the Nelson valley were the Beaker Folk, an early Bronze Age culture. They introduced the practice of individual burial in round barrows, later developing the cist, a primitive tomb consisting of a stone coffin or a cavity lined and covered with slabs of stone. A cist found at Llancaiach Isaf Farm contained the remains of a child, some bronze ornaments and a beaker. The beaker is now in the care of the National Museum of Wales, Cardiff.

102

The area was occupied by the Roman forces based at Gelligaer Fort a mere 1½ miles away and their influence is still to be seen.

Just as the heights of Mynydd Eglwysilan now provide an ideal site for various radio transmitters, so they would have given ideal viewpoints too from which to mount watch for marauders coming by land or sea, and the fold in the slope on the Nelson side would have given excellent protection from anyone following the Taff Valley northward. The name of this area is Llanfabon, 'Llan' – land which has been consecrated to or by the saint, 'fabon' a mutation of Mabon, said to be the brother of St Teilo, Bishop of Llandaff AD 572.

On the original sacred enclosure a monk's cell would be built and in later times would be replaced by a church. The site of the present parish church has been a place of Christian worship ever since the placing of that monk's cell at the side of what may have survived of a Roman road.

The present parish church was designed by John Prichard (1817–1886) who was appointed Diocesan Architect in 1847. Apart from the restoration of Llandaff Cathedral itself, he was responsible for the restoration and building of many churches in the diocese. His work has the reputation of being based on true scholarship and as a rule features excellent detail. In this case his work has been enhanced by the provision of some fine stained glass windows.

The growth of the Nonconformist tradition can be seen in the chapels of the village. From 1787 to 1843 the early groups of Nonconformists belonging to the Welsh Congregational Cause met to worship (illegally) in a room in local farms and cottages. In 1843 Mr. Thomas, squire of the Llechwen estate, built at his own expense Zoar Fawr on Llanfabon Road in the hamlet known as Tai'r-Heol. After a disagreement, the building ceased to be used as a chapel and some members met in a top room of the Dynevor Arms until 1857 when Penuel Chapel in High Street opened. Zoar Fawr came to be used as a barn and was eventually demolished shortly before the First World War, its stones to rise again in the form of the terrace of villas at Tai'r-Heol.

Until Calfaria chapel was opened in 1878, the Baptist congregation went to Berthlwyd Welsh Baptist church above Quaker's Yard and baptism took place in the stream at the Bwrlyn on the west side of the present Welsh Water office block in Pentwyn Road. The first Primitive Methodist Chapel, Salem, was built in 1859. It was rebuilt in 1894 to accommodate the much larger congregation. Bethel Evangelical Church, Heol Fawr was originally Ebenezer Methodist Chapel which opened in 1875. The vestry was the earlier Methodist Church opened in 1832.

Many of the buildings in the area reflect the vernacular styles of the mid to late 19th century. But some, particularly the farmhouses, predate that time, many being longhouses dating from the 17th century. The area

103

has three listed buildings. Llancaiach Fawr (Grade I) is one of only seven Grade I listed buildings in the county. Built in the 16th century as a semi-fortified late Tudor period manor house for the Prichard family it eventually passed to the Wingfield family who were farmers and was thereafter used as a farmhouse until bought by the Rhymney Valley District Council and restored by them. It is now a superb living history museum set in the Civil War year of 1645 with costumed stewards re-enacting everyday scenes showing what life was like in a genuine Civil War stronghold. Today it is a very popular tourist attraction.

The two Grade II listed buildings are Llancaiach House and the remains of the cottages at the side of the Handball Court.

The first geological resource to be exploited was the existence in the area of a remnant of the upper coal measures, the Grovesend Beds. The seam at the base of those measures, the Mynyddislwyn seam, was very near the surface.

Many mines were worked, officially or unofficially, well into this century. In the region of Llancaiach House the seam was worked from the pits of Gelligaer colliery (later known as Powell's Works). In the slopes above Gelligaer colliery there was an outcrop of an even higher seam, Big Rider (known elsewhere in the coalfield as No. 1 Llantwit).

The coal from these two collieries and from Top Hill colliery (just to the north-east of Llancaiach Fawr) converged on the hamlet which became Nelson.

The pits of Gelligaer colliery and Llancaiach colliery closed in 1881 but working from levels in the vicinity continued for some time as the Mynyddislwyn seam was reputed to contain the best house coal in South Wales. The only masonry remaining of the Gelligaer colliery is the base of the substantial stone engine house of its Cornish pumping engine (1869).

Fortunately Nelson had a second string in its geological inheritance, the Pennant sandstone between the upper and lower coal measures. With the expansion of towns all over the area, this beautiful building stone was much in demand and some of the small quarries which had so far satisfied local needs, expanded considerably. The largest, Park, Pandy and Berthgron, each had their own tramroads to railway transfer facilities which survive to some extent in footpaths and trackways.

A substantial amount of stone was exported as paving slabs, and small trainloads of dressed stone went regularly to the Midlands. This was an era in which the quarry masters built themselves substantial houses of beautifully dressed stone e.g. Penlan, Pentwyn Road, and Llwyncelyn, although equally fine stonework with heavy quoins is to be found in many parts of the village e.g. Springfield Terrace.

But the most beautiful walls abound in the older houses, utilising the natural fault lines of the material where the orange-red iron stains have percolated deep into the rock and furnished a flat surface of delightful colouring which could be turned to the outside of the wall. Many boundary walls survive in the village with these characteristics.

Much of Nelson's history and 'specialness' is embodied in the large Conservation Area which defines the original settlement, consisting of the lower end of High Street enclosed by cottages linking The Square with the group of religious buildings. With the Industrial Revolution, development took place radially from the tiny hamlet at The Square. Sadly the pre-industrial cottages have gone. Many of the houses in the High Street are typical 19th century terraced houses. Some of them were the shops of the developing village before Commercial Street became the centre.

Neither the chapels nor the church stand empty; congregations still attend for worship and special events, reflecting the importance they have always had in the religious and cultural life of the village. St John's church, built in 1888 in the late Gothic revival manner, dominates the upper end of the Conservation Area, surrounded by large houses including the rectory, reflecting stages of development in housing and building styles. The open spaces of the church and rectory grounds and the gardens of the large houses contrast with the terraced groupings at the lower end of High Street.

The present Llanfabon Infants School is newly built and opened in January 1992. The original school still stands behind the High Street. It was originally a National School.

One of the most prominent features of the village and which stands in the Conservation Area, is the Handball Court. This three-walled structure was built in the 1860s by the landlord of the Royal Oak Public House. There used to be another, older court attached to the Lord Nelson Inn but all that remains is part of a garden boundary. Originally, in the 18th century the game was played against the north wall of a church as churchyards were then social meeting places and adapted as playgrounds. By the 19th century games were no longer allowed and the first handball courts were built. The game became the recreational sport of manual workers. In 1913 the Handball Court was given into the care of the people of Nelson.

The ancient game of handball has taken on new life with the recent formation of the locally based Welsh Handball Association. The Annual Handball Championship is held on the Handball Court in the Square, Nelson, in August.

Newton (Porthcawl) 🐚

Newton village is built on and around Clevis Rock, and for the last 800 years St John the Baptist church and the green have been the centre of village life. In 1147 land was given to a knight, Richard de Cardiff, and a typical Norman village was born.

Originally the church tower was flat roofed, serving the Normans both as a place of worship and defence against the Welsh. Church dignitaries met in the stone seated porch. Today the stone altar survives. There is also a very rare stone carved pulpit and a font carved out of a solid block of sandstone. The Elizabethan chalice presented by the Queen in 1580 is the most treasured possession of church plate.

At the lower end of the green is Sandfords Well which, together with a well by the bakery cum post office in the main street, was the villagers' water supply a hundred years ago – the lassies filling their earthenware pitchers while the lads playfully teased and pushed them down the steps.

Sandfords Well remains. It once had a reputation for magical properties, because when the tide on Newton beach is out, the well is full and when it is in, the well is empty. Local physician, Dr Hartland, set up a spa and dispensed the alleged healing water.

In the 1500s there was a small creek extending inland. Ale houses abounded. The old Red House near Newton point was supposedly the haunt of smugglers and wreckers. Mussels, crabs, lobsters and prawns

Clevis Hill, Newton

106

were gathered on the foreshore. Later a steamship plied across the channel. Porlock oak furniture was brought to Wales and lime sent back to Somerset. By the 1930s numerous holiday huts sprawled across the dunes. Today wild flora and fauna still abound, the evening primrose, thyme, harebells and orchids together with rabbits and curlew.

The Pyle Mail Coach, the brewhouse drays and gigs no longer clatter past the Crown. Closeknit village life deteriorated with the coming of the buses. No longer was it necessary to walk to Porthcawl to catch the train – Pine's carriage only used if one had luggage!

No more can the constable, tradesmen, straw bonnet maker, blacksmith and lamplighter be found, or Pine's horse-drawn hearse, the sawmill, brewery and slaughterhouse be seen. Gone too are the travelling fairs, the Mabsant Feast in June with accompanying stalls, roundabouts and morris dancers, the Boxing Day Meet, and the Christmas appearance of the 'Mari Lwyd'. Guy Fawkes bonfires on the Green disappeared by the early 1960s.

Today village life embraces Victorian fayres, flower festivals grace the church, and the Ancient Briton, Jolly Sailor and the Globe welcome modern day drinkers. Speedboats and windsurfers flash across the bay.

Moorlands private school has closed, but the schoolroom still nestles alongside the green. Today it houses the Sunday School children. The local shops still draw villagers for a gossip and village life continues to flourish.

Newton (Swansea)

Newton is situated to the west of Swansea and includes the beautiful bays of Langland and Caswell. There are the ruins of St Peter's Holy Well and Chapel in Caswell Valley, which was recorded in 1128. Its water was good for the eyes and many people visited it for its curative properties. Services were held on Lady Day and Easter. There was a windmill on Caswell Point.

Newton used to be a small rural village with most of the villagers working on the many small farms. Milk was delivered to the houses in cans and measured out to customers into their jugs at their doors twice a day.

Ploughing was done with two horses pulling a one furrow plough. Hay was collected by horse and cart and corn was cut by scythe, bound into sheaves and stood in stooks – six sheaves to a stook. These were collected and taken to the farm yard, where a steam engine pulling a threshing machine came in October and threshed the corn. All the farmers would help each other.

The roads were swept regularly by the roadman and were lit by gas standard lamps which the lamplighter, who walked from Mumbles with his pole twice a day, lit and put out. A stream of water ran down the main road in a deep gutter from the common. After heavy rainfall it would gush down and into a culvert. The houses on this side of the road had paving stone bridges to enable people to cross in and out. There were several pumps in the village.

The two public houses, the Rock and Fountain (which brewed its own beer) and the Ship and Castle (now the Newton Inn) were frequented by pirates and smugglers who used donkeys to move cargoes plundered from ships lured to their doom on the rocks off Mumbles and Langland. The bounty was shared out in these Inns. Some donkeys had to walk through the houses to get to their sheds in the back gardens.

One of the old Newton customs was the 'Bidding Wedding'. When a couple got married, a barn was set aside where they would go to receive gifts of kind and money. Their path would be chained by a rope and flowers and they would have to scatter coins to 'buy' their way to the barn. Money was also 'heaved' (lent to them) which they would return once they were on their feet. They would then spend the rest of the evening celebrating by eating, dancing and drinking local brew.

The local women gathered seaweed from the beach at Langland for manure for the potato fields. They would also meet in Mary Twill Lane at the pool, formed from the fresh water stream, to do their washing.

The outlying areas consisted of a few large houses where the business-men of Swansea lived. Pony and trap was used for transport. Poorer folk working in Swansea had to walk down to Oystermouth each day to catch the old Mumbles steam train and walk back again at night.

Many famous people are connected with Newton. John Wesley preached in a barn in the village in 1758. Oliver Cromwell picketed his army on the village green which is now called 'Picket's Mead'. Francis Ridley Havergal lived here and wrote the famous hymn *Take my life and let it be; Consecrated Lord to Thee*. It is said that Henry VIII stayed here on his way to Weobley Castle. Dylan Thomas' parents were married in Paraclete Chapel, which was built in 1818 and Dylan often came to stay at the Manse with his aunt and uncle, who was the minister there.

The first school in Newton was recorded in 1743. Newton National School was established in 1860 and was a Church school. They used oak apples for counting. The head teacher lived in the school house Monday to Friday and went home for weekends. The children used to march from the school to the church for services and always had a half day's holiday for Ascension Day. From 1882 it had piped water from the fresh water springs at Caswell and flush toilets. A sewage system came to Newton in 1910.

The Glynn Vivian Home for the Blind was built in 1907 and Belgian refugee children stayed there in 1914 and were enrolled in the local school. In 1924 Prime Minister Ramsay Macdonald and his wife visited the Home and all the local children were taken by their headmistress to see them arrive.

St Peter's Church was built in 1903 with beautiful stained glass windows, paid for by the gentry of the village.

Newton is now a suburb of Swansea, but it is still one of the loveliest parts of Wales, and retains its village atmosphere.

Norton 🦚

En route to the Mumbles between Blackpill and Oystermouth, lies the village of Norton. The centre of the village is known as Norton Cross. The reason for this is that it was situated at the convergence of no less than four roads, namely Norton Road, Glen Road, and the main road running through to Oystermouth around the Castle.

In days gone by and before the present Mumbles road was constructed, Norton was a very busy and important village. Glen Road, then a narrow country lane, was the route to Murton and Bishopston. Norton Road ran down directly on to the foreshore, while the road running north of Norton Cross was the route to Killay and that running south of Norton Cross was the route via the Castle to Oystermouth.

Norton Cross residents take great pride in their village and despite the passage of time the village atmosphere has been retained by carefully up-dating houses and little cottages, the gardens of which are a great delight and provide a riot of colour at all times.

The village pub, known as the Beauport, plays an active part in the life of the village, not only as a hostelry but also for the renowned generosity of the landlord in participating in all charitable activities concerned with the area.

Norton village has three lovely old mansions, all of which stand proudly in their own grounds, beautiful examples of the craftsmanship and quality of days gone by. Today they are no longer family homes. Norton House is a very well known high class hotel, the stables and coach houses transformed into providing extra accommodation. Norton Lodge, home of a former prominent Swansea solicitor, was taken over

109

by Swansea City Council as a Rest Home for the elderly. Norton Villa, family home of a prosperous coal exporter named Mr. Spencer Thomas, today serves as a clinic for mothers and babies and chiropody treatment for the elderly, having been taken over by the County Council. So we see that the basic changes to Norton village are that country lanes have given way to roads and that stately homes have been put to community uses. Many older residents once worked as maids and cooks in these mansions.

The greatest and most recent change is the demolition of the old Norton Mission Hall, a corrugated sheet building which had stood on the site for 77 years and is now replaced by the new and attractively designed Norton Village and Church Hall. Despite some grants this project naturally needed funds, and so it brought the whole community together – the church group, the Residents' Association and Norton WI members – two of whom serve on the Hall management team.

Nottage 🐝

Nottage is a district of Porthcawl.

The Great Well (Ffynnon Fawr) is at the bottom of Nottage Hill near the traffic roundabout. It forms one of a line of wells which follow a fault line extending from Porthcawl breakwater to St David's Well. Ffynnon Fawr has played an important part in providing the old village of Nottage and the new town of Porthcawl with water.

St David's Well owes its importance to the supposedly curative powers of its water and the sanctity bestowed upon it by a visit of its patron saint. The presence of the stone tablet placed there by the National Association of Monumental Masons in 1962 is an indication of the prestige associated with this quiet dell of Dewiscumbe. This well was mentioned in a 12th century Grant of William Earl of Gloucester.

Along the road from St David's Well is Cuckoo Bridge which carried the Great Western Railway line over Moor Lane. The line of the railway to Ty Talbot Farm and through a tunnel underneath the village can still be seen. The remains of Nottage Halt can also be seen. It was very popular and often referred to as the Golf Station.

The Rose and Crown Hotel takes its name from two cottages which stood on this site, Rose Cottage and Crown Cottage. The remains of Rose Cottage can still be seen behind the barbecue area. Crown Cottage had a long association with the Burnell family and was the last ale house to be licensed in the Bridgend area.

Ashcott Villa is next to the Rose and Crown. This villa was the site of the ancient church. A 1630 Manorial Survey indicates there was a church in the village which may have been associated with St David's Well or Noge Court Grange.

Groes Cottage was so named because the old village cross is reputed to have stood on this site. More recently this was a village shop and post office. The post office is now situated in the stores next to Elm Tree Cottage. The village bakery was next to Groes Cottage, at the rear of the Farmer's Arms.

The Village Green was dedicated to the community by Nottage Court Estate in 1983. The end wall was known as Labourers' Wall, where men lined up for work – generally on May Day. At one time the green contained a barn, two milking sheds and allotments. When the railway tunnel was dug underneath the village, human remains were found at the eastern end of the Green. It is thought that this area was a graveyard associated with the old Celtic church or the church frequented by monks at Noge Court Grange.

The Swan pub was built in the garden of an old cottage. The name Swan applies also to fields in the Long Acre area of Nottage.

Nottage was one of the earliest centres of Nonconformist activities in Wales. John Miles preached in Nottage in 1657. After the Declaration of Indulgence 1662, two licences were issued by Charles II allowing Walter Craddock, Independent, and Howell Thomas, Baptist, to preach. Howell Harris in 1743 formed a Methodist 'Society' in Nottage. Baptists leased a cottage on the site of the present chapel and were received into the Association by 1789. Differences over doctrine divided the Baptists, and the church became Unitarian.

Tudor Cottage is white with black beams. At one time in the 16th century this was West End Farm, and alongside the butcher's shop is the farmyard, pound and stables. Elm Tree Cottage is the oldest in the village. It is the only building registered as an ancient monument. In 1846 there were three cottages on the site – Elm Tree, Apple Tree and Pear Tree. It has now been extensively renovated.

St David's church was an ex US Army barrack hut which was consecrated in 1948. Before this, Holy Communion Services were held at 'Redlands', West Road. In the late 1950s a building fund was started, but it was not until 1989 that this was intensified under Canon David John, and in November 1992 the new St David's was consecrated on land originally given by a deed of gift by Mr Blundell of Nottage Court.

West Park primary school was built in 1971 on a field which previously had been a market garden, due to expansion of the West Park Estate.

Nottage Court (Noge Court Grange) was listed as one of the Wheat Farms administered by the Abbot of Margam. It was then known as Noche Court. When the monastic lands were sold during the Dissolution of the Monasteries, Noge Court Grange was included in the sale of land to Sir Rice Mansell, 1540. In 1545 the Lougher family acquired the property and the house was rebuilt in 1570. The new building was built in the Elizabethan style and the original beams still support the roof structure. The original stone mouldings around the windows, doorways and fire places are still there. For many years the building was known as Ty Mawr, but after extensive renovations in 1855, the gentleman in residence – the Rev Henry Hey Knight, re-named it Nottage Court. The Rev Knight was the son of the Vicar of Tewkesbury and he arranged for a tapestry which had been in Tewkesbury for 350 years to be hung in Nottage Court. During excavations at Nottage Court, evidence of Roman and pre-Roman cultures were found in the form of Medusa and clay images. In the Court grounds are fossilised footprints of a bronto-saurus and the Gondianius stone which has Roman inscriptions. Set inside the walled surround of Nottage Court, Garden Cottage has replaced the old Lamb Cottages. On the entrance wall is the cement engraving of a lamb. This plaque was at one time set into the gable end of the Lamb Inn which stood in the garden. The inn was owned by the Guest family and at one time parish vestry meetings were held there.

The village pond used to be at the road junction of West Road and Florence Street. The bus shelter was built by public subscription. The chestnut tree was planted in 1902 to commemorate the coronation of King Edward VII. Nottage Forge opposite the bus shelter, is now used for making wrought ironwork. Daven on the hill next to Kenfig Cottages, is a house built over the exact spot where the railway tunnel emerged from under the village.

Ogmore-by-Sea

Ogmore castle has been in ruins for hundreds of years. The first castle on this site was not of stone but of timber. The stone castle was begun by the Norman, Sir William de Londres, the first Lord of Ogmore, around the beginning of the 12th century. This castle consisted of the central keep, built of large irregular boulders set in brown mortar. Around the keep was the inner ward. The detached building on the east side of the inner ward was probably built in the late 12th century, and the curtain walls which surrounded the inner ward, together with the great hall in the northeast of the inner ward, date from the beginning of the 13th century. The other detached building in the outer ward, nearest to the farm, is believed to have been the court house, and dates from the 15th century. It would seem strange that a castle should be built on what appears to be an unsuitable site, but, strategically, it is an important site. When the Normans came into Glamorgan, about 1093, they advanced westward and built castles to defend the lands they had conquered against the Welsh, who resented the Norman intrusion into their land. With the river, and the castle's own defences, and the high ground behind from which to observe the western approaches, Ogmore Castle was on a better site than would at first appear.

William de Londres was succeeded at Ogmore Castle by his son Maurice, who also had a castle at Kidwelly. Whilst away at Kidwelly, he left Ogmore in charge of his steward, Arnold le Botiler. Ogmore Castle was attacked by the Welsh, and Arnold defended it so well that Maurice rewarded him with the Manor of Dydryfan, on condition that, whenever the Lord of Ogmore visited there, he was presented with chalices of wine. The name Le Botiler became Butler, and their coat of arms contained three golden chalices on a blue field. The castle was restored in 1928–1929 by the Ministry of Works, and is now looked after as an ancient monument by Cadw.

The name of the Pelican inn is taken from the Coat of Arms of the family of Carne, once owners of Ewenny Priory. After Henry VIII had caused the Dissolution of the Monasteries, Ewenny Priory was first leased to, and later purchased by, Sir Edward Carne. His coat of arms included an ancient heraldic device known as 'a pelican in her piety'. This depicts a female pelican, with wings half-spread, and with a brood of young at her feet. She is plucking her own breast and the drops of blood are falling into the open mouths of the pelican chicks. Thus, she is feeding them with her own blood. This is a very old device in heraldry and can be found in many places, including on a bronze door in Cologne Cathedral, in Germany, and on the tower which sits on top of Glaston-bury Tor in Somerset.

Crossing the road from the Pelican, we come to Ogmore Farm. This is one of the oldest farms in South Wales, and was originally the manorial farm to Ogmore Castle. We believe that the first farm house was built here as long ago as the 13th century, and the present house dates from as long ago as the 16th or 17th century, although it has probably been altered since then. We know from old documents that the farm was part of the castle lands, but in the year 1490 it was leased to John Walsh, as tenant farmer, for seven years at £54.7s.8d per annum. First in the hands

113

of the Lord of Ogmore, the farm later became the property of the king, as part of the Duchy of Lancaster. Today it is still an active farm, run by the Williams family.

In the old days before bridges were built across shallow rivers and streams, stepping stones were often placed in the water to enable people to cross whilst keeping their feet out of the water. The stones in the Ewenny river have been there for very many years. There are many more stones than can now be seen in the water as some are buried by years of mud and grass on each bank. We do not know when the stones were placed there but we think they are at least 400 years old. In fact, the first stepping stone may have been placed in Norman times or just a little later as this was the only route from St Brides Major through Merthyr Mawr and towards Pyle and Laleston before the roads were built. Baptisms have taken place from these stones in the river, and a more lighthearted custom has occurred here, that of young men racing across the stones (usually after several drinks in the Pelican inn near by) to cross in the fastest time without falling into the river.

Tuskar Rock is a large rock in the Bristol Channel off Ogmore-by-Sea and has claimed many a ship in storm tossed water. One ship, *The Mellany*, built in Portmadoc in North Wales, sailed on a regular run with coal to Valparaiso in South America.

Before the fateful night the captain and his wife stayed the night in an hotel at Cardiff, when they were awakened in the early hours by a sound in their room. The next morning they arose to discover a little mouse had drowned in the wash basin. Because of this occurrence the wife wouldn't sail with her husband. The *Mellany* set sail and off Lundy Island met a severe storm, made to return to Cardiff but foundered on the Tuskar Rock. All aboard were lost.

In the 1950s some new housing began to be built on the West Farm Road area of Ogmore-by-Sea. One of the first home owners recalls life in the village then:

'On my solitary walks with the pram, I noticed other bungalows nearing completion and I waited eagerly to see if there might be another young Mum to talk to. I knocked at doors and invited them for coffee. Friendships were formed and have lasted to this day. We had no play groups, no cars, and we walked, in convoy, to the baby clinic at St Brides Major. We called back at Verity's Cafe in Southerndown for a cup of tea. We made our own playgroups, most afternoons we met in turn at someone's bungalow and shared ideas and recipes. When the weather was good we took the pushchairs to the beach. We had such good times, although we had very little money.'

We are very fortunate to live in beautiful surroundings of sea and

114

countryside. Quite a large portion of Ogmore Down is taken up by the Southerndown Golf Club. It is of international standard and reputed to be one of the driest and finest photogenic courses.

Ogmore Vale 🦢

One enters the Ogmore Valley via Bryncethin, Blackmill, Pantyrawel and Lewistown. After passing through Lewistown, rounding the curve of the road, before you lies the Ogmore Valley which includes Ogmore Vale itself, Wyndham and Nantymoel.

The mountains to your right are covered with fir trees, now being sectioned and felled to make way for the newly planted young firs. The head of the valley is dominated by the Bwlch mountain. The road leading up to the Bwlch brings you to a junction which divides with the Llynfi Valley to the west and to the east, Treorchy and the Rhondda valley. Meandering down the centre of the valley is the river Ogmore on its way to the coast at Ogmore-by-Sea. We are fortunate to have the beauty of the mountains and be in easy reach of the coast.

The face of the valley has changed considerably over the years. The mines no longer exist, landscaping has created vast pastures stretching across the valley. At one area a small industrial estate, Penllygwent, exists, but apart from these small businesses and shops there is little else offering employment. A few farms are scattered on the mountainside, also the remains of old farmhouses, long since fallen into ruin. One farm however, has been saved from such a fate. Aber Farm, reputed to be early 15th century, has quite a history. It was purchased by Byron Evans and repaired in an effort to restore it to its former glory. Mr Evans and family now live in and work the farm, preserving our heritage and converting an eyesore into a delightful working farm. Another farm, Nantymoel Farm, is over 300 years old and is unique in the valley with its wonderful stone-work steps leading to bedrooms and the arched window and sills.

Education within the valley is to eleven years old then children migrate to comprehensive schools outside the valley. Many schools built at the beginning of the century have been neglected or put to a use which has led to their dereliction, such as the old secondary/grammar school at Wyndham, and the Tynewydd Boys School at Ogmore Vale. One school at Nantymoel however, has been converted into sheltered accommodation called Dinan Close. Another sheltered complex built at Ogmore Vale opposite the site of the old railway station and the Gwalia Stores is called

Gwalia Close. The Gwalia grocery stores have been taken down and rebuilt at the Welsh Folk Museum at St Fagans.

For many years the Gwalia played a large part within the community of Ogmore Valley. Up to the time of closure in 1979, to step inside was to step back in time to the early days of shop keeping at the beginning of the century, with the succulent smell of fresh cheese, butter, dried fruit, bread and bacon on the slicer all ready to weigh, wrap and sell from scales, with their brass weights on the wooden counters topped with marble.

Nestling together along the row were other shops, chemists, draper/ outfitting and the ironmonger all belonging to the Gwalia.

Initially it was a company store owned by the mineowners, Cory Bros. It was later purchased by Mr William Llewellyn JP who also owned streets of houses. One such street named after him lay at the foot of a mountain overlooked by Gorwyl House, Mr Llewellyn's mansion. Servants were employed to look after the house and family which grew to include four sons and one daughter. One of the sons sustained an injury during childhood which resulted in permanent blindness, this boy was destined to become the Rector of Llandow (near Cowbridge) and the grandfather of Dr David Owen – now Lord Owen. It was fitting that Lord Owen opened the rebuilt Gwalia Stores at the Welsh Folk Museum on 13th July 1991.

The new health care surgery at Ogmore Vale is built on the site of the Workmen's Hall. The hall suffered irreparable structural damage and had to be demolished. The surgery has two doctors, a nurse and staff and is run on a more business-like system than years gone by, when one waited for hours in a small packed waiting room desperately keeping a watch to see you didn't miss your turn.

Clubs and public houses abound within the valley. One can join skittles, darts, bowls and quiz teams. Many social groups run by the church and chapel fellowships, meet regularly. We have a male choir and ladies choir. The younger element have their centres at Nantymoel, Wyndham and Ogmore Vale. The Ogmore Valley WI hold their meetings at the Aber Youth Club at Ogmore Vale and have liaised with the youngsters on occasions, to find the association very rewarding.

At one time there were over 20 churches and chapels in the valley, now there are probably nine to ten at the most in use, some on a part time basis. Two were converted into furnishing establishments while another accommodates The Baden Powell Centre. A newly named 'Christchurch' is the result of the coming together of four previously independent denominations, an amalgamation which hopefully will be united and strong in future years.

Oxwich 🌿

Oxwich, a small seaside village, is situated twelve miles from Swansea to the west of a magnificent three mile sweep of sand.

The one street of ancient cottages is now punctuated by modern houses and the old hedges of blackthorn have been replaced in most instances by fences or walls. But in parts it still retains some of the old village charm.

One tends to think that the Oxwich of the last century was idyllically peaceful. Not so, because what is now a beautifully wooded point rising above the beach and sea was the scene of a busy limestone quarry, owned by the Penrice Estate. Most of the limestone was shipped to Devon where it was converted to lime for use on their acid soils. The links with Devon were shown by the one time dominance of Devon surnames such as Ace, Grove and Tucker. There was in many of the Gower villages a distinctive Gower dialect, having much in common with the West Country.

Oxwich probably existed as a settlement since early Celtic times. The original church was founded in the 6th century by St Illtud, which suggests that some sort of settlement was present at the time.

Legend has it that the original village of Oxwich was grouped around the church on the cliff edge and that it was gradually destroyed by the sea. There is, however, no evidence to support this theory, although it is possible that over 4,000 years ago there was a settlement on the coastal marshes, when the sea level was lower than it is today.

The church is in an isolated position so it is easy to understand why the legend arose, especially as the original rectory, which was situated below the church and very close to the sea, was destroyed by a violent storm in 1805, necessitating the building of the new rectory, which is now an hotel.

Oxwich has a history of 'wrecking', in common with many coastal villages. One of the earliest recorded wrecking incidents occurred in 1557, giving rise to what became known as 'The Affray of Oxwich Castle'. A dispute arose over a wreck of a foreign ship. A fracas ensued under the gateway between the Herberts and the Mansels (the castle was built by Sir Rice Mansel in about 1550 and its ruins are today in the care of Cadw). An aunt of the young squire, who had been left in charge of the castle, was struck by a missile and killed.

In 1794 the rector of Oxwich recorded that 'Poor Thomas Matthews died of drinking too much smuggled gin'. Oxwich church was full to pay their last respects to poor old Thomas.

Parkmill 🌿

Come for a walk through Parkmill village, the gateway to South Gower and its magnificent bays. At the start we pass Kilvrough Manor with its high curving boundary wall. The original manor was built in 1585 by Rowland Dawkins, but the present house is late 18th century. There are now only six acres of ground around the house which includes the round folly. The manor is now owned by Oxfordshire Education Authority and is run as a holiday and training centre for young people.

As we pass wooded slopes on either side of the road we come to the Gower Inn. This was the natural meeting place for local farmers coming to and from Swansea market. It was and still is one of the 'great institutions in Gower'. Adjacent to the inn is the gate to the 'cwms' (valley) through which the stream (remembered as Killy-Willy) meanders to Ilston – partly underground. About half a mile into the 'cwms' we come to a 17th century ruin of a building claimed to be the first Baptist chapel in Wales, founded in 1649. As we retrace our steps back to the road we come to the 100 year old school – now bought and used by the Girl Guides for outdoor pursuits. Further along we pass the old and new police houses and the post office which, unfortunately, like a lot of other village post offices has closed. This was once the hub of the village, where villagers gathered to buy their groceries and exchange news and gossip. As the road narrows we pass the well-used chapel.

Before arriving at the Green Cwms and Giants Graves, on the left one can walk over the hill to Three Cliffs Bay – where in 1917 wine barrels were washed up on the shore and the whole of Parkmill congregated on the beach and imbibed of the wine – although it was a Sunday!

The 14th century mill fell into disrepair for a time but has recently been restored and the wheel is turning once again. The area has been made into a craft centre and the stream now runs clean and unpolluted across the field to Parc-le-Breos.

Now modern traffic causes congestion during the summer months. Not so long ago, a quiet Sunday walk through this delightful village, with a stop at Shepherd's shop for an ice-cream, was a way of life.

Penarth 🌿

Penarth possibly derives its name from Pen – a head, and Garth – a ridge. This headland was used long ago for a beacon on which a fire was lit to warn the county of invasion by the enemies at sea. Signals were repeated on the Garth mountains, Castell Coch and on to Merthyr Tydfil, Breconshire and Carmarthenshire. Beautiful views of the Bristol Channel and Somerset coast are seen from the headland. The church of St Augustine stands out on the headland and is a prominent landmark, especially for those at sea in the Bristol Channel.

In the 19th century the population of Penarth was under 100 but its rapid growth was due to the building of its dock, opened in 1865, to extend facilities for the export of coal from the valleys to Cardiff docks.

From the recently constructed 'Penarth Mariner', one can walk along the pebbly–sandy beach to Penarth pier when the tide is out. During the summer months one can enjoy a boat trip on Campbell's steamers from Penarth Pier to Weston-super-Mare, Ilfracombe, Lynton and Lynmouth on the Devon coast and also to the Gower coast at Swansea, or just sit and enjoy the yachts sailing from the Penarth yacht club.

Penclawdd 🌿

Nestling under the hills on the North Gower coast lies the village of Penclawdd. Facing the Burry estuary, with the many changing colours of its tides and marshland, it is the only Welsh speaking community in Gower.

Up to the end of the 19th century it was a thriving port with coal, tinplate, copper and brass being produced. However, since the port died, the only industries remaining are cockle gathering and, on a smaller scale, farming. Penclawdd is renowned, even on the Continent for its cockle industry which has been in existence in the area since Roman times. Up until the 1970s women were the main gatherers, and were a hardy lot, noted for their endurance and ability to withstand all weather conditions on the sands of the estuary. Nowadays more men take responsibility for the gathering because of the decline in employment previously provided by factories and collieries in the area. Over the years villagers have seen the cockle gatherers' transportation change from the donkey, to the horse and cart, and now to the landrover.

It may be difficult nowadays for visitors and younger inhabitants to

119

realise that within living memory Penclawdd was a thriving commercial centre for much of North Gower. Many still remember that there were no fewer than twenty grocers, three drapers, three barbers, four fish and chip shops, a forge, railway station, three chapels; a church, a cinema and at one time, for those so inclined, eleven pubs! Also the village had its own undertaker who could often be seen working late at night because all coffins were hand made from planks of timber.

A feature of village life has been and still is the Whitsun walk undertaken by chapel members. This is part of a large Whitsun celebration spread over three days with singing festivals.

The spirit of community and the capacity to work together has always been a characteristic of the village. This is reflected in the achievements of its cultural activities ranging from successful choirs and brass band to equally successful football teams.

In recent years the village has greatly expanded. The North Gower coast, and Penclawdd in particular, has proved to be a popular area for many young as well as retired newcomers. It is not difficult to be accepted in a village like Penclawdd which has always been noted for its friendliness. The recent establishment of a new and thriving Community Centre, with its many diverse activities and educational courses, is already proving its worth, not only as a meeting place but as a base for further cultural development.

Penclawdd has had, and does have much to offer.

Pencoed

Pencoed means 'Woodend' or the 'end of the wood', and according to old records it would appear that there were dwellings here at least 600 years ago. It lies five miles north east of Bridgend. To the north is the long ridge of Cefn Hirgoed with St Mary Hill to the east and Coed-y-Mwster to the west. According to a map printed in the 16th century, Pencoed was once spelled 'Pencoyd'.

Prior to 1850 there were only a few houses scattered around the village with farms and small holdings on the hillsides. In 1850 the only place of worship was at Salem chapel and the parish church was St Crallo's at Coychurch about two miles distant. The village at this time would have been comparatively self-supporting. Corn was grown on the farms and taken to a cornmill at Melingroes on the outskirts of the village. There was a woollen factory and a malt house. Stones, timber and lime were obtained locally. Coal was mined within two miles of Pencoed at

Pant Hirwaun and Cribbwr Main. Most of the villagers kept pigs and poultry. Corn was bought from local farmers and the majority of men worked on local farms or as casual help during harvest. Others found work in coal mines, quarries and lime kilns in the parish. Welsh would have been the dominant tongue among the people in their homes.

There were two turning points in the history of Pencoed. One was in 1850 when the railway was built through Pencoed and a station was constructed. The second was the mining of coal to the north of the parish. These two facts were the main reasons for the increase in population at this time and helped to establish Pencoed as a thriving community. It has grown ever since.

With the development of coal mines in the area, an influx of people came from Somerset, the Forest of Dean and Border Counties to look for work. Where Welsh had been the only language spoken, English became the first language. As more houses were needed this led to the opening of the brickworks, and Pencoed Foundry was opened to supply tools and trams for the collieries.

The first place of worship in Pencoed was Salem chapel built by the Methodists before they dissented from the Anglican Church and became a Nonconformist movement. The Rev David Jones, the Rector of Llangan, which is about five miles from Pencoed, was largely instrumental in setting up Salem in 1775. He was the foremost Methodist leader of that time. A notable characteristic of the Methodist Movement was that in the early years converts were grouped into societies and such a society had been formed by 1747 in Pencoed. Eventually a meeting place was needed, so Salem chapel came into being. It was the first Methodist chapel in Glamorgan. However, by 1830 a larger chapel was built on the same site and it was reputed to have a seating capacity of 500 and opened on 27th December 1830. This chapel was used until 1887 when yet a larger chapel was needed for the increase of population in Pencoed. On 16th June 1886 the foundation stone of the present chapel was laid and it was opened on 1st June 1888.

Anglicans living in Pencoed at this time attended church services at St Crallo's church at Coychurch, 2½ miles away. The present church in Pencoed, St David's, was built in 1862 and was first used as a National School run by the church. This is the reason why the altar is not in the correct position in the church – it faces in the wrong direction. It was granted a licence to perform divine service on 15th September 1915.

Tregroes House has had quite a varied history. It was for about four centuries the Squire's residence of the village. This was the largest house in Pencoed and stood on a site of an earlier house, and was inhabited by the Thomas family until 1870. They were a well known Glamorgan

121

family of their time whose motto was 'nil desperandum'. Early records of the family refer to Robert Thomas who in 1661 was charged at the Great Sessions of Glamorgan with the murder of Edmund Thomas in a duel fought on Cefn Hirgoed, not far from Tregroes, on 4th February 1660. He was outlawed and his lands and possessions taken from him. In 1669 he was pardoned with a restitution of lands and goods. The present house was built about 100 years ago.

After 1870 several gentlemen owned the property until the Bevan family sold it to Glamorgan County Council in 1925. It soon afterwards became a demonstration farm – locally known as the 'Dem' for short, then it was taken over by Pencoed College of Agriculture and Horticulture and today is called simply Pencoed College.

It has been recorded that an eisteddfod was held at Pencoed as early as All Souls Day, 2nd November 1733. Lewis Hopkin (1708–71), a famous poet in his day, explained that the eisteddfod was not for the dead but for the living, that its object was to foster the Welsh language and poetic art. These very words are being said today, over 200 years later.

Pencoed has always been proud of its band. Pencoed Silver Band was formed in 1902 as a brass band. In 1946 all instruments were re-silvered. Band practices were held in the Britannia Inn for many years. This inn was opened in 1850, on the day the first train ran through Pencoed. Today the silver band is sponsored by the British Legion Club.

In the 1930s Pencoed was a small sleepy little village with a close community spirit where the only car owners were the doctor and two garage owners. The majority of men and boys worked in local coal mines, so it was a common sight to see the miners return from work covered in black coal dust.

The highlight of the year was the Sunday school outing, the only time most children got to see the sea and travel in a charabanc (a coach with a soft top, which would be rolled back in the sunshine). Sunday School and Band of Hope were very important to the children. On Tuesday nights they queued to see the magic lantern show. This was still pictures relating to Bible stories.

Another favourite time was when Dads, in their spare time, helped the local farmers to cut and gather hay and children were allowed to help.

Pencoed was a nice village for children to grow up before the Second World War as it was quite rural. We had a large Public Hall situated at the top of Glossop Terrace, where dances, drama, variety shows and picture shows were held. This hall was a delight to people of Pencoed, young and old alike. Sadly it burned down many years ago.

At the beginning of the Second World War a hostel was built at

Pencoed with 1,000 beds to accommodate workers employed at the Ordnance Factory at Bridgend, a few miles distance. This is now an Industrial Estate. Hostel accommodation was also given to Polish miners who had come to work in the coal mines in the area. Much good agricultural land was lost to this project. Today the hostel has been demolished to make way for housing.

During the Second World War schoolchildren were able to have a hot meal at lunch time at the British Restaurant which was sited in the grounds of Trinity Chapel. The children were marched each lunch time to the restaurant which was nearby. Otherwise if children lived too far to go home at lunch time they would bring a packed lunch to school.

Also at this time there was an American Camp at St Mary Hill, a small village about two miles from Pencoed. Every evening American soldiers visited the public houses in the village and many young girls from Pencoed became GI brides. Often these American soldiers were invited to various homes for afternoon tea, especially on Sundays.

During the past three decades the population of Pencoed has grown rapidly, as a number of housing estates have sprung up.

Because of the increase in population over the recent years Pencoed was given town status in 1982.

The recent acquisition to the area has been the building of the Sony factory on the edge of Pencoed near the M4 interchange. This factory provides much needed employment, and manufactures electronic equipment making it a very modern, clean place to work.

Pencoed has twinned with Waldsassen in Bavaria and exchange visits have taken place during the past several years and many new friends made.

Pendoylan

Pendoylan is situated in the rural area of the Vale of Glamorgan. The parish covers 3,500 acres, which includes 56 acres of lake water. The current population numbers 1,000 plus – quite different from that of 1938 when it was about 350! The villagers are proud of their numerous successes in winning the Best Kept Village in the Vale of Glamorgan competition (twelve times since 1958), including two occasions when it also won the National Competition. The parish is laden with history and legend.

In the centre of the village is the very old Red Lion Inn. Pendoylan Church in Wales Primary School meets the educational needs, being a gift of Miss Mary Fothergill of Hensol Castle in 1873 and replacing the earlier school which was held in 1, Church Row – a row of tiny cottages that were once known as almshouses.

Between the inn and the school there stands the ancient parish church dedicated to Saint Catwg. This is a substantial building with chancel, nave and south porch. Its massive western tower dwarfs the church and contains six bells. Inside this Norman tower, which served as a refuge for the local population in the turbulent past, there is a flight of narrow, twisting, stone steps. When threatened with raiders from outside, one person armed with a sword could stand on the narrow steps and prevent any enemy reaching the people. In the churchyard there are two ancient yew trees, and local legend claims that the army of the Black Prince cut their arrows from these trees!

Pendoylan has two wells, one in the south of the parish dedicated to Saint Teilo ('Ffynnon Deilo'), and the other in the village, dedicated to Saint Catwg. The latter well comes through a rock, and it is said that in 1922, during a fire in Church Row, much water was obtained from this well to extinguish the blaze.

Bethania chapel is situated between the village and Clawdd Coch, and is used by the Presbyterian Church of Wales. Originally this was the Calvinistic Methodist Chapel and was built in 1870; associated with its building were the Morgan brothers from nearby Gwern-y-Steeple, and Evan Edwards, a local tax collector. The present 'Bethania' replaced a smaller chapel which was on the site of a burial ground. The latter still exists. Interestingly, there used to be a large sycamore tree at Clawdd Coch, where the Latter Day Saints held their services.

Nowadays, a meeting place for the parish is the Pendoylan War Memorial Hall, situated between Bethania and the village. It was opened in 1933 and is dedicated to the ex-servicemen of the parish.

A couple of miles in a northerly direction from the village there stands the impressive Hensol Castle, the ancestral home of the Jenkins family. Judge David Jenkins was a distinguished lawyer and a Justice of the Western Circuit of Wales. He was born in 1582 and is said to have been 'a man of forceful ability'. He was a strong supporter of Charles I during the Civil War, and this adherence resulted in him being taken prisoner in 1645 at Hereford by the Parliamentary Army. He was confined in turn at Newgate, Wallingford Castle, Windsor Castle and the Tower of London. Upon being arraigned at the Bar of the House of Commons he refused to kneel in respect and was fined £1,000 for contempt. Being impeached for high treason he declared his intention of 'dying with the Bible under one arm and the Magna Carta under the other.' He was, however, pardoned and released in 1656, eventually returning to Hensol.

His son, David, inherited the castle, followed by *his* son, Richard, the last of the Jenkins of Hensol, and a well-known harpist. Later the property passed to the Earls Talbot of Hensol. The Talbot family left Hensol at the close of the 18th century.

Samuel Richardson was the next owner. He was a pioneer in agriculture and carried out great improvements on land drainage on the site. He introduced the threshing machine, replacing the old flail method of extracting the seed from corn.

Later, the Crawshays of Cyfarthfa bought the castle. The Crawshays were followed by another family of ironmasters, the Fothergills of Abernant.

The estate was sold to the Glamorgan County Council in the 1920s. It is now a hospital for the mentally handicapped, under the administration of the Mid Glamorgan Area Health Authority.

Llanerch vineyard at Hensol which is about one mile from Pendoylan, is the largest vineyard in Wales, producing estate-bottled wines.

Llanerch Farm when acquired by Peter and Diana Andrews in 1978 was in a dilapidated state and has been extensively conserved and restored and the buildings rebuilt to a very high standard. The farm embraces 20 acres of land, woods and lakes. A six acre vineyard of carefully selected vines now thrives where once was pastureland.

In 1988 the first vintage from the vineyard of 200 bottles were used at a family wedding. In 1990 the production increased to 10,000 bottles with a potential of 30,000 bottles per year when the vineyard is fully matured. Labelled Cariad Wines, cariad meaning 'darling' or 'lovely', its logo is the Celtic Cross with four wine glasses on a plate of grapes. The grapes include both German and French varieties. The visitor centre includes a vineyard shop and refreshment area, eight acres of woodland and lakes and six acres of vines.

Penllergaer

Our village, situated four miles north of Swansea, has grown from a small hamlet to a much populated area. Industry, by means of collieries, steel and tin works surrounded us in the old days. They are now replaced by factories including the large 3M Company, famous world-wide.

The mansion of Penllergare (as spelled by the family) was the home of the village squire Sir John Dillwyn Talbot Llewelyn. His father created an extensive wooded garden with lake and cascades there in the 1840s. The manson was demolished and the local authority offices of Lliw

Valley Borough Council occupy the site. The Observatory has been retained for its association with J. D. Llewelyn's early photographic activities. Other parts of the garden, including the orchid house are now the subject of survey and reclamation. The Llewelyn family was very well respected in the village, their help to many villagers in times of need was immense and greatly appreciated.

There have been many changes over the years and with the increase in traffic, the M4 motorway was constructed which necessitated the removal of the bridge over the river Llan.

Part of the grounds of the mansion home now comprise the new motorway and a large estate of modern properties where once stood our village cricket ground. The flowers in summer time were a delight to see and many Swansea schoolchildren were brought here and entertained to tea parties 'on the green' prior to the Second World War.

The school celebrated its centenary in recent years and St David's church also celebrated 150 years in 1992. A flower festival at the church for a week will always be remembered. The remaining descendants of Sir John's family were invited to attend in the church celebrations and their presence created tremendous interest.

A commemorative stone is sited near Garngoch Hospital to commemorate the Battle of Gower which took place on the 1st January 1136.

A force of Welshmen led by Hywel ap Meredudd of Breconshire battled to defeat an Anglo-Norman army, which was advancing from the Gower Peninsula. So many were killed in the battle, that the area became known as Garngoch which translated means the red hoof, so called because the hooves of the horses were bloodied in the gory battle. It is thought that the circle of trees at Bryndafydd Farm is the burial place of those that fell in the battle.

Penllergaer means 'top of the fort', the fort being a Roman fort that was situated on the corner as one turns into Garngoch Hospital from the present Julians Superstore.

The proposed hospital road improvement scheme involved its re-alignment to bridge the new Llanelli/Swansea link road and it is now considered that the earthworks do not unduly affect the site of the Roman earthworks which is a scheduled ancient monument at Garngoch.

The 'dip' in the road as one approaches CEM Day's from Gorseinon was an area that was walked by people to and from Swansea on market days. There the people were often waylaid and robbed, hence the place became known as Cwm Lladron – the valley of thieves.

Penllyn 🦋

The village Penllyn is just two miles north west of Cowbridge.

There has been a castle at Penllyn since the early 12th century as the Normans realised the strategic value of the site. Part of a wall of the 12th century square keep still exists behind the present house. Some of the family names associated over the centuries with the estate of Penllyn include those of Le Norris, Turberville, Seys and Stradling.

A Miss Gwinett was bequeathed the estate in the 18th century. She had the house rebuilt in its present form and added a great deal of land to the estate which was subsequently bought in 1846 by Mr John Homfray of Llandaff for £30,000. He had further interior alterations made to the house, rebuilt Penllyn Chapel at the entrance to the castle grounds and added trees to the woodland on the hill around the castle.

The estate remained in the hands of the Homfray family until 1961 when the castle was sold to Mr Christopher Cory. It is now a private mansion, still owned by the Cory family and can be seen from the A48 Cowbridge to Bridgend road.

Near the roadside by Penllyn Court are two wells (now sadly overgrown) provided for domestic supplies for local people by Dr William Salmon who came to live at the Court in 1816. Dr Salmon landscaped the estate and built a science laboratory there. Various men of science, including Michael Faraday were visitors at the Court.

During the drought of 1887 people travelled from Cowbridge and surrounding villages to the wells for water, and on VE Day at the end of the Second World War an open-air thanksgiving service was held at the wells.

An inscription on one of the wells reads: 'Dwr, Rhodd yr Hollalluog Dduw' – Water, gift of the Almighty God.

Dr Salmon died in 1896 at the age of 106 – the oldest person in Wales and the oldest doctor in Europe.

In the 1920s Penllyn had a postwoman who would cycle or walk from Graig Penllyn to Pentre Meurig in the early morning to collect the mail brought by cycle from Cowbridge. She and the postman would sort out the mail in the porch of the (then) police station at Pentre Meurig. She would then deliver the mail, on foot or by cycle, first to Penllyn Castle, then to the farms at Vistla and Moorlands, around the two villages of Penllyn and Graig Penllyn and finally to Fferm Goch, a settlement just north of Penllyn. It took her many hours to deliver all the mail.

It used to be the custom at Easter for the children of the village of Penllyn and Graig Penllyn to take bunches of primroses to the church

Penllyn Village

for the Penllyn Castle gardeners to use in decorating the church for Easter Day. The children's reward was an Easter egg, given to each of them by Mrs Homfray, wife of Colonel Homfray of Penllyn Castle.

The first Penllyn and District Horse Show was held on a Wednesday in August 1924, in the beautiful grounds of Penllyn Castle (the residence of Colonel H. R. Homfray). This has become an annual event and is still held on a Wednesday in August, but since 1953 it has been known as the Vale of Glamorgan Show and is still held in Penllyn Castle Park. In April 1963 there was a lot of controversy in Penllyn when an avenue of 106 trees lining the road into the village were condemned to the woodman's axe. The Minister of Housing and Local Government at that time revoked a preservation order placed on these trees by Glamorgan County Council. An objection to this order had been made by Major Frank Homfray, owner of Penllyn Estate, on whose land the trees stood. Apparently the trees concerned were showing signs of rot. They were all between 80 to 120 years old and could become dangerous, particularly as they over hung the road.

The estate planned to replace trees which had been felled on the eastern side of the road to the village. The trees felled were made up of oak, ash, beech, sycamore and chestnut and had been bought by a timber merchant. However, another 68 acres of woodland on the Penllyn Estate and adjoining estates were safe under the preservation order.

Penmaen & Nicholaston 🖾

If you stand at the eastern end of Cefn Bryn moorland known as the 'backbone of Gower' you see, to the north, Parc-le-Breos, to the south the Bristol Channel and the spectacular Three Cliffs Bay, and to the west the ancient oakwoods of Nicholston. The whole area lies within the Gower Peninsula – the first designated Area of Outstanding Natural Beauty and much is under the protection of the National Trust.

In this magnificent setting lie the villages of Penmaen and Nicholaston. The old farms and cottages are scattered along the spring line and the later large houses take full advantage of the beautiful views of sea and cliffs.

The post office, school and general store have closed but there are still two active churches sharing their rector, a village hall, a hotel and a nursing home called Glan-y-Mor. During the Second World War, the latter, a large group of white buildings on the shoulder of Cefn Bryn, became a temporary home for families bombed out of their homes in Swansea. It had been built as a workhouse in the 1860s. The threat of being sent 'Up Penmaen' was often used by mothers to frighten naughty children.

For many centuries farming has been the main occupation. Patterns here changed but the basis of success has always been the mild climate, the southerly aspect and the fertile soil. Most of the best land grows early vegetables and soft fruit but sheep and cattle are raised and arable crops grown. Even the rough grassland of Cefn Bryn allows grazing for cattle, sheep and ponies.

Penmaen Burrows is a large area of sand dunes on top of the 200 ft cliffs. Ancient man has left his mark – a megalith between 4,000 and 5,000 years old. Some say that a village known as Stedworlangs lies buried beneath the sand. In 1861 the Rector of Penmaen found a piece of painted glass while walking on the burrows and this discovery led to the uncovering of a lost parish church. Within its walls four human skeletons were found buried beneath the floor of the chancel. These may have been plague victims, which would account for the walling up of the chancel and the subsequent abandoning of the village in the 14th century.

129

The present church of St John in Penmaen has 14th century foundations. Its living lay in the possessions of the Order of Knight Hospitallers
of St John of Jerusalem and its register dates from 1765. Sadly little trace
of the early Gothic fabric remained after heavy restoration in the 1850s
at the cost of £500. The same is true of St Nicholas in Nicholaston,
restored in 1895 at the sole expense of Miss Olive Talbot. However, it
does have an ancient bell cast by Aven Von Won in Kampen, Holland.
The inscription reads 'I am cast in the year of our Lord 1518'.

In the reign of Henry I, the lands of Gower were occupied and
colonised by Norman lords. William de Breos was a great favourite of
King John and Gower was added to his extensive possessions in 1203.
About 1230 his descendant, John de Breos created a hunting park, Parc-
le-Breos, within this estate. It still exists today although its woodlands
are now largely owned by the Forestry Commission. As late as 1912, by
which time the estate was owned by Admiral Walker-Heneage-Vivian,
the annual bag of pheasants was 2,000.

Part of the parish lies within a National Nature Reserve and the whole
area has a rich and varied flora due to the wide range of habitat. In 1992
the local WI undertook a survey of the flowering plants in the parish and
324 species were identified, including unusual plants like herb paris,
caper spurge, cranesbill and stinking hellebore.

Glanymor Old People's Home, Penmaen, was formerly the Gower
Workhouse. The Poor Law Amendment Act of 1834 provided a central
authority to regulate the relief of the poor throughout England and
Wales. Parishes, grouped into Unions, were represented by elected poor
law guardians who were required to make provision for relief in workhouses. In response to this the Gower Union Workhouse was built at
Penmaen on land purchased by the Guardians from C R M Talbot, in
1860. The building was erected in 1862 at a cost of £3,397 to house 50
paupers.

Unfortunately no minute books from the Gower Union prior to 1896
have passed into the custody of the West Glamorgan Record Office, and
therefore it is not possible to construct a detailed history of this workhouse from primary sources. However, the minutes of the guardians
meeting in May 1904, commenting on the conditions in the workhouse,
stated that it was 'clean and in good order'. This was in marked contrast
to the conditions in the Swansea workhouse at Mount Pleasant, which
were frequently criticised. Indeed, conditions in the Gower workhouse
were generally considered to be an improvement on those in Swansea
and Neath. For example, beer was usually given to the inmates by the
Gower Board of Guardians at Christmas, whereas the Swansea and
Neath Guardians were reluctant to allow alcohol at any time.

One well-known character who spent the last years of his life at Penmaen, was the ballad singer Phil Tanner, 'the singer of Gower'.

As a result of the Local Government Act 1929, the duties of the Boards of Guardians were transferred to the county boroughs and county councils on 1 April 1930. Following the National Assistance Act 1948, the workhouses ceased to function as such, and the Gower workhouse became known as Glanymor.

Pennard 🌿

Before there was a main road from Swansea to the village, the road ran from Swansea only as far as Bishopston. Travel to Pennard was by means of horse and carriage, or cart, and these were driven along the sands from Oxwich to Pennard, and then down Hael Lane, past Hael Farm, through Bishopston Valley to what is now Pyle Corner. This route is now designated as a bridleway.

Hael Farm was a beautiful old farmhouse, built more than 200 years ago, with a genuine inglenook fireplace. It had no water laid into the house, but had a big catchment tank outside. There was no electricity, oil lamps being used instead, and the floor was made of stone flagstones. Before the Second World War, the 75 acres were farmed by Trevor Jones and at harvest time, the whole village turned out to help. A tractor was hired to thresh the corn and twelve men came to help. Trevor's wife would carry flagons of cider and jam tarts out into the fields for the men. During the war, when permission had been granted for a lamb to be killed, this was served up as a veritable feast.

There were ducks on the pond in those days and wild daffodils in abundance in one of the fields. Local children would gather those to give to their mothers on Mothering Sunday. One of the most amusing reminiscences of those days was of their two pigs called Mutt and Jeff who used to stroll up Hael Lane every day, one on either side of the lane, as far as the village green (now the bus terminus). A few minutes later they could be seen toddling back down the lane again to the farm.

Sadly, the farmhouse today is falling into decay. The roof tiles are being blown off and the windows have long since gone. The wind whistles uncannily through the old house and one thinks nostalgically of the happier days when it was a real home to the Jones family.

In the 1950s our postman was Bob Davies who lived in Parkmill on the hill behind Shepherd's shop. Bob had lost an arm in the First World War and this had been replaced by a hook. Despite this, and despite having a large area to service, Bob made all his deliveries on a bicycle. So prompt and reliable was he that one could time one's clock by his visits.

His delivery route took him right through to High Pennard and then down to Pwll Du Bay where there were, and still are, only two houses. The owner of one of these houses would not agree to a box being placed at High Pennard where Bob could have left his mail. Instead, 'Old Bob' had to go down a very steep track down to the Bay, leave the mail, and then climb the steep hill back to the top where he had left his bicycle!

Penrice ༄

Penrice village was once the foremost village in Gower with twice weekly markets and four fairs a year.

On the village green is the base of the old cross which is known as the 'Crying Stone' because it was used by the village crier.

The Norman church with its large porch has a huge and ancient oak door jamb surrounding the door. A seat, donated by the Oxwich and Penrice WI is set against the churchyard wall from which there are wonderful views over Oxwich marsh, the bay and on clear days, the North Devon coast.

Out of the village, down the hill are the ruins of a mill and mill pond. The woods are open to the public. The entrance to the woods is situated on Penny Hitch Hill, so named because it was possible to hire a horse for one penny to carry heavy loads from the mill to the top where today one can see, across the fields, the ruins of Penrice Castle (not open to the public). The area is a haven for birds and flowers abound the year round.

Pentyrch ༄

Pentyrch is a hillside village situated on the lower slopes of the Garth Mountain. It is about seven miles from Cardiff and, having good access to the A470 and the M4, is now largely a dormitory village for the capital with a population of about 2,500.

The centre of the old village is the church of St Catwg. The present church is of Victorian construction and is dedicated to St Catwg who was a famous Welsh Saint of the 6th century. It seems likely that there was a religious foundation at Pentyrch from this time. There is certainly

St Catwg's Church, Pentyrch

evidence of a church at Pentyrch from the 12th century onwards as there is mention of the church in Papal Bulls of the time, so the existence of a community at Pentyrch for many centuries is indisputable. Even before the 6th century there exists evidence that neolithic people were living in this area from the discoveries of tumuli on Garth Hill, a flint axe head at Cefn Colstyn Farm and a cromlech at Creigiau.

From the 16th century onwards Pentyrch became an important centre for the production of iron. Iron ore was mined on the lower Garth Mountain. Pentyrch was also on the southern edge of the South Wales coalfield and several small coal mines supplied the ironworks. The Mathew family owned and worked a furnace and forge in the locality from 1565–1625 and guns to fight the Armada are reputed to have been made in Pentyrch. The ironworks fell into disuse after 1625 but were revived in 1740 by the Lewis family of Van and by 1805 they had become part of the large Melingriffith works, which provided employment for the inhabitants of Pentyrch for many years.

Pentyrch now has a mixed population of old village families and many people who have moved in from other areas as new houses have been built and the village expanded. The village was at one time largely Welsh speaking. However, this is no longer the case, although there is a Welsh Society, a Welsh play group and a branch of Merched y Wawr (a women's organisation, similar to the WI). There are two chapels and the church with connected associations. The rugby club is flourishing and on the same fields are a tennis club, cricket and bowls club.

The modern village hall is the centre of village activities and houses the WI, the Guides, and Brownies, the Welsh and English speaking nurseries, a mother and toddler group and Darby and Joan club. Near the hall is the surgery and post office and several shops. The village school caters for primary education and a youth club on two evenings a week. Last, but not least, there are two public houses. The oldest, The King's Arms, was said to have been a meeting place for Cromwell's men before the Battle of Saint Fagans.

Penyfai 🍃

Penyfai could be mistaken for a sleepy little village. In fact from the main Bridgend road it is hardly noticeable at all, with houses clustered around the church and chapel and then up a steep hill to the newer parts, the commonland and the M4 motorway. We have to delve back into its history and find that Penyfai is made up of the very old and the very new.

Parts of the village date back to the 12th century. The local manor house Cwrt Colman had close links with the Cistercian Order of Margam Abbey and the oldest farm was Ty Mawr Farm (changed in 1967 to the 'Pheasant Pub').

Cwrt Colman has had many owners, including Robert Sidney in 1585 and Colonel Llewellyn and his family. The last owner was a retired headmaster, Mr George Morgan, who reluctantly sold in 1981, as parts of the manor were very dilapidated and there was a lot of dry rot. The manor is now restored to its former glory and is a thriving residential hotel and restaurant.

In the late 19th century Penyfai boasted Mrs Minty's school, where local children received basic education for the princely sum of two pence a week. The church school was provided at the beginning of the century when the new church was built. Later, with the arrival of more houses and young couples with children, the present primary school was built in 1963.

It seems incredible today but there was a certain place in Penyfai where footpads laid in wait for unsuspecting travellers and a band of robbers known as the Cefn Riders roamed.

In Elizabethan times iron ore was mined in Penyfai, smelted at Angletown (Glanrhyd) which is near by, and most of it was exported to England. There was a quarry which provided stone for local buildings; notably the Baptist Chapel built in 1706, which is one of the oldest chapels in Wales. Wesley was said to have preached there on several occasions. Angletown Asylum (known as Glanrhyd Hospital now) was also built of Penyfai stone in 1865.

There was also a malthouse in the village to cope with the locally grown barley, and beer was brewed in the Tavern and sold for two pence a pint in 1840.

The village really started to grow in size and character in the 1950s, when houses were built on the main road near the church in the lower part of Penyfai. Later in the 1960s the large High View development of 333 houses took place. In the 1970s and 1980s even more houses were built, especially with the advent of the M4 motorway and easy access to Cardiff and Swansea and further afield. In fact some members of the community sold their houses in Bristol, came to live in Penyfai and commute daily over the Severn Bridge!

Times are changing. The 1841 census showed 119 persons, most of them miners, farmworkers or workers on the Cwrt Colman Estate. Today there are about 1,450 on the electoral list. There are no miners and the majority of people work well away from the village with the help of the easy access to the M4 motorway.

Local associations are very keen to keep Penyfai as it is now. There was a threat recently to cut down Coed y Wernlys woodlands to build more houses but this was opposed with a petition and letters to notable people, including HRH the Prince of Wales, and help was sought from our local County Councillors.

People were very community minded when the village was small. There were lots of activities with the church and chapel, the cricket club and the scouts and guides movement.

Over the last few years several organisations and clubs have made great efforts to get the community together again. The WI was formed four years ago, the church and chapel have clubs and recently a Community Association was formed which organised dances and coach trips. They are striving very hard to get a village community centre for everyone to be able to use.

The local pub also provides quizzes and special event evenings and fireworks displays. Most of all we want Penyfai to be a real village again. With the help of school fetes, the children's sports day in August and the scouts' fun weekend in September we shall surely succeed.

Penygraig 🦋

In early days Penygraig was a typical mining village, its houses slanting up the narrow streets, and colliery hooters blaring at the start of every working shift – their noise enough to wake the dead. A metamorphosis has occurred over the intervening years as the area is now denuded of coal pits, reverting to the original green valley. Trees are being planted and leisure areas created where once King Coal reigned supreme.

The resultant clean air means that the lives of the women of Penygraig and district have gone through dramatic changes, particularly in recent years. In 1914 for instance, coal fires were the norm, meaning that all water was heated by iron kettles and boilers for all domestic purposes. Most cooking, too, was over a coal fire, although bakehouses were available for the baking of home made bread, etc. Fireplaces were blackleaded daily and brass candlesticks polished. Ashes were collected daily, as also all household rubbish. Every housewife scoured her front door step and swept the area outside her house, so there was very little rubbish about. Shopkeepers too were very clean and even policemen cleaned their stations. Ironing was done on a well scrubbed table with the irons heated before a red hot fire. Clothes were washed on a scrubbing board. The housewife worked in as arduous a manner as her menfolk, if not as dangerously.

The advent of electricity and gas here has made life so much easier for women. The National Coal Board installed pit head baths and changing rooms, so eliminating the necessity of the colliers bathing at home. Medical centres were set up, all opening up a new world for the populace, giving women more leisure time for their own interests.

This area has always enjoyed an excellent standard of education, with Miners' Institutes and libraries, a Mining School at Treforest and a Technical School at Pentre, giving bright boys good opportunities in industry. Penygraig was in the catchment area for Porth County and Porth Secondary Schools, also Tonypandy Grammar School for boys and girls attended by scholarship pupils. Qualifications were obtained in these schools for entry to Universities, Teachers Training Colleges, Hospitals and the Civil Service.

The Anglican Church of Llanfair-ar-y-Bryn was commissioned to be built in 1889, and was originally a church that conducted its worship entirely through the medium of Welsh.

Throughout its history it served as the parish church for Dinas and Penygraig and has been a distinguished landmark on Amos Hill for a number of generations.

In recent years, the parish has had to face a number of practical difficulties, including being grouped with the neighbouring parish of Williamstown and therefore sharing the vicar, and also mounting repair costs to Llanfair and St Barnabas.

The final services were held on Pentecost Sunday, with the congregation moving to St Barnabas, Dinas, and St Illtud, Williamstown.

The site of Llanfair will be used for the development of four houses.

If you visit Penygraig you cannot avoid 'The Big Chapel' on the square, as it was called many years ago. The work commenced on the building on 1st November 1831 and on 2nd February 1832 the first Soar Ffrwdamos chapel was completed at a cost of £300. In 1868 it was rebuilt at a cost of £739 and in 1905 it was again rebuilt at a cost of £5,705 including the beautiful pipe organ which was one of the finest organs in the valley. In 1910 and 1911 oratorio concerts were held with Mr Griff Davies as conductor. In 1928 concerts restarted with Mr Davies and when he died Mr T J Hughes of Tonypandy became the conductor. Well known artists who performed were Ceinwen Rowlands, soprano, David Lloyd, tenor, and of course our own Gwyneth Morgan from Carn Celyn Farm.

As the congregation became smaller and chapel members moved to other parts of the country, it was decided that members of Soar would hold their services in the vestry. In 1979 the chapel was donated to the community and is called Penygraig Community Project. It is a voluntary organisation registered as a charity.

Music has always played a vital role in Penygraig and its environs; eisteddfodau, cymanfas, male voice choirs, children's concerts, etc., flourished during the decades. The Women's Institute has fostered this, joining with two other Institutes in 1988 to form an excellent choir for a Christmas concert which was of a very high standard and was well attended.

Sports have always proliferated in the area. In early days games were played on Miners' Welfare Grounds, with cricket, tennis, bowling and hockey. Penygraig Rugby Football Club has been in existence for a century, first using Council ground and changing in the now defunct Butchers Arms, a very large hotel much used for meetings. A great transformation took place in 1970 when the committee and members opened a new clubhouse and a first class field on the site of the old Naval Colliery, which had easy access to the main road. Wives and friends helped by providing meals for the players and visitors.

Mr Joby Churchill, a local man, was trainer for the famous Tonypandy boxer, Tommy Farr. Many other boxers trained and were well known in the area.

Women, generally, were not greatly involved in sporting activities, although most schools had their own hockey and netball teams. Bowls has become quite popular. Night classes in flower arranging, cookery, pottery, sewing, etc., have always been available, also dancing classes. Co-operative guilds and Labour section meetings were another source of interest for women.

Another great change in our area is the up-dating of our homes. Grants have given many householders the opportunity of installing new bathrooms, etc, as well as improving the fabric of the houses. Colourful paintwork and new roofs create a kaleidoscope of colours, replacing the old Rhondda grey. New estates have been built by the Council since the Second World War, over 300 houses in Penygraig itself, and with the

Peterston Super Ely

demolition of many old buildings and colliery sites, etc, small privately built estates have arisen.

The friendliness of the people and the green hills replacing the old coal tips, make this area a good place to live today. Unfortunately local employment opportunities are few.

Today many people travel out of the area to business and industry. Modern transport and the new roads mean that Penygraig is only twelve minutes away from the M4 motorway.

Our forefathers faced adversity with courage. Hopefully this generation will meet the present challenge which will give our children and their children a bright and happy future in this now green and pleasant land.

Peterston-super-Ely 🐚

The village lies a mile or so off the main A48 road about seven miles to the west of Cardiff. It is divided into two main parts, separated by the river Ely. To the north is the hub of the community: the parish church, post office/shop, garage, The Sportsman's Rest, The Three Horseshoes and the primary school. The southern part is a residential estate – Wyndham Park – reached by the White Bridge (originally a road bridge but now pedestrians only with the defaced notice stating 'orses pro'ibited). This estate was originally agricultural land owned by John Cory of Duffryn (whose statue graces Cathays Park in Cardiff). In the early 20th century he was influenced by the garden village/suburb movement (e.g. Welwyn, Bourneville) and planned a similar development, to be known as 'Glyn Cory'. The scheme envisaged homes for about 6,000 people, a park, golf course and other amenities. Only a fraction of this grand scheme came to fruition, which is the pleasant, leafy Wyndham Park of today.

The original village, in Welsh Llanbedr-y-Fro, was once a sub manor of St Fagans and was held by the descendants of the Norman knight Peter le Sore, who dispossessed the last Welsh Lord of the area, Meurig ap Hywel, in about 1091. The remnants of the castle of the le Sores may still be seen near the church. Parts of the church date from the 12th century.

Slightly apart from the centre of the village is Croes-y-Parc, still in use and one of the earliest Baptist chapels in the Vale of Glamorgan, although the nearby river is no longer used for baptism.

The original school is now a private house. The new school occupies a spacious site on the edge of the village and has recently inaugurated an outdoor classroom – the quality of which led to a special prize being awarded in recognition of the efforts of the pupils, staff, parents and friends.

In May 1648 thousands of men passed through Peterston-super-Ely on their way to and from the Battle of St Fagans – the Parliamentarians against the King's army. Many present villagers remember another war, against Hitler. Bomb craters can still be seen, there was a searchlight battery at Palla Farm and Americans were based on the Cottrell estate. An American hospital was built at Rhydlafar and many local women helped out by joining the WVS. Wounded soldiers were invited to local homes. After a village dance, a jeep crashed at St Brides. On the lighter side, conkers were collected to make glue.

The railway has been important to the village and sounds of steam and shunting must formerly have filled the air of the now peaceful countryside. There used to be a very large siding where coal was transhipped from the Great Western Railway to the Barry Railway en route for the docks. Three signal boxes were manned round the clock. Today, the siding and station are no more, although the houses of Station Terrace still look out on the passing Inter-City Swansea to London trains.

Employment in the village has over the years declined. But, if community spirit may be measured by the number of voluntary organisations, the community is thriving. There are nearly 20, ranging from mothers and toddlers, through brownies, guides and youth club to the over sixties. The WI, now over 50 years old and with 40 members continues to play its part.

Pontarddulais 🦡

Before the Industrial Revolution, Pontarddulais and district consisted of a few farms, and a small number of whitewashed cottages. At the time the only buildings of note were the old church on the marsh, Capel Iago, the newly constructed railway station, and The Red Lion coaching station. The church (of Llandeilo Talybont, to give the name of the ancient parish), with its medieval wall paintings, has been removed to the Welsh Folk Museum at St Fagans where it will be rebuilt.

The population of the village increased with the opening of the Hendy tinplate works. Many people moved into the area, and although they became an integral part of the community the natives always referred to them as 'Dynion dod' (infiltrators). So according to custom, they were christened for identification with the name of the place they came from, such as Jack-y-Cardi (came from Cardiganshire), John Caerfyrddin, Dan Kidwelly. Due to similarity in christian names this custom of nicknames had always prevailed amongst the natives. Some were tagged with their mother's name such as Shoni Harriet, or after their homes – Twm Ty Crwn. A few were named after their form of employment such as Billo Crudd (cobbler), others after their peculiarities like Dan Pen Oen (Lamb's Head) because he was partial to a lamb's head soup and Jackie Milgi (Greyhound) due to his long legs. A colourful character of this era was 'Dai Born Again', a regular customer of the local pubs, who always tried to convince his audience that he was in a state of reincarnation by quoting experiences in his previous life on earth.

During the development of Teilo works a row of workmen's cottages was built nearby. Here lived a mixture of personalities; the good, the bad and the indifferent. The street eventually got so notorious, that it became known as Jug and Bottle. It was customary during those days for wives to take lunches (including a jug or bottle of beer) to their husbands in the works. Every morning the women proceeded to the Farmer's public house to have the jugs and bottles filled with beer. Invariably on the way back the women would gather for a gossip around the village pump, a favourite rendezvous for the scandalmongers. Star turns at these assemblies were 'Marged Knowall', and 'Nanny Carry Beer', both residents of the infamous Jug and Bottle street. Marged knew everyone's business, and all the scandal of the village. Her fertile brain could exaggerate issues, spreading a great sense of stimulation amongst the women. In the excitement the women would take sips of their husband's beer, and more often than not the jugs would soon be empty before Marged's tale of passionate and illicit romance ended.

Due to lack of education, many people were illiterate and naive. They were short-changed, cheated, and exploited and women were cowed with their efforts to make ends meet. They all in turn took their troubles to a character called 'Ann Chwarae Teg' (Ann Fair Play). She always pacified her visitors with the words 'I'll see that you get fair play.'

The unscrupulous landlord who owned all the houses in the street, regularly increased the rent. In the interests of fair play Ann refused to pay, with the result that she was eventually taken to court. With a very despondent attitude in the dock, she sobbed, pleaded poverty, degradation, and put on a performance worthy of a Hollywood movie star. It brought tears to the Judge's eyes and the final episode in her performance touched the Judge's heart, when she broken heartedly said 'My husband is a sick man (although he was at work every day), he already has one leg in the grave and the other has no business to be out.' Verdict – case dismissed, with a warning to the landlord that unless a reduction in the rents of the tenants was forthcoming he would be liable to face the consequences. So by fair means or foul Ann was always there to defend the right of the underprivileged – 'Chwarae Teg iddi' (fair play to her).

Today Pontarddulais is a very active village with various choirs and dramatic societies. The Pontarddulais Male Voice Choir is well known throughout the country and was formed many years ago. Pontarddulais also has a silver band which is over 70 years old.

Pontyclun 🌿

Pontyclun is a large village and owes its origin to the former Llantrisant railway station. It has now had its own railway station for many years. It is on the main line which links West Wales via Cardiff to London.

The name Pontyclun may mean Meadow Bridge, or alternatively 'bridge over the river Clun', which here flows into the Ely.

Coal, iron, lead, and limestone were found in abundance in former times. No industry remains, and it is now largely residential, farmland and lovely hills. It is a district of most attractive walks of endless variety and is centrally placed for Cardiff, Pontypridd, Cowbridge, Bridgend and the Rhondda Valleys.

Noteworthy events and notabilities of the area were Sir Leoline Jenkins (1623–1685), who became Principal of Jesus College, Oxford; Sir David Evans (1849–1907) who became Lord Mayor of London in 1891, and Mr G. T. Clark (1809–1898), engineer, Public Health commissioner, resident trustee of the Dowlais Iron Company, authority on medieval Glamorgan, a noted author and antiquary. Mr Clark bought a mansion at Talygarn near Pontyclun for his home. Near to Talygarn is St Anne's church which he refurbished in memory of his wife. Recently a 10th century Byzantine mosaic, depicting the head of an apostle, in the church was identified as originally from the west wall of the Cathedral Santa Maria Assunta on the Island of Torcello, near Venice. This mosaic was taken to Sotheby's in London and sold to an American collector. Both the Church in Wales and St Anne's Church, Talygarn, benefitted financially from this sale.

In early years Pontyclun continued to expand and Mr Clark built the Pontyclun Institute (now known as Pontyclun Athletic Club), for the benefit of the residents, providing sports e.g. bowls, tennis and other indoor sporting facilities.

In 1923, Talygarn mansion was purchased by the Miners' Welfare and used as a convalescent home for sick and injured miners, then subsequently converted into a Rehabilitation Centre. It is now proposed to use it as a Nurses Training College.

Pontyclun has become a thriving and developing community with a number of various types of shops dotted along the main road leading through the village.

Pontygwaith 🦢

Our village can be said to be a typical Welsh mining valley settlement of some 600 dwellings, dating from the early 1900s.

The church was consecrated on 6th July 1896, having cost £3,348 to build. It was to a design of the architect George E Halliday, and on a site which was part of the Penrhys Isaf Farm, the property of the Llewellyn family of Baglan Hall. The church was built entirely at the expense of Mrs Madeline Llewellyn, the then owner of the estate. The church stands in Madeline Street.

No colleries exist here today, but the area bears striking evidence of the coal mining industry. All around we see mighty tips of spoil, now mostly covered in grass though sites of pitheads with winding gear, drams and coal wagons etc have disappeared. Coal mining here, on a commercial scale, came and went within 100 years. It may be coincidental that this industry has departed in the reign of Queen Elizabeth II but was first recorded in Pontygwaith during the reign of Elizabeth I.

The valley in those days was heavily wooded with dense vegetation. Iron stone has been mined in Hirwaun since 1575. Anthony Morley, a Sussex ironmaster, brought the industry to Llanwonno and Merthyr Tydfil. There is possibly a strong connection between Pontygwaith (workman's bridge) and Furnace Road where Morley's furnace was situated. There was also a forge nearby.

Furnace Road was the old parish road to Llanwonno. The river was the boundary between the ancient parishes of Llanwonno and Ystradyfodwg. There is documentary evidence (1620) that charcoal was produced from trees felled from the Penrhys Isaf Estate. Since the charcoal for smelting was made on the Ystradyfodwg side of the valley and had to be brought across the river for the smelting process, there was need for a bridge. A site near the old brook from Penrhys was selected, near today's Bridgend Hotel and remains the site today for Pontygwaith – The Bridge of Work.

Pontypridd 🦢

Pontypridd, the gateway to the Rhondda Valley is situated at the meeting place of the Taff and Rhondda rivers and the Rhondda and Merthyr railway lines. It is surrounded by hills that are always visible in the valley. Years of reckless industrial development have left their scars on these hills and in the valleys. Pontypridd owes its existence to coal. Prior to the development of the mines, it was a rural area and farmers crossed a ford at Pontypridd, driving their stock to Llantrisant market. The sinking of the mines in the late 19th and early 20th centuries saw a dramatic expansion of Pontypridd. Houses for miners were built in long straight lines running parallel with the mountainside. The famous 'Old Bridge', constructed in 1786, outlived its usefulness and a three arch bridge was built alongside in 1857 to facilitate the passage of people and goods. The surrounding area became known as Newbridge but was changed to Pontypridd after the post office came into existence to avoid confusion with other Newbridges. The owner of the Great Western Pit, anxious to use the Glamorganshire canal to transport his coal to Cardiff Docks, built the Machine Bridge over the river Taff in Treforest and a weighbridge was established on the bridge to weigh the coal before being loaded onto the barges. These barges of coal travelled to Cardiff, pulled by magnificent shire horses and returned to Pontypridd laden with grain, flour and timber.

The population exploded and by the 1920s it reached a peak of 48,000. Pontypridd had become the social and recreational centre for the surrounding districts.

The railway was an important means of transportation. By the First World War, Pontypridd dealt with 11,000 passengers a day and 500 trains, both passenger and mineral were passing every two or three minutes in the daytime, making Pontypridd one of the busiest railway centres in Great Britain. The 510 yard long platform was reputed to be the longest in the country, although in recent years the platforms have been shortened. The station was a familiar sight to innumerable Sunday School outings going to Barry Island each summer. The train travelled the old Barry line through the countryside of Efail Isaf, Creigiau and Cadoxton before reaching Barry and the sea. Sadly this railway is no more.

Electric tramcars commenced running from Treforest to Cilfynydd in 1905. Road subsidence and flooding created serious problems and the electric trams were replaced by the trolley buses which were later replaced by buses.

After the General Strike of 1926 and the Great Depression, thousands of people migrated from the area and, in an effort to create jobs, the Treforest Trading Estate was established. The Duke of Kent opened it in 1938 and 6,900 people were employed there initially, rising to a massive 17,000 during the Second World War. This Estate has held a chequered history in terms of employment. Many of the original factories have been and are being demolished and modern hi-tech units are going up in their places.

In the late 1910s Pontypridd boasted many places of worship. Thousands flocked to them each Sunday and during the week they were hives of activity.

Choristers attended for choir practice, drama groups practised their plays. Bible groups came together regularly, prayer meetings, Band of Hope and many other activities made them focal points in their communities. Regretfully, many are now struggling to keep open. Membership has declined and many have closed their doors for ever. Carmel chapel was pulled down and the site was used to build flats for the elderly.

Some of the residents there today may remember that special day of childhood associated with Carmel Baptist chapel.

'Summer heralded the Sunday School Anniversary for which we had prepared our recitations and songs for many weeks. That was followed by the Sunday School Trip to Barry Island, truly a red letter day. In the late 1920s and early 1930s so many children attended Sunday School that the LEA awarded a day's holiday, usually in mid June, so that children could attend their trip. That day was special over any other trip to the seaside because we went as a group with our friends. We sat in a large circle on the beach, near the end where the pool used to be and had a wonderfully happy day, paddling or swimming in the water, catching crabs, playing games, sometimes watching the concert party. We always took sandwiches for lunch. We took bottles which we filled with water from the tap beneath the Gwalia Tea Rooms and to this we added orange or lemon oxade cubes. Our Mams had trays of tea with jugs of hot water from the tea room.

At tea time all the children gathered at one of the big tea rooms above the beach. There we sat at long trestle tables and ate paste sandwiches, bright yellow slab cake or seed cake all washed down with tea served from an urn. On the way back to the train for home we walked through the fair. We all had been saving for months and most had been given spending money by generous grandparents, aunts and uncles. We were very careful to choose rides which gave good value for money. We always bought Barry Island rock and nougat to eat on the train home. We usually bought a rock for Dad too. One of the highlights of the journey home was the passage in the dark through the old Wenvoe Tunnel.'

Tabernacle chapel, standing alongside the Old Bridge, has been turned into a very fine Heritage Museum and Historical and Cultural Centre. This has been carried out by members of the Pontypridd Historical Society. The conical pipe organ has been restored and now recitals and other concerts are held there.

The Glamorgan Mission to the Deaf and Dumb was founded in

Pontypridd 100 years ago. Glyntaff Crematorium, built in 1924, was the first in Wales. This together with the Round Houses near the Common and the obelisk in the small garden opposite Castle House in Forest Road, Treforest, remind us of the eccentric Dr. William Price who promoted cremation by attempting to burn the body of his baby son. At the Old Bridge we can remember the remarkable William Edwards who, despite initial failures, built this single arch bridge in 1755. The old Crawshay Home, Forest House, Llantwit Road, is now home to an expanding University of Glamorgan, with approximately 5,500 students. There is a mixture of full time, sandwich courses and part-time students, many or whom travel thousands of miles to study in our midst.

Familiar sights around Pontypridd were the men with horses and carts selling their various wares and calling to attract attention. Tom 'Cockles' had sold cockles from the age of 14. He had a wooden leg and it was believed that if he rode his cart with the wooden leg inside it was going to rain, but if it hung outside it was a sure sign of fine weather. On a musical note there was Madame Muriel Jones, the famous choir mistress, who visited royalty 20 times to entertain them with her magnificent ladies choir.

Future plans for a leisure centre to supplement the much patronised one at Hawthorn, and the improving of shopping facilities with traffic free streets should help to continue to keep Pontypridd a good place to live.

Port Talbot

In the 1890s C. R. M. Talbot of Margam Castle, donated the land surrounding Court Farm, part of the Margam Estate, for dockyards, machine shops, factories etc. The extensive fields gradually became streets of houses – among them Grange Street, Cwrt Ucha, Maes y Cwrt, Courtland Terrace and of course Courtland Place. In deference to the Talbot family this area became known as Port Talbot. Modern Port Talbot and ancient Aberavon now merge into one modernised pedestrianised town centre.

From ancient documents and periodic excavations, we can deduce interesting historical facts about Aberavon. In the 5th century in the *Book of Llandaf* and in the *Book of Morgan*, a town known as Nantavon is mentioned as being 'one of the six oldest towns in Morganwg'. Historians believe Nantavon and Aberavon to be one and the same.

Excavations near the New Docks, not far from Court Farm, revealed a mass burial ground of Celtic origin. Locally this site is known as 'Platch yr Eglwys', which suggests that it may have been the site of a Celtic church, or a church built later by the monks of Llantwit.

The Roman invasion of Britain in AD 43 was fearlessly resisted by the natives of Wales under the leadership of Caractacus, but the final Roman conquest and occupation meant that forests were cleared, moorlands were drained and reclaimed land was cultivated. Iron, tin and lead deposits were mined. Clay deposits were used for pottery. Roads linked walled towns and ports were made. The 'Julia Maritima', the road from Glevum (Gloucester) to Moridunum (Carmarthen) passed near Aberavon.

Between the departure of the Romans in AD 410, and the Norman invasion of Aberavon in the late 11th century, its history is one of internecine warfare, of invasion by Saxon and Danish hordes, and devastating floods which buried much of the town beneath the sand on the seashore.

When the Normans eventually subdued the natives, they built abbeys, churches and castles. Wisely they gave the Lordship to Afan to a Welshman – Caradog. He built a timbered castle where Castle Street now stands. This was later replaced by his son Morgan, in true Norman style. Morgan, a pious Catholic, built a church to St Mary the Virgin in 1199. This remained a Catholic church until the Reformation. The living was sequestered in 1649 by Cromwell, and restored in 1660. The first Protestant incumbent was a Welshman named David Jones Leyshon Thomas. Devastating floods caused much damage in 1768. Present day St Mary's was restored in 1859–61.

'Dic Penderyn' who took part in the notorious Merthyr Riots, was hanged in Cardiff in 1831 for a crime of which he was innocent. He is buried in St Mary's churchyard, at the entrance to the church.

Early in the 19th century Nonconformity spread throughout the area. The original Carmel chapel was built in 1810 and Ebenezer as it now stands, in 1836.

Catholic worshippers met in a house in the old Mountain Row, building later by sacrifice, hard work and dedication the old church of St Joseph. In 1931 the present day St Joseph's church was completed.

The Ancient Borough of Afan may have become the modern Port Talbot, but its history remains.

Federation House, the home of WI life in Glamorgan, is at 13 Courtland Place, Port Talbot.

Radyr & Morganstown

Radyr and Morganstown lies about six miles to the north west of Cardiff, west of the river Taff. Mostly situated on the high ground above the escarpment which rises from the river, it is now essentially a pleasant residential area. There are good rail and road communications with Cardiff, and easy access to the M4 motorway which crosses the north end of the village. There has been much post war housing development which has changed the appearance of the village significantly. Fortunately a village atmosphere remains despite the increase in size.

The church of St John Baptist is of medieval origin. The growth of the population near the railway station meant that by the 19th century the majority of parishioners lived at some distance from that church. To allow for this, a second church called Christ Church was built in 1904. There is a Methodist church in Radyr and the Bethel Presbyterian church in Morganstown.

Two primary schools and a comprehensive school serve the educational needs of the area. The Adult Education Centre offers tuition in a wide variety of subjects. Sporting activities are well covered with cricket, football, golf, tennis and rugby clubs. There is a choral society and a drama group. Other amenities include a well-stocked library, a health centre and dental surgeries. There is a small shopping centre where a useful range of goods is supplied by friendly shopkeepers.

The community is 'twinned' with Saint Philbert de Grand Lieu, France.

Church of St John Baptist, Radyr

149

To keep residents aware of what is happening in the village a local newspaper, *Radyr Chain* (taking its name from the old turnpike chain on the road to Llandaff) is distributed free to every home, approximately every two months.

The Old Church Rooms at Radyr was erected as a National Society School in 1880. It continued to be used as a school until 1896 and then became known as the Church Rooms. During the late 1980s the hall was bought by the Radyr Community Association for the use of the community in general. Radyr and Morganstown WI was formed in 1957. A lively and thriving group holds its meetings here.

Most villages produce 'characters', but some are particularly memorable. We had a doctor who lodged in the village of Morganstown, but whose surgery was in Taff's Well. A large gentleman, he always wore a dark overcoat, black hat and black boots. He had an outstanding skill; an ability to ride his bike very, very slowly whilst holding an open black umbrella over his head. All the children found this fascinating. He was known to carry forceps wrapped in brown paper sticking out of his pocket ready for any eventuality. His nickname was 'Bread Poultice' as this was his favoured remedy for all exterior ills, while most interior maladies were treated with a sixpenny bottle of pink medicine.

Another well loved member of our community was the village cobbler, Bert Chapman. He was a fund of knowledge and his dark little workshop was a real meeting place. He always promised that your shoes would be ready on a certain day, but when you called to collect them he would say 'I just have to give them a final polish.' This meant that he had an opportunity for another chat about village or world affairs. It was a sad day when he finally gave up work in the late 1970s.

Radyr Court, sited near the old church of St John Baptist, was the home of the famous Mathew family. Sir David Mathew of Llandaff Court was standard bearer to Edward IV. He was killed in a riot at Neath and buried at Llandaff Cathedral.

Edmund Mathew prevented an attempt by the Chancery Court of James I to take the mansion house of Radyr and some of his lands. Edmund was a sheriff of the county and was an early iron founder. Later his son George was to sell Radyr Court and move to Ireland.

Resolven 🦚

The village of Resolven (derived from Rhos-haf-lyn – 'Moor of the summer lake') is situated in the Vale of Neath, six miles north-east of the town itself. Ynysfach ('Little island') was in existence long before Resolven, the latter being built on its site. Resolven Mountain, to the northern side, was once the base of a large Iron-Age hill fort and later of 1st century Roman camps. 'Henllan' Mountain, to the south, also boasts the remains of an Iron-Age fortress, but also earlier evidence of a cairn (burial mound) complex, in existence before 600 BC. Until the coming of Christianity and due mainly to the settlement of the Celts in the Vale, Ynysfach and its rural neighbours had the composite reputation of being the 'Fairyland' of Wales – the home of Gwyn ap Nudd, Lord of the Underworld, and focal character for many pagan legends which still abound under the colourful banner of Resolven folklore.

By the 12th century, the Cistercian monks of Neath Abbey had established an extensive sheep grange on Resolven Mountain, but this was attacked by marauding locals in 1227 and ultimately given to the Earl of Warwick in 1452.

Ynysfach relied on its old south-western road and pack-mule trains for transporting goods until the the 1750s. Melin-y-Cwrt Iron Works and Furnaces, on the outskirts of the village, proved to be an extremely successful local industry, but it was the Neath Canal (1795) and Vale of Neath Railway (1851) which encouraged and established the longer-lived coal industry in the area. Consequently, many of the streets which composed the newer 'Resolven' were constructed by pit owners and bear their names, most notably J. W. Lyons and the omnipresent Cory Brothers. The latter founded the prosperous Glyncastle colliery, which enterprise became synonymous with the history of coal mining in the area. Only after the Second World War did Resolven coal enterprises decline, and the newer concerns of Rheola Aluminium and Cam Gears become the centres for local employment.

The industry-backed growth in Resolven's population in the 19th century led to a boom in local chapel-building, although Capel Melin-y-Cwrt is the oldest surviving. Methodist Zion (1821) was followed by St David's Church (1850), by Baptist Sardis (1864) and Bethania (1875), and by Jerusalem (1876). The latter gained fame as inspirational home of the hymn-tune *Rachie* and as the first chapel to broadcast Welsh religious services nationwide.

Although Ynysfach had lived through the 19th century cholera epidemics, the new village of Resolven was severely hit by a 'Great Flood'

151

when the river Clydach burst its banks in 1911. But no natural disaster conquers the spirits of Resolvenites, as the village-based eisteddfods of the 1950s seemed to prove!

Resolven today has a population of some 4,000, and is looking forward to the resurrection of its historical past as part of the new wave of tourist-based industries in the Vale of Neath.

Reynoldston 🦢

Mansel Jack and his friends are a group of standing stones. Reynoldston has a claim to one of Jack's friends, who now lives at Stouthall. Jack and his closest friends are all near Oldwalls, within a short walk of each other, two are near Burry and one in Knelston.

Jack is variously Mansel or Samson Jack, but none of the other stones have acquired any familiar name, through all the thousands of years that they have stood upright. In Bronze Age times it must have involved a huge community effort to erect them. The stones are the local Bryn stone, an old red sandstone conglomerate, usually called a puddingstone from the large number of round pebbles dotting its greyish-pink surface. This tells us that the stones are probably local. So many areas of Gower are still strewn with boulders that it is easy to imagine how our ancestors took the largest and erected them, rather than just moving them into the hedges and walls, out of the way.

Reynoldston is in the middle of the Gower peninsula, approximately 15 miles west of Swansea. It was formerly the capital of Gower. A lovely caring village, its inhabitants are fairly evenly divided between families dependent on their living on Swansea and people enjoying their retirement. The village has increased greatly in size since the Second World War. There is no industry here.

St George's church was built in 1867 in the same position and to much the same plan as the previous church erected in the early 13th century. The present church contains a font made from a block of stalagmite probably from the South Gower cliffs and believed to date from the 13th century. A pillar cross stands beside the chancel arch and, as one of the earliest Christian monuments in Gower, is now a registered ancient monument.

Rhondda 🦁

The people of the Rhondda are a singing people who have spent their lives with coal and have contributed not only industrial wealth to the world but are an example of community life at its best. They are a friendly people; welcome is always on the Rhondda mat. If you are a stranger, a pat on the back and a greeting are acceptance into their society. The Rhondda and its people are known all over the world.

Rhondda grew great at the end of 19th century with the opening up of the coalfields. The story of the inter war years is a sad and tragic one when unemployment existed on an unprecedented scale and many of the young and virile were compelled to look further afield for employment, resulting ultimately in the migration of some 55,000 people from the area.

Rhondda's record as a reception area during the Second World War is one which will be remembered for all time. The homes of the people were thrown open to the less fortunate persons who were compelled to seek rest and shelter from heavily bombed areas. The warmth of the reception and hospitality extended to evacuees from the large industrial centres of the country was a natural manifestation of a people who had been taught to rely upon the splendid virtues of fortitude and courage throughout their lives.

On 28th April 1955 Rhondda was granted a charter of incorporation by her Most Gracious Majesty Queen Elizabeth II. It was presented to Councillor Ivor Idris Jones (Charter Mayor) by His Royal Highness Prince Philip, Duke of Edinburgh.

Rhondda can look back on many hazards and difficulties overcome, and go forward to the future with the same confidence and resolve that they will as far as it is in their power, prevent a recurrence of the conditions endured in the past, when coal was king.

Rhoose 🦁

Rhoose, just three miles from Barry, is a coastal village. On a fine day the coast of Somerset can be seen quite clearly. Rhoose is twelve miles south west of Cardiff.

The settlement can be traced in documentary sources from the 16th century. Work was mainly agricultural with lime-kilns scattered around the area, and it was from the then thriving port of Aberthaw, a few miles distant, that the agricultural produce and limestone was shipped to parts of South Wales and south west England. Today there is no longer a port here. By 1912 the limestone became the basic raw material for the Aberthaw and Bristol Channel Cement Works. The limestone from this area was used in the construction of the docks at Sebastopol and in the Eddystone Lighthouse at Plymouth Hoe. Today when one thinks of Aberthaw one immediately thinks of the cement works and the power station which still survive. The area where the port used to be is now known as The Leys.

In the Rhoose area three large farms formed part of the original settlement. These are Lower Farmhouse, Malt House and The Barn – Rhoose Farm.

The Cardiff-Wales Airport which celebrated 50 years as an airport in 1992 is situated on the edge of Rhoose village. The airfield had been built originally during the Second World War by the Air Ministry for use as a satellite aerodrome and operational training unit for RAF Spitfire pilots. During the early 1950s it was decided to use the airport for civil aviation development and Rhoose Airport was established in 1952. At this time it was managed by the Ministry of Aviation. In the early summer of 1952, the Irish carrier, Aer Lingus was granted permission to operate a service to Dublin. By 1954 the airport had been renamed Cardiff (Rhoose) Airport and saw the start of the Welsh airline, Cambrian.

Facilities were soon added to the site near the edge of Rhoose village to include a new terminal and hangar and new services and aircraft were introduced, with links to the South of France, Belfast and Cork. By the close of the 1950s major rugby 'airlifts' to Dublin and Paris had helped to increase the number of people using the airport. Holiday charter business to prominent resorts of the Mediterranean also increased.

During 1965 control of the airport transferred from the Ministry of Aviation to Glamorgan County Council who re-named it Glamorgan (Rhoose) Airport. With the advent of larger jet aircraft, Glamorgan County Council constructed a new terminal building and control tower and doubled the main runway to 7,000 feet. On completion in 1972 the terminal was opened by HRH Prince Philip, Duke of Edinburgh.

In 1974 the airport was taken over by a consortium of West, Mid and South Glamorgan County Councils and yet again re-named for the last time to Cardiff-Wales Airport. 1979 saw the start of the charter flights from Cardiff to Toronto in Canada which still continue.

During the 1980s passenger levels increased steadily each year with more holiday makers seeking the sun. Once again a longer runway was required to take larger aeroplanes so it was extended to 7,725 feet. Then in the summer of 1989 the first charter flights to the USA – New York and Florida.

Cardiff-Wales Airport has grown steadily since its early days with many prominent tour operators creating popular holiday packages out of Cardiff.

The spacious and modern three-storey terminal has a large range of facilities available to passengers in an attractive and comfortable setting.

Adjacent to the airport a dedicated group of enthusiasts has established Wales' only Aircraft Museum, and the Museum's administrators hope that it will also play an important educational role for schoolchildren.

Rhossili

About 18,000 years ago, the body of a young man was coated with red ochre and interred in a cave at Paviland, overlooking a sea of grass, where now waves crash on the rocks below. Two chambered tombs of rock were made on the landward slope of Rhossili Down by Stone Age men, 6,000 years ago. It was in the Bronze Age that, on the ridge of the same Down, men buried their dead under stone cairns. In about 500 BC Iron Age forts were built across the base of many Rhossili cliffs. The Vikings arrived by ship and left their names: 'The Worm's Head' for the serpent-like tip of Gower, 'Middleton' and 'Pitton' for hamlets which are part of Rhossili.

The original village was built on the 'raised beach' behind Rhossili Bay, beside a flowing stream fed by a spring on the Down above. In 1979, a long-house, part of this village, was revealed by flood and 'rescue archaeology' unearthed both this building, with curved ends, and a church dating from about 1150. This was Norman built, but almost certainly replaced an earlier construction on the same site. Part of the inside wall was decorated with a mural of leaves and tendrils, excellently preserved. In the early 14th century, fierce storms swept the coast and buried this original village in sand, so the people moved to the top of the cliff above and built a new church, taking with them, so legend says, the font and the arch from the door of the church below. Certainly the arch of St Mary the Virgin, Rhossili, is slightly askew and seems older than the rest of the building. Like all the cottages, the church was thatched, as can be seen by the height of the stone gable. One corner of the churchyard was used as a burial place for unknown sailors wrecked below the village, while within the church is a memorial to a famous son

155

of Rhossili, Edgar Evans, who travelled with Scott to the South Pole in 1912 and died on the return trek across the ice.

Farming has always been the staple occupation of the villagers. The 'vile', on Rhossili headland, was divided by grass banks into narrow strips so that people could have several strips in different areas, getting a fair share of good and bad land. These strips were still in existence until recently, being shown on the 1979 Ordnance Survey map.

Limestone quarrying was mentioned in 1672 and continued until 1899, the stone being shipped to North Devon by boats precariously moored to ledges in the cliffs. Smuggling and wrecking were less virtuous occupations, discouraged by John Wesley. He preached at Great Pitton Farm, using a pulpit chair which is still on the premises. Wrecks occur without the aid of wreckers, however, the most obvious being the *Helvetia*, a barque laden with timber, which grounded in Rhossili Bay in 1887 and is still clearly visible on the beach.

John Wesley's visit caused the Beynons of Great Pitton to build a small chapel on their land. The new Methodist chapel was built by the villagers beside the road into Rhossili in 1887.

Tourism began in about 1850, and a later visitor was Dylan Thomas, who, in 1930, wrote that he wished he could live always on Worm's Head. Now, most visitors come for a day or weekend, many hang gliding from Rhossili Down or surfing in the waters of the bay below.

Farming continues, but many villagers commute to Swansea for work, or have come to the village to retire.

Rudry 🌿

Rudry is situated in a rural area at the northern apex of a triangle formed by Cardiff, Caerphilly and Newport. The name itself has at least three different spellings; Rudry, Rhydri, as used in the Welsh language or Ruddry as on the 1843 tithe map.

At the beginning of the 19th century only two major roads existed. One followed the river Rhymney and dates back, in parts to Roman times. The other, known as a ridgeway road, ran from Caerphilly past St James' church, overlooking the village. Communication otherwise was by paths and trackroads. One such path linking the village to the railway halt at Waterloo, when repaired in 1897 by the new Parish Council, was named the 'Diamond Jubilee Path' in honour of the 60th anniversary of the accession of Queen Victoria and the name has stuck to this day. Unfortunately the rail link has not. Today, thanks to the motor car and new roads, it is more easily reached from all parts of the country.

Evidence found in old documents show that the church of St James dates back to 1254, taking the form of a wayside shrine used by pilgrims on route to worship at shrines abroad. The parish's own records date back to 1627. Perhaps the most notorious priest to live in Rudry, though he never served as curate, was the Reverend William Price. He was said to be insane and his behaviour raised many a comment and complaint.

The most famous of his children was Doctor William Price, the pioneer of cremation, who it appears inherited his father's eccentricities. It was in 1914 that St James' Chapel-of-ease was raised to the status of parish church and it is now united with that of Bedwas and Trethomas. A chapel, Capel Ebenezer, also serves the people. This was built in 1821 although the first prayer meetings began in 1798. It has since been extended and with restoration work carried out, is in use every Sunday.

The Church Hall was originally the home of the Rudry National School founded in 1835. This flourished as a seat of learning and with the introduction of the new Education Act in 1902 a Board School opened in new premises which still caters for all primary school age children. The change enabled the Church Hall to be the centre of all the community's social activities which also included use as a HQ for the Rudry Platoon of the Home Guard formed in 1940. After the opening of the Parish Hall in 1957, built following ten years of fund raising and hard work, the Church Hall was confined to church meetings only. It still stands but nowadays is a private house.

There are four public houses in Rudry, namely the Griffin inn, the Maenllwyd inn, the Greenmeadow inn and the Rudry hotel. Of these the Griffin is the oldest with recent alterations revealing some medieval masonry. Being adjacent to the church one theory has it that it might have been used as a pilgrim hostel.

The Maenllwyd dates back to the 17th century and a 'Mari Lwyd' once stood in the public bar. The Rudry Hotel is known locally as the

Capel Ebenezer, Rudry

Monte Carlo of Rudry or 'Monte'. It acquired this nickname during the industrial era when men were paid wages at the public house and subsequently drank and gambled them away.

Although situated in the countryside, Rudry was known, until fairly recently, more for employing men in industry, than in agriculture. Little evidence remains today of the geologically related industries of the past centuries – brickworks, collieries, iron mines, forges, tin plate works, corn mills, and, further back still, lead and silver mining dating from Roman times. The land has gradually returned to the basic industry of farming. The woods which were decimated by the iron workers for charcoal to smelt the iron ore, are now managed by the Forestry Commission with a programme of felling and replanting. Walkers through these woods and hills on the trails and footpaths will still find some remains of these industries and of the mansions built for their owners.

The future will bring change, not least the influence of new people from the commuter belt housing as it spreads ever wider from the towns. The welcome, so much a tradition of village life, will be warm.

St Athan ✺

The village of St Athan, near Barry has a traditional ghost story which has been handed down through the ages. Sir William Berkerolles of St Athan went on a Crusade to the Holy Land. His wife was utterly dismayed and could not be pacified. His return home was full of pomp and ceremony and much rejoicing. It was during the magnificent banquet that a Norman Lord informed him that his wife had been unfaithful. He was furious and decided to punish her severely. Even though she protested her innocence, she was locked in a damp, dark, rat infested room to starve. Loyal servants smuggled food to her, despite threats of extreme punishment if caught.

One day in a fit of outrage and anger Sir William ordered that his wife be buried up to her neck on the boundary between St Athan and Llantwit Major. Early in the mornings, before anyone stirred, her sister would run through the fields, her long dress dragging and soaking up the dew. As she came upon Her Ladyship she let her suck the moisture retained in the hem to quench her thirst. Death came ten days later. With her dying breath she pleaded her innocence, still wishing a blessing on the person who had ended her life so cruelly.

A year later, on good authority from relations at Penmark, Sir William

Berkerolles learned that the stories of his wife's infidelities were completely untrue. Advances had been made to her by the Norman Lord, but she had rebuked him and he had sworn revenge. Distraught at these revelations Sir William took to drinking heavily. He would beat the walls of his room in an uncontrollable frenzy at the knowledge of the dreadful deed he had executed. For days his voice would be heard for miles as he called for his beautiful wife. Eventually he died, insane.

Walking in the ruins of this Manor House on a still summer night, you may hear a rustle, glimpse a movement, or sense a presence. Don't be afraid, it is only the ghost of Y Ladi Wen, the White Lady of St Athan.

A more tangible reminder of the Berkerolles family of East Orchard castle are the effigies of Sir William (d. 1327) and Sir Roger (d. 1351) and their ladies, on their tombs, bright with heraldic colour, in St Athan church.

St Athan has a history of smugglers and wreckers, an occupation very popular here in times past. One young airman at Royal Air Force, St Athan, had cause to know of this old village activity as he patrolled the perimeter fence one evening with his guard dog, Target.

He was walking parallel to a turgid, oily stream which served as drink for the cattle which grazed in the field opposite. Suddenly Target gave a low growl and crouched to the ground, his teeth bared and his ears down, peering towards the road. There was nothing to see and no sound to be heard in the darkness but the Corporal felt ill at ease. He retraced his steps, looking for familiar outlines, but seeing none. The high chain-link fence and the outlines of houses had disappeared and he found himself standing on a stony road with high hedges on either side. It was then that he heard the muffled sound of horses' hooves. He crouched with Target against the hedge, as he heard low voices in tones which sounded strange to his north-country ears. There was muffled laughter too. Then, in the fitful light of the moon, he could make out dark figures, walking in line along the single track. They came, not from the main road to the village, for that seemed now to have been swallowed up by fields and hedges, but from the steep and narrow single-track, which present-day villagers use as a scenic walk to the beach.

There were four sturdy little Welsh mountain ponies, each one led by a cloaked figure, and laden across the back with small barrels and rolls of cloth. When they reached the brow of the hill, they did not immediately turn in the direction of Cowbridge but, as if by mutual arrangement, they followed the stream for a hundred yards or so, until they reached the pool where the clear water sprang from underground. Now, the water sparkled and rippled along, crystal-clear.

Two more shadowy figures joined them at the well and the Corporal

159

thought that he could discern the raised voices of bargaining and hear the chink of coins.

He felt no sense of time, and Target remained crouched and motionless, even when the little procession, now refreshed, pattered back to the road and slowly went from sight, along the track towards Cowbridge.

As the sound of hooves died away, as if by arrangement, the clouds parted and the Corporal could see again the familiar houses and the boundary fencing. Target leapt to his feet with a vigorous shake and strained at his leash, wanting to be on his way again. When the Corporal looked at his watch, he was amazed to see that only minutes had passed since it all began. Was it all a dream?

When dawn spread light across the airfield, he made one last journey along the perimeter, by the stream. Something shone in the mud, by the pipe where the well had once been. He stooped to pick up a coin, and cleaned it with his sleeve. It was worn and thin, but of real silver, not like any coin he had seen before. He knew then that this was more than a dream.

The Corporal said nothing of his experience to his fellow airmen, but in the days which followed, he made visits to the local library and to the old Blue Anchor pub at Aberthaw. He learned that Aberthaw, which lies in the parish of St Athan at the point where the river Thaw joins the Severn Estuary, had, for many centuries, been a busy port and boat-building centre, even as far back as when the Vikings invaded Britain.

Ships from all over the world called here and smuggling was rife. The Blue Anchor Inn was used by the smugglers as a hiding place for their contraband and there is reputedly an underground tunnel which led from the inn down to the harbour.

The Corporal now knew for certain that for a brief time he had been privileged to see ghosts from the romantic age of the smugglers. He would forever remember St Athan as it really was, all those centuries ago.

His fingers caressed the smooth, cool coin in his pocket and he was glad.

St Brides Major ✿

There are a number of natural sandpits in the parish. How we have progressed from the days when sand was used on the floors in the cottages in our area, and children had to walk miles to collect 'marl' for whitening doorsteps and hearths.

Tree-planting has taken place in the village of St Brides Major for many years, the first being chestnut trees at the bottom of the village, called 'The Pant', planted by Countess Caroline of Dunraven, to commemorate General Picton's departure from the village farm Tyn-y-caeau to the Battle of Waterloo. Since that time, trees have been planted to mark special occasions – Coronation of George VI, Queen Elizabeth's Silver Jubilee, wedding of Prince Charles, etc. The clump of trees planted to commemorate the Coronation of George VI, 1937, is recorded in the Royal Record of Tree Planting. These were presented and planted by St Brides Major Coronation Committee.

At the far end of the village, at Pitcot, lies the pool – edged by Pool Farm, which is reflected in the calm waters. In winter, this pool has been the highlight of skating parties, and in latter years has become the home of families of swans, duck, and coot.

In the early 1800s the Mormon missionaries were very active in the district and were so successful that they captivated practically the whole of St Brides Major. One such missionary was John Pritchard Jones, born in St Brides Major on 7th April 1828. At the age of eleven he gave up school to become an apprentice tailor and obtained a good education by studying at home. At the age of 21 he married Mary Bevan of the same village.

In his early youth, John Pritchard Jones received the Gospel and organised Branches in St Brides and Wick, a neighbouring village. He rented a hall for his meetings in the White Lion Hotel at Bridgend and was assisted by Elders from the surrounding villages of Ewenny, Wick, Llanfey, Ogmore and Corntown, also from many other places in South Wales, with wonderful results.

On 17th May 1864, John and his wife and five children, following a Meeting of the Faith, met for the last time in 'Crofta', St Brides Major to organise a large party to emigrate to Salt Lake City, to join Brigham Young in the Mormon faith.

On 19th May 1864, they boarded a ship at Liverpool to begin their long journey to Salt Lake City, America. They arrived in Salt Lake City on 4th October 1864. He worked very hard at a number of jobs to get food for the family, and was a stock raiser and farmer.

In 1870, he organised a law school and was a director of the First National Bank of Spanish Fork. He was a Justice of the Peace for 16 years, and was one of the organisers of the Welsh Eisteddfod in the State of Utah.

At the age of 71 he returned to his native Wales to visit, and died two years later at the age of 73, in 1901.

On the 10th of May 1981 descendants of John Pritchard Jones arrived in St Brides Major trying to trace their forebears. They were his great

161

grand-daughter and her little son of eight months, Frank Llewellyn Jones.
They produced a copy of their family tree which was self explanatory
– Mary Jane being the grand-daughter of John Pritchard Jones' eighth
child.

St Fagans ✍

St Fagans is four miles west of Cardiff, on the A48 and is on the edge
of the beautiful Vale of Glamorgan. Although times have changed the
village is still picturesque with thatched cottages just underneath the
castle walls which are very eye-catching.

There is a church, chapel, school, cricket ground, bowling green, post
office cum shop and village hall. The village pub is called the Plymouth
Arms, retaining its original facade. The interior has been modernised in
a dignified caring manner. Whilst the pub is one of the oldest buildings
in the village, the main claim to fame that St Fagans has is the Castle, as
it is known to the older inhabitants, but known to most as the Welsh
Folk Museum. It is an Elizabethan manor house built by John Gibbon
on the site of a former manor house. The beautiful gardens descend in
terraces to three large fish ponds, which are fed by a clear stream guarded
by a female statue. The castle and the grounds were given to the National
Museum of Wales in 1947 by the Earl of Plymouth.

Buildings have been brought from all over Wales and re-erected by
the Museum staff in the extensive grounds. There are farmhouses, a
blacksmith, mill with working wheel and recent additions are the Gwalia
Stores (which sells farmhouse butter, cheese, eggs, and bacon to the
public and ironmongery, in a way new to the young, but well remembered by the older generation), and a tailor's shop. A terrace of six cottages
from Rhyd-y-car, Merthyr Tydfil, have been furnished, re-creating styles
of furnishing over six decades.

Derwen Bakery, which is near the Toll House, bakes bread and cakes
every day in wood fired ovens, including 'bara brith', a currant tea loaf
which is cut and spread with butter.

Gareth Lloyd, the potter, is always on hand and is willing to give a
demonstration of his skill on the potter's wheel.

Marvin Morgan, the miller, will entertain with snippets of poetry and
displays his walking sticks which he cuts from the hedgerows.

Llwyn-yr-Eos, on the edge of the museum grounds, is one of the
farmhouses which has not been re-erected, but was always part of the
village. When the farmer retired, the Museum included it in their com-

Castle Hill, St Fagans

plex and now, on Wednesdays the kitchen comes to life when local ladies make Welsh cakes on the 'planc' (bakestone) using the coal fired range, also bread, 'bara brith' and other traditional fare. Although these are not for sale, 'tasters' are always available from the ladies, who are members of St Fagans WI.

There is plenty of livestock for the children to see; chickens, ducks, geese, pigs and, in summer, horses, which are harnessed to carriages and are used to take visitors around the museum grounds.

A delightful chapel is situated in the grounds, where at harvest time and Christmas services are held. At Christmas the museum is open in the evenings when traditional Christmas pastimes are shown and toffee is pulled in Llwyn-yr-eos kitchen.

The parish church of St Fagans is dedicated to St Mary the Virgin and was founded in the 12th century. The development of the church in its present form occurred in four stages. First, the Norman foundation, next the change to the Decorated style in the 14th century, then the addition of the tower early in the 18th century and lastly the Victorian restoration with the addition of the north aisle and vestry in 1860. The bells were re-cast and tuned at this time. These bells were taken down and replaced with two small bells from St James' Church, Leckwith on 6th November

1988. The churchyard is entered from the west through a lychgate given to the church by Mr Robert Forrest in 1885, then agent to the Earl of Plymouth, and rector's warden 1874–1910, in memory of his four year old son.

Nearby is the War Memorial to the men of St Fagans who died in the two World Wars. The Calvinistic Methodist Chapel was erected in 1837. It was re-built in 1900 at a cost of £450. Sadly the chapel is now in a dilapidated state.

The present school was built in Cardiff Road in 1860 for 111 pupils and is built from stone taken from Coed Bychan quarry situated in the village. Throughout the years the school has educated many hundreds of pupils to a high standard, but sadly, due to new educational requirements, it will close in 1993.

The Battle of St Fagans was fought here in 1648 between Oliver Cromwell's troops and those of King Charles I, the Roundheads being the victors. Lower Stockland Farm and Tregochas were in the thick of the fighting with the two armies drawn up between the two houses. Both are mentioned in historical documents. The nearby brook, Nant Dowlais, which marks the boundary of St Fagans with St Brides-super-Ely was said to be running with blood.

St Hilary 🌿

The village is situated two miles south east of Cowbridge on rising ground and has a beautiful view of the Thaw Valley and surrounding countryside. The village of St Hilary celebrated 900 years of the existence of the church in 1990.

The electoral roll in the 1920s numbered less than 100, most people making their living from the land.

During the harvest, meals were carried to the hay fields in baskets, together with demijohns of cider. After the harvest the threshing machine came to the farms. It was known as the engine and drum. The machine pulled into the rick yard often with a great deal of shouting and manoeuvering and the throbbing of the engine could be heard many miles away.

Lady Franklen, who lived in the Cottage, possessed the first motor car in the village. It was nicknamed the 'coffee pot'. Parker the chauffeur sat outside and the passengers sat behind under cover and spoke to him through a speaking tube.

At Christmas time the pagan custom of the 'Mari Llwyd' was kept and everyone stayed behind locked doors to prevent the Mari Llwyd, (which was a horse's skull covered with a sheet and dressed with ribbons), from entering and biting the occupants and causing general mayhem.

On Boxing Day the Glamorgan Hunt met up on the Stalling Down and many visitors came along to see the spectacle and give the Hunt servants Christmas boxes. When the hunt moved off, many of the villagers would follow on horseback or foot.

The roads and verges in the village were beautifully kept by a Council road man, Alf Shaw, who worked exclusively for the village.

Village children played games in the surrounding fields and especially in Beaupre Woods, where there were old silver and lead mines. Stones were thrown down the shafts to produce echoes and splashes in the water at the bottom.

Most weeks a whist drive or social was held in the Mansel hall and there would be a fancy dress party for the children and adults at Christmas.

In the evenings after dark the village would be in darkness, except for the glow of the lamps from the windows. One night as the sexton, John Rees was coming out of church with his lantern, he heard a tramp, who had emerged from the Bush Inn, staggering about in the dark just outside the churchyard. Seeing John Rees' lantern, the tramp called out, 'Where am I?', John answered 'Among the living'. The tramp then asked 'Where are you then?', John answered 'Among the dead'. The tramp fled shrieking in terror!

St Nicholas

The Cory family of Dyffryn House and the Mackintosh family of Cottrell between them owned all the houses in the village and employed most of the villagers.

Dyffryn House and its associated manor of Worlton have a history that extends to over 1,000 years. The manor was originally given by King Judhail to Bishop Oudoceous and his successors as Bishops of Llandaff before the year AD 640 in thanks for being saved when he fell from his horse. The original moated house (no longer standing although the moat still exists) was built a little to the south west of the site of the present Dyffryn House and remained in the possession of the Bishops of Llandaff for nearly 900 years until it became the property of the Button family sometime in the mid 16th century.

The first house on the present site was possibly built circa 1571, perhaps by Miles Button whose fourth son, Thomas, went to sea in Queen Elizabeth's navy and achieved note as an adventurous sailor and Arctic explorer. He was knighted and appointed Admiral of the King's Ships on the coast of Ireland by James II. Thomas Button discovered the Nelson river and was the first navigator to reach the coast of America via the Hudson Straits.

The fine stained-glass window in the Great Hall at Dyffryn House depicts Button's contemporary, Sir Walter Raleigh and Queen Elizabeth I.

During the 18th century the estate became known as Dyffryn, St Nicholas, changing its name from Worlton, and it was during this century that the estate passed from the Button family at the death of the Martin Button who left the estate to his heir-at-law, Robert Jones of Fonmon. The Button family had remained loyal to King Charles I during the previous century and it is said that debts incurred as a result of service in support of that monarch ultimately led Robert Jones to sell the estate to Thomas Pryce of Court Carau.

Dyffryn House was rebuilt by Thomas Pryce and on his death, it passed to his daughter Frances Anne, and then the estate passed to Thomas Pryce's kinsman, John Knight Bruce-Pryce. His second son, Henry Austin Bruce, served as a Member of Parliament from 1852 to 1873. He became Home Secretary in 1863, ten years before being created the first Baron Aberdare.

John Bruce-Pryce's eldest grandson, Alan, eventually sold the estate in 1893 to John Cory, eldest son of Richard Cory of Cardiff, a ship owner.

Dyffryn House was again rebuilt and at John Cory's death in 1910 passed to his third son, Reginald, who was a distinguished amateur horticulturist – largely responsible, with the landscape architect Thomas Mawson, for creating the important gardens that surround Dyffryn House today. Reginald Cory's bequest to the University Botanic Garden, Cambridge has enabled that garden to flourish and expand whilst his bequest to the Royal Horticultural Society of London enabled the Society's Lindley Library to acquire a number of important books.

The estate of Dyffryn House and the surrounding gardens were leased to Glamorgan County Council in June 1939 for a period of 999 years for use as a botanic garden and conference centre. The historic gardens of some 55 acres and plant houses, with their collection of rare and unusual plants, are still open to the public and well worth a visit. It is in the garden grounds that the Everyman Theatre holds its Open Air Festival of Entertainment each year.

The village school and schoolmaster were feared by many of the children. They would race to school every morning so that they wouldn't be late, as the bell would ring any time between 8.30 am and 9 o'clock. It was quite usual to be in school long after 3.30 pm too, as they were set either a spelling test or an arithmetic problem just after 3.30 pm. No one was allowed to leave until they had answered correctly.

The shop, post office and saddler's shop were all in the same house. Milk was delivered on foot from a local farm and the surplus taken to Ely in churns by horse and cart driven by the farmer's daughter. The local cobbler knew every shoe he repaired. He collected and delivered the repaired shoes every Saturday evening. The Coffee Tavern was where men used to play darts and billiards but where no females were allowed and no intoxicating drink.

Long summer childhood days were spent watching Mr David, the royal thatcher, repairing the thatch roofs, or playing on the swing and seesaw, and watching football and cricket matches in Cae-Pentre. Haymaking time was busy, when men who had worked hard all day found time and energy to help the farmers in the evenings. Grass was cut by scythe and hook and a roadman, who took pride in his work, kept his length of road immaculate.

There are no big Estates now. The majority of people have had to leave the village to find work and housing they can afford, but there are a few of us left who have wonderful memories of days gone by. We would not want to live anywhere else.

Sker 🦡

Sker House was built by the monks of Neath Abbey in the 12th century. It was used by them as a retreat for the religious contemplation demanded by the Cistercian Order. The name derives from Ysgair, meaning rocky outcrop.

At sea countless people have lost their lives as a result of the activities of the wreckers who used Sker as a base from which to lure ships onto the rocks, but many ships have foundered simply as a result of the elements. The 1947 wreck of the *Santampa* with the loss of 39 hands and the consequent loss of the Mumbles lifeboat with eight men is seared into the history of Sker.

Religion, too, has taken its toll. The martyred priest, Phillip Evans, was captured at Sker. He was later hanged, drawn and quartered in Cardiff. The Roman Catholic leader, Lord Stafford lost his life in 1680 as a direct result of the Popish plot in which a member of the family at Sker played a leading role.

Sker House

Today, Sker House is no longer inhabited and has fallen into disrepair. However it seems that there may be plans ahead to restore the house to its former state by Cadw, the association which promotes the conservation of historic buildings and ancient monuments in Wales.

R. D. Blackmore, author of *Lorna Doone*, whose mother came from nearby Nottage Court, also wrote *The Maid of Sker* which he based on Sker House, the countryside around and its people. It was purported to be his first book as a writer.

Isaac Williams occupied Sker House between 1797 and 1831 and had two beautiful daughters, Mary and Elizabeth, who loved dancing in the Town Hall of Kenfig. A resident harpist named Thomas Evans of Newton Nottage, who was always in great demand, met Elizabeth and fell in love with her. When her father heard of the association he was furious. After all, he was a gentleman farmer and Thomas Evans a mere carpenter, no matter how good a musician. Undeterred, the harpist continued meeting Elizabeth secretly. One night he hired a coach and horses to elope with her. Unfortunately, when approaching, the house was disturbed by the barking of the dogs. Thomas thought it better to retreat. Her father locked his daughter in her room and did not allow her to leave the house for a long time. Although she still pined for Thomas Evans, she was forced to marry a Mr Kirkhouse of Neath. Nine years later she died of a broken heart.

It is said that the ghost of the Maid of Sker walks in the upstairs room in which she was imprisoned.

168

Southerndown 🍃

Southerndown is five miles from Bridgend and has not changed in size as much as most villages in the Vale of Glamorgan, as there has been no large housing development. A few houses have been built in the bottom of the village and a few at the top end. Several buildings have changed their use. The Residential Home for the Blind was originally the Dunraven Arms Hotel, and later becoming a Miners' Convalescent Home and then during the Second World War it housed evacuees from London. Sunshine House, which is now a private house was originally the Marine Hotel, then became the Sunshine Home for Blind Babies. It operated as such for many years, until there were too few babies to justify its upkeep. The Little West Residential Home was for many years a private hotel (The Little West), where members of local organisations enjoyed their annual dinners and functions.

The Three Golden Cups public house has remained the same and has not changed in its use and character.

All Saints Church was built in 1969 when the old church was demolished in order to widen the road through the village. One house, Castle View, was demolished also at this time. The church was originally a Reading Room where daily papers were provided for locals and visitors to read. In the last 30 years we have lost our post office and the only two shops that were there. They have become private dwellings and a restaurant.

Southerndown has a lovely sandy beach in a beautiful cove surrounded by cliffs 150–200 feet high. Hundreds of visitors flock to this area each summer but we, the locals love to walk the hard sands and explore the rock pools all the year round.

Now demolished, Dunraven Castle was a beautiful landmark. The castle was given by the Lord of the Manor of Ogmore for services rendered in defence of Ogmore Castle. In the past the village of Southerndown and local village life had been centred around the Dunraven family whose family seat was in Ireland. The grounds and gardens of the castle are now managed by the The Heritage Coast Project who have set up a centre to record the history and geography of the area.

Sully 🌿

Sully is a long narrow parish, extending along the shores of the Bristol Channel between the Edwardian seaside town of Penarth and the popular seaside resort of Barry and seven miles from the city of Cardiff.

At a casual glance, Sully appears as a modern village, with new estates of houses. In fact, its growth has largely taken place since the 1960s. But there is still plenty of evidence that the Romans and Norsemen formed settlements in the parish.

The de Sully family, medieval lords of the manor, built the nowruined castle and founded the church which is dedicated to St John the Baptist, and a church still stands in the same spot today. It is a small, attractive church, well kept and well attended. It is the focal point of the village and of a lively and active Anglican congregration of all ages.

Sully is well known for its 300 bed hospital. It stands on the foreshore and is designed so that all the wards face the sea. Pioneer work was done there in the curing of tuberculosis and it was one of the best equipped chest hospitals in Britain. Nowadays, it still deals with some chest cases, but it is recognised now for giving the pollen count to hayfever sufferers, from its asthma and allergy research bureau and it has an acute psychiatric unit, elderly mentally ill unit and stroke unit.

The beach at Sully is mainly pebble with sand at the low water line. Bedrock stretches from the low water mark to the pebbles. On the bedrock below the hospital, in the 1980s, dinosaur footprints were discovered and authenticated. Some of these are now on show at the National Museum of Wales, Cardiff.

Sully Island is a unique feature of the area, due to that fact that the causeway is only uncovered at low tide. The sea attacks the island on the Bristol Channel side and the currents around the causeway are treacherous.

Across the Channel and opposite Sully, is the Somerset coastal town of Watchet. There are two islands visible in the channel from Sully, Steepholme and Flatholme. The former is a well known bird sanctuary and the latter is the famous island that Marconi used, to relay the first wireless message across water.

Many years ago Sully House, situated near the sea shore at Swanbridge, was tenanted by a sea Captain who traded from Sully to foreign parts in his own vessel. On one of these occasions he was accompanied by his wife. During the voyage the wife died. Knowing the sailors' superstition about keeping a corpse on board ship, the Captain doubled up her body and hid it in a lead-lined box. When the ship returned to

Swanbridge, the captain buried the box in the woods behind Sully House until he had arranged for a coffin and burial.

When the Captain returned with the coffin, he found that the box containing his wife's body had disappeared. They were never found. It is supposed that someone, maybe a member of the crew, had witnessed the burial and had dug up the box, thinking it was treasure. The ghost of this poor lady was said to walk between the house and the woods, seeking her resting place.

There is a sequel to this story. Some years ago the stables of the old house were being renovated and when some stone flaggings of the stable yard were removed, the doubled-up skeleton of a woman was discovered underneath. The story ends; the skeleton was buried, and the ghost was never seen again!

In 1977, the Captain's Wife public house and restaurant was opened near the spot where the old Sully House stood.

Taffs Well 🍂

Six miles north of Cardiff, following the famous river Taff, at the mouth of the narrow Taff Gorge lies the village of Taffs Well. The surrounding area is dominated by high hills and the beech and alder clad limestone gorge. The mighty Garth mountain, 1,000 ft high, overlooks the village and gives its name to the neighbouring village of Gwaelod-y-Garth. On the top of this mountain ancient burial mounds have been found. Throughout history the village of Taffs Well has been important to the development of Cardiff and the surrounding iron and coal industries.

Due to its location in the narrow Taff Gorge, Taffs Well has always had an important role in communications. During its history the village has seen, amongst other things, a canal, two roads, and four railways, in addition of course to the river Taff.

From archaeological discoveries in the area, it is thought that the Romans set up metal workshops in the immediate vicinity, making use of the alder copses to produce charcoal for metal smelting purposes.

In 1767 the Merthyr ironmasters decided to build their own road from Merthyr to Tongwynlais. The idea was to join their road with an existing toll road which led into Cardiff at the 'Old Furnace', i.e. the Ynys Bridge south of Taffs Well. This new road was also to be a toll road with tollgates at Tongwynlais, Portobello, and Cross Keys Inn at Nantgarw. It is interesting to note that at this time, Taffs Well was referred to as Portobello on all existing plans e.g. the Yates map of Glamorgan 1799, and was called that for some time, the Portobello being an inn in the village.

In 1794 the section of the Glamorganshire canal through Taffs Well was opened. Its most important feature was the triple locks at Glan-y-llyn. Unfortunately all that remains of the structure is the lock house which stands by the side of the present day A470 trunk road. In 1836 the canal carried half a million tons of coal, iron and foodstuffs between Merthyr and Cardiff. It fell into disuse with the coming of the railways, finally 'came to rest' in the 1940s and in the 1960s was filled in to make way for the A470.

The first railway of any commercial importance to be built in Wales was the Taff Vale Railway. The section between Cardiff and Abercynon was built by Brunel in 1840, Taffs Well being one of four stations. In 1858 the Rhymney Valley line joined the Taff Vale at Taffs Well and the station became known, as did the village, as Walnut Tree.

In *Worrells Directory of South Wales* of 1875 we find:

'Taffs Well is a rapidly improving village in the parish of Eglwys-ilan. ... It takes its name from an ancient well which is said to possess medicinal properties of a very high order.'

However, there is evidence of the existence of a thermal spa in Taffs Well many years before that. It is said that the floods of 1799 laid bare Roman masonry adjoining the well and knowing the Roman habit of bathing it seems possible that the well was used by the Romans. In fact investigations have shown that the waters of Taffs Well are of the same chemical make up as the Roman baths at Bath.

In 1891 the well was acquired by a certain Mr Morgan who enlarged it and provided accommodation by building a stone hut over it. However, by 1929 the well had fallen into disuse until a public meeting was held to revive interest in it. A number of local residents had cleaned out the spa and bathed in it and told the meeting how invigorated they felt having so done. In the latter part of the year there were floods again and a large portion of the well house was destroyed. Not to be outdone, the well was once again cleaned and was used by many people in the area.

During the 1930s the village decided to have its own swimming pool and incorporated the spa into it. The writer H. V. Morton visited the well and was enchanted by the spa which he thought had potential. In 1935 it was used as a swimming pool by school children from as far as Radyr and Llanbradach. Local people remember using the pool as late as 1958 when it was used daily by mothers and children from May to October, heated naturally by the thermal springs.

In 1960 a flood destroyed the baths and the spa but not beyond repair.

172

The spa and the land was bought by a local man who decided to do something with it for the youth of the area. It was cleaned up, once again by the youths and a double decker bus was purchased to be used as a club house and changing rooms. However, a second major flood completely cracked the foundations and finished off any project ideas.

The land and spa was sold to Taff-Ely Borough Council for a nominal sum on condition that they would develop the site as a leisure amenity. Plans were drawn up and shown to the people of Taffs Well but as yet they have still to be put into practice.

Taffs Well was one of the centres for the manufacture of chains and anchors. The close proximity of the canal made it easy for the distribution of these to Cardiff docks and for the delivery of raw materials. One of the descendants of these factories is South Wales Forgemasters which is still in production in the village. There has been a factory on the site since the latter half of the 19th century which made anchor chains and was later involved in the manufacture of war equipment.

Today Taffs Well is a dormitory village for Cardiff with new housing estates springing up and ever-increasing traffic problems. But older residents can remember a very different way of life here.

The Whitsun March was a big event. The Brass Band headed the march; starting with the Welsh Church, picking up children from the other two churches, and seven chapels; all marching through the village, and on the return journey dropping off at the various church/chapel halls for the tea; sandwiches and always plain cake, jam and cream (known as tram line cake) and favourite seed cake. After the tea all denominations went to the field where sports took place.

Shopping was done at Liptons, Home and Colonial, Maypole and Thomas and Evans. All had a person who would weigh the butter, then with two wooden paddles, knock it into an oblong shape, then with a paddle with grooves on it mark three sides, the other was for the paddle with the flower emblem. All dry goods were weighed to the amount you required. Biscuit tins had glass tops and you could see the biscuits. The bottom of the box always had broken biscuits and these were put into bags, all mixed, and one could buy these much cheaper. Cobblers did the shoe repairs in their front rooms, and it was fascinating watching them, with a mouthful of nails, tap the shoes, taking the nails out of their mouths, hammering them into the shoe, never missing the rhythm, putting the wax round the sole, and polishing afterwards.

It was quite usual in the mornings for mountain ponies, sheep and geese to parade through the streets knocking over dustbins, and being a general nuisance; and at the same time every evening returning to the mountains.

173

Tongwynlais 🐚

To some people Tongwynlais is a village at the gateway to the Taff Valley and five miles north of Cardiff, but to very many more it is the village with the fairy castle – Castell Coch.

Castell Coch overlooks the village of Tongwynlais and is just off the main road A470 to Merthyr Tydfil. It nestles on a wooded hill and reminds one of a medieval castle but this is not so, as this castle was only built in the late 1870s. However, there was an original castle here built in the 13th century by a Norman Lord of Glamorgan, Gilbert de Clare, to guard the entrance to the Taff gorge. Sometime in the 15th century it was destroyed and the ruins remained standing for centuries. Castell Coch or 'Red Castle' derived its name from the red sandstone from which the original castle was built.

In 1871 the third Marquis of Bute, who was a very wealthy man, commissioned the architect William Burges to rebuild Castell Coch. The Gloucester builder A Estcourt was engaged and work begun in 1875. When Burges designed the conical turrets of the castle, he was influenced by the Swiss castles at L'Aigle and Castle Chillon on Lake Geneva. The castle was rebuilt in limestone from local quarries.

The castle has a triangular layout with three circular towers capped by conical roofs which gives it the romantic appearance of a Rhineland castle. Burges even included a working drawbridge complete with port-cullis at the entrance and this is the only way into the castle, which is approached through the village of Tongwynlais. This entrance leads into a small courtyard encircled by towers, galleries and apartments. Inside the apartment wing and keep tower, Burges indulged in the extravagance of Victorian decoration. Steps lead up to the first floor banqueting hall which is decorated with scenes of saints and martyrs and has a heavily sculpted fireplace. The octagonal drawing room is a wonderful two storey area with an encircling balcony and a colourful rib-vaulted ceiling. The walls are brightly decorated with scenes from Aesop's *Fables*.

The interior of the castle was finished in 1891.

When Lord Bute decided to rebuild Castell Coch he intended to use it as a country retreat but he seldom did and his descendants even more rarely. The castle passed into the hands of the Department of the Environment and then to Cadw – Welsh Historic Monuments. It is valued as a magnificent example of high Victorian Gothic architecture at its most exuberant and as a fair representation of a medieval castle from an idealized past.

The setting of the castle is as romantic and enchanting as the building itself. On the one side is a sheer rock face and on the other a beautiful wooded hillside. The woods were planted for Lord Bute when the castle was rebuilt; oak, ash, sycamore, hornbeam and beech are now well established.

The cliffs on one side of the castle are often used by rock climbers in the early stages of training. The woods beyond the castle grounds are in the care of the Forestry Commission and walks continue through them.

One of the old family houses in the village was the mansion built in a Gothic style called Greenmeadow House. This was the home of the Lewis family, one of the most influential families in Glamorgan. The main branch of the family owned vast estates in South Wales including St Fagan's Castle. The house stood at the entrance to Tongwynlais from the direction of Cardiff. Greenmeadow House which had been empty for many years following the death of Colonel Henry Lewis, eventually became so dangerous that it was demolished in the 1940s and a housing estate was built in the grounds. Two of its streets are known as Greenmeadow Drive and Cae Lewis in memory of the Lewis family. This family also gave a plot of ground for building a church in the village. This was called St Michael and All Angels and was built in 1877. There was a private path from the house to the church which the family used.

With the coming of the Glamorganshire Canal – and houses being

Castell Coch, Tongwynlais

175

built for the boatmen, Tongwynlais became a thriving village, with a bustling weekly market. People also came from miles around to visit the annual Boatman's Fair.

Although Tongwynlais has been taken into the City of Cardiff, it is still very much a village in which many local activities take place. Our prize winning silver band is over 100 years old, and our choral society has been re-formed after a lapse of some years. They and other worthy organisations, including the WI are well known for their charitable works.

Tongwynlais was in the forefront of the evangelical movement in Wales – thanks to the visits of the well known revivalists, Christmas Evans and Evan Roberts. The sign that we are a united village is shown by the church and chapels joining together in the Witness March around the village every Whit Sunday, headed by the village band.

Tongwynlais is still a village in which we are proud and happy to live and it is a much quieter place since it has been bypassed by the A470 roadway.

Ton Pentre 🦡

Ton Pentre is situated near the top of the Rhondda Fawr valley, two miles from Treorchy and eight miles from Pontypridd. The village grew as a mining community and at the beginning of the 20th century at least three colleries were working, namely Maindy, Ton and Easter Colliery, but these closed over 50 years ago. Today there is no industry and many shops have closed, including the popular Co-operative Stores. Many long rows of houses were built to accommodate the miners and their families, straggling the valley floor and the hillsides.

Ystradfodwg church was built on the first Christian site in Wales. In the 6th century this was a link for travelling monks between Llanwynno and Llantrisant. There were also many thriving chapels in Ton Pentre but sadly these have now closed.

The famous Cory Workman's Band was formed in Ton Pentre in 1884. At this time it was known as the Ton Pentre Temperance Band, but changed its name when Sir Clifford Cory (coal owner) offered to subsidise it. The band has won many national competitions and is still thriving today.

Between Ton Pentre and Cwmparc are situated the Gorsedd Stones. These were erected when the Welsh National Eisteddfod took place in Treorchy in 1928.

St Peter's Church, Ton Pentre

Tonteg 🌿

Tonteg is a village which is approximately ten miles north of Cardiff and three miles from Pontypridd. Tonteg lies on a ridge high above the river Taff which flows from Merthyr Tydfil to the sea at Cardiff. The village is in the parish of Llantwit Fardre and in an area which can trace its history back to the Bronze Age.

A large earth mound, previously known as 'Coed-y-Twr' but today called 'Tomen-y-Clawdd' is the remains of a typical Norman motte and bailey castle. This had been built in this area to provide defence for the Taff valley against any Welsh chieftains who wished to attack the Normans. The earth mound has a flat top about 20 metres in diameter and the sides are covered with grass and trees, which makes it very attractive when the trees are in leaf. During the early years of the 20th century it still had a moat surrounding it, but today there is only a circular ditch covered with grass. The local inhabitants call it the 'Monkey Tump' and it used to be a popular place for children to play. But this is now discouraged as it is scheduled as an Ancient Monument. Today it is in the centre of the pleasant Oaklands Housing Estate and the residents there enjoy watching the changing colours of the trees.

The village has no focal point as such. The main road from Pontypridd to Llantrisant passes through with housing developments on both sides of the road. This road (A473) was built originally in 1839 by Francis Crawshay the well known ironmaster who lived at Treforest, as a way to his country house at Hensol Castle. His house at Treforest is now part of the Glamorgan University.

Prior to 1950 it was a very small rural village with a few small shops and farms dotted around. The only new houses which had been built were by the local Council and formed a very small housing development surrounded by farmland. After the late 1950s the farms in the area gradually sold their land for housing development.

Consequently the old farmhouses were demolished. However, one well known farmhouse is still standing, Maesmawr Farm. It is reputed that Charles I in 1648 spent the night at Maesmawr Farm and one room was known as the King's room. The land has been farmed by the same family for over 500 years.

Since 1960 Tonteg has expanded rapidly and is now more urban. However, there are still a few green fields within easy reach and pleasant places to walk. It is still an attractive place to live as there is no industry, just a small garage, a petrol station, two car showrooms, a sub-post office and a few shops of various kinds. Today many of the quaint old cottages have been demolished including the old Greyhound inn which according to an old photograph was frequented in 1900 and was situated on the main road near the crossroads. The only public house in the village is The Three Horseshoes. The village hall is a wooden building known locally as 'The Hut' and is used for various social functions. It has stood on this particular spot for many years.

In 1912 a hospital was opened at Tonteg as an Isolation Special Care Unit because this was then out in the country and considered a healthy place. Today the hospital only has one small ward caring for elderly patients and is no longer in the country but surrounded by attractive houses.

One of the first open plan schools in the area was built in the village. It opened as a primary school in January 1967, then in 1969 a separate infants school was opened adjoining it. Under the guidance of the headteacher and the PTA, funds were raised to build a swimming pool at the junior school and this was officially opened on 16th April 1977. In 1978 Ysgol Ty Coch opened as a residential special school for physically handicapped children.

Two railway lines used to pass on the edge of the village and Tonteg boasted a halt. One line travelled from Pontypridd to Barry, owned by the Barry Railway Company, which villagers used regularly in the summer on their excursions to the seaside at Barry. The other railway was from Pontypridd to Llantrisant. This line closed in 1951 and the Barry line in 1958. Both lines today have been demolished and parts are overgrown with grass and brambles.

There is neither a church nor a chapel in the village. The parish church of Llantwit Fardre is St Illtud's church and serves all the villages in the parish which includes Tonteg. It is situated about three quarters of a mile away at Upper Church Village. Salem, the Welsh Baptist chapel is at Church Village which is about three quarters of a mile from the centre of the village and is the other place of worship. Salem has been a popular venue for carol services and sacred concerts as well as a place of worship.

John Hughes, composer of the hymn tune *Cwm Rhondda*, was born at Dowlais in 1873. He moved with his family to Hollybush, Church Village in 1874.

He started work at 12 years of age as a door boy at Glyn Colliery. Later he served as a clerk and subsequently as an official in the Traffic Department of the Great Western Colliery. He married Hannah Maria David in 1905 and they came to live at Tregarth, Main Road, Tonteg, where he remained there until his death. John Hughes died on 14th May 1932, and is buried at Salem chapel.

He composed a number of Sunday School marches, anthems and hymn tunes. The most famous was *Cwm Rhondda* originally known as *Rhondda*, which he wrote in 1907 for the anniversary services at Capel Rhondda, Pontypridd. He set the tune to the English words of William Williams, Pantycelyn. His only surviving descendant, his granddaughter, Miss Ann Webb, unveiled a commemorative plaque at Tregarth, Tonteg, on 25th October 1987.

Tonyrefail 🍃

Two hundred years ago Tonyrefail was a tiny hamlet, scarcely qualifying to be called a village. It stands at the head of the Ely Valley, surrounded by green, gentle hills, scattered with farms. To the north lies the steep sided narrow Rhondda Valley, while to the south the valley leads some four miles away to the fringe of the Vale of Glamorgan. The name of our village is more commonly translated as 'the smithy of the sloping field'. It is likely that the smith was the focus of the life of the village since his skills would be of value to the farmers and the millers.

Our village has made its mark on national history. Edward II was born at Caernarvon Castle and was enthroned in 1307. He was an agreeable figure, of mild disposition but indolent and fond of pleasure. He made many enemies, foremost of whom was his wife, Queen Isabella. She raised an army against Edward which routed him and his supporters. Edward fled to South Wales but when making for the safety of Llantrisant Castle, he was betrayed and captured on the fringe of Tonyrefail. A tablet commemorating his historic capture was erected some six centuries later on the very spot, but has since been removed for safety to a local school. The place where poor Edward was taken is named, aptly, Pant y Brad – the hollow of treason.

Near where Edward was reputed to be captured lie the ruins of an old Quaker Meeting House, with an adjoining cemetery, now sadly much overgrown and difficult to find. In the middle of the 17th century, the Meeting House was the centre of a flourishing Quaker movement. Prominent in the movement were the Bevans of nearby Treferig House, a family of ancient Welsh lineage, who became great friends of William Penn. They followed him to Pennsylvania, in search of a strict and sober atmosphere in which to bring up their children. John Bevan became very well known and active in his adopted country.

In time, however, he became disillusioned with the schisms within the movement and he and his wife eventually returned to South Wales, leaving some of their children to settle and marry in America. John and

his wife Barbara died early in the 18th century and are buried in the
overgrown Quaker cemetery with other Friends. Their graves have all
but disappeared although the ground is still owned by the Quakers. It is
sad that such an interesting part of our local and national history has
been neglected, but we can feel proud that, through John Bevan, descendants of ancient Welsh kings are part of present day American life,
shaping the history of that vast country.

Life in Tonyrefail, in its idyllic rural setting, went on quietly for
hundreds of years. With the coming of the coal industry great expansion
took place but now the coal industry has come to an end. It has left its
scars but nature, as is her wont, has worked her silent magic and the
scars have almost disappeared. Let us hope that the spirit of our village,
unlike the scars, will never fade.

Treharris ⚜

Treharris lies at the lower end of the Merthyr Valley above the old village
of Quakers Yard, on a hillside which shelters the valleys of the Taff and
Bargoed rivers about 350 ft above sea level.

Its story begins to unfold in the year of 1870 when two strange
gentlemen arrived at Quakers Yard station. They made their way to fields
belonging to Twyn-y-garreg Farm. They walked to and fro for a long
time conversing with each other. Something of great importance was
being debated. They then retraced their steps and caught the train back
home.

Great was the talk and conjecture about the visit of the strangers. The
news that a company was going to sink a mine on land belonging to
Twyn-y-Garreg Farm electrified the atmosphere of the district. A company under the chairmanship of F W Harris was formed. Thus did F W
Harris bestow his name on the village.

On the first Monday in February 1873 the first sod was cut for the
sinking of the pit. 1879 saw the first coal being brought up to the light
of day. In 1881 coal was raised from two pits, named the Harris Deep
Navigation Pits. But after a seemingly good start a cloud descended on
the valley with the news that the collieries were to close. Rumours were
wrong and the collieries were taken over by the Ocean Coal Company.
The area thrived with the colliery the centre of the community. The next
rumours about the closing of the Deep Navigation were unfortunately
true and on Good Friday 1940 the whole village gathered to watch in
sadness as the Salvation Army Band led the last working miners from
the pit.

The area of Quakers Yard and many of the streets of Treharris, however, get their names from the Quaker Movement, a group of Nonconformists who met at Berthlwyd chapel (one of Wales' five oldest chapels), in the 17th century. A large piece of land in the area, known as Pantanas Estate, was owned by Mary Chapman, widow of Hambden Chapman of St Mellons, Cardiff. When she died in 1700 she left the Quaker Friends a piece of land to be used as a burial ground. Burials have taken place here at intervals since, the first being Lydia Fell and the last being the infant son of Thomas and Sophia Litten in 1891. Today only one tombstone remains and that is in memory of Thomas Edmund who died in 1802 and his wife Mary who died in 1810.

Although few Quakers now live in the area, many of the streets bear tribute to the movement. Fox Street was the first street to be built in Treharris and is called after George Fox who visited the area. Penn Street is named after William Penn, Founder of Pennsylvania. Fell Street is named after Lydia Fell, the first Quaker to be buried here.

Treherbert 🐚

Treherbert is a former coal mining village situated at the base of the Rhigos Mountain and Pen Pych, the highest mountain plateau in Northern Europe.

Prior to coal being found in the area at the end of the 19th century, this was hill farming country, but, with the advent of coal came the Taff Vale Railway (later to be GWR) and access to Cardiff and Barry Docks, and also the Swansea Bay Railway which was carried through a tunnel in the mountain at Treherbert and then gave direct access to Port Talbot, Neath and Swansea.

As Treherbert was the 'end of the line', sheds were erected for the housing of the railway engines. Here they were cleaned and 'fired' and made ready for work. Coal trucks were built and maintained on the colliery sites. With six collieries in its immediate area and the engine sheds, Treherbert became a destination for work-seekers from many counties of the British Isles.

Dr AJ Cronin was once a GP in this area and Treherbert was disguised as 'Trenethi' in his famous novel *The Citadel*; and for readers of that novel, legend has it he really did blow up a sewer whilst working here.

The collieries have long since disappeared, their sites are now landscaped and our mountains are covered in trees; albeit Norwegian Spruce, but our valley is green once more.

Isaac Jones came to the Upper Rhondda in 1868 and in 1872 established a business as a printer, publisher and stationer at Bute Street, Treherbert. He was a native of Caio, Carmarthenshire, a district which was alive with musical and literary activity and moved into one where his natural bent could find full scope.

During the last quarter of the 19th century the eisteddfod gained popularity and the Welsh concert solo was developed as a form of art. Tonic sol-fa notation became common but Isaac Jones was able to set old notation himself.

He soon became one of the most renowned printers in the Principality, issuing many important books, magazines and musical compositions, perhaps the most popular and well known of them being *Myfanwy* by Dr. Joseph Parry, Merthyr Tydfil.

Treorchy 🌿

Treorchy is situated near the top of the Rhondda Fawr Valley – here the valley is at its widest. Before 1860 the Rhondda Valley was mainly rich meadow and wild picturesque mountains, but with the coming of coal, 'The Black Gold', long lines of terraced houses were built like 'stone caterpillars' crawling over the lower slopes of the valley. Today it has a bustling shopping centre with a weekly market. This tradition of a market in Treorchy goes back to the 1930s. Amongst its many attractions it is the home of the famous Parc and Dare Hall which houses a fine cinema. This splendid building, the most prominent in the centre of Treorchy, with a name that is known throughout Wales, now belongs to the Council who have restored it to its former glory. The Station Road frontage of the Hall was built in 1903 as a Working Man's Institute, the construction being paid for by the miners at a rate of a penny in every pound that they earned – and take-home wages at that time were less than £2.00 per week.

From the start the Parc and Dare was packing in the audiences to see films starring Buster Keaton, Charlie Chaplin, the Keystone Cops and Rudolph Valentino. Stage performances too were featured with a Semi National Eisteddfod each Whitsuntide. Drama Festivals were a highlight with entries for the event coming from all over the country. Today the Parc and Dare which is still undergoing improvements, has an auditorium that has been fitted with 900 seats, lighting and public address systems, and a modern stereo cinema. As well as screening films, the theatre stages productions by local amateur companies and by such touring companies as the Welsh National Opera, the London Festival Ballet and the Scottish Ballet.

South of Treorchy beyond the railway station is the Pengelli–Ystradfechan recreational complex with playing fields, bowling greens, tennis courts and an attractively arranged children's playground with paddling pool. Treorchy Rugby Club currently playing in the prestigious Heineken League attracts large crowds to all their home matches at their ground The Oval. Also in this area is the new Community Hospital, opened in 1991 by the well known Rhondda man Lord Tonypandy, who as George Thomas MP was the former Speaker of the House of Commons. The hospital now carries his name – Ysbyty George Thomas. Another local landmark is the local comprehensive school built in the late 1960s and one of the most modern in the valley whose facilities include an indoor swimming pool and which prides itself on its talented brass band.

Over the last 25 years the language of Wales has been kept alive in the flourishing Welsh school where children up to the age of eleven years are taught, later to carry on with their education at the new Welsh Comprehensive School at Cymmer Porth – a few miles away.

Treorchy has a strong cultural tradition and is the home of several bands and choirs which includes the Treorchy Royal Welsh Choir, the oldest in Wales and the famous Treorchy Male Voice Choir. The Treorchy Royal Welsh Choir was so named after performing before her Majesty Queen Victoria on 29th November 1895. The present Treorchy Male Choir is very active with many performances in this country and numerous tours abroad. In 1928 the Royal Welsh National Eisteddfod was held in Treorchy and the large stones of the Gorsedd Circle remain to mark the occasion. The local library, with its excellent reference section, hosts many varied exhibitions which are well attended by the people of Treorchy.

The first Co-operative Store in the Rhondda was opened in Treorchy in 1868 which proved a life-saver to the community during the General Strike of 1926 and the depressed 1930s. Unemployed miners and their families were allowed goods 'on tick' for up to six months so that they could have food. Sadly the Co-op no longer exists as a friendly store but as a supermarket at the lower end of Rhondda.

Treorchy had two collieries and two levels at the height of the coal industry in the Rhondda. The ugliness left by the disused coal workings has been covered by the thousands of pine trees planted by the Forestry Commission. The uniformity of the trees is not to everyone's liking, nevertheless they hide the damage left by the coal industry which scarred the most lovely valley in Glamorgan. Today Treorchy is still thriving.

Troes 🐚

Troes, four miles from Cowbridge, is an old village, in the past a pretty village of thatched cottages coloured pink, white and grey. The thatched roof village pub, Malthouse and Granary, was the star. There were watermills alongside the river where farmers took their grain for grinding, whose relics are to be seen today. Older villagers recall winters when they were marooned by floods, with candles and oil lamps their only light.

Nonconformity was introduced here in 1831 principally by W Griffiths of Llanharan, meeting in an old barn. Before long the building was bought by three gentlemen, David Jones, Lewis Jenkins and David Owen, together with the next door garden, from Edward Mordecai of Troes for £30 for the purpose of building a chapel. A regular Sunday chapel was established and became very successful. In 1841 a new chapel was built 40 ft by 30 ft at a cost of £240 which won favour among the people. It soon became too small and a beautiful oak gallery was added at the cost of £100. Mr Rhys Saron Jones, a former student of Brecon College, was appointed minister and was described as a popular well loved man. He ministered until 1871, when he emigrated to America. The beautiful chapel remains, much as it was. Extensive repairs are needed and paid for by money raised by villagers and donation from the Community Council. Villagers continue to worship here, and have christenings, weddings and burials.

There have been many changes over the years to the village. An Ack Ack battery was sited on the moors in the Second World War. The pub is no longer spit and sawdust but has been modernised and is congenial. Old farm houses and cottages have been updated, electricity, gas and main sewerage introduced, barns converted to dwellings and modern houses built. The Community Hall, created by the villagers, has been enlarged to meet the present day needs of the village; nursery class, brownies, youth clubs, young at heart, WI, whist drives, dances, parties. Funds for its upkeep come from rents, a village lottery and the Community Council. It is administered by a nominated committee. WI members play a vital part in organising functions.

Additional amenities are a tennis court and our village green. A converted barn is our village shop and our post office a converted house garage. We have green fields around us. Cows, horses, chickens, pheasants, rabbits, foxes and other small wild animals traverse our streets.

We have a daily village bus and we have cars, but we also have the quietness of the country and the friendliness of village folk. What we fear most is that the fast encroaching industry will destroy all this.

Waunarlwydd 🌿

The village of Waunarlwydd is situated between Fforestfach and Gowerton, approximately five miles from the city of Swansea. It is mainly enclosed by the hill called Craig y Bwldan, rising to 450 ft on the south side and the railway line to the north.

The village has a strong religious tradition. It has three chapels: Zion Welsh Baptist founded in 1860, Sardis, an Independent chapel, also founded in 1860 and Bethany, English Baptist, founded in 1875.

Before 1750 all the menfolk worked on the land or had occupations closely connected with the land. These were farmers, farm labourers, blacksmiths, millers and weavers. With the coming of the Industrial Revolution more and more collieries were opened to meet the increasing demand for coal to work the steam power in works and factories. The men, hoping to earn higher wages, left the land to work in the mines, tinworks and steelworks that were established where Gowerton now stands. Waunarlwydd was a village before Gowerton came into being.

Around 1860, the London, Midland and Scottish Railway line was built and later the Great Western line. Many new residents came to seek employment in the new industries, and some came to maintain the railways.

Many of these were English speaking people from Somerset, Devon, Cornwall and Pembrokeshire. This had a marked influence on the Welsh-speaking village of Waunarlwydd.

Waunarlwydd in the present day is an active suburb of Swansea, with two schools, post office, village shops, Chinese take-away, hairdressers, garage, newsagents, nursing homes, plus three public houses and a rugby club. The church and chapels are still in use. The old Welfare Hall (to which the miners used to contribute) has been replaced by a new building which houses various meetings most days of the week.

Numerous organisations for all ages are actively enjoyed by the villagers, and the village is growing daily with the influx of people to the new housing estates built in recent years.

Ynysforgan & Ynystawe 🍂

We live in a very rural area surrounded by fields, woodlands and hills in the Swansea Valley. Houses have been built on what was previously good farm land – two adjoining farms in neighbouring villages Glyncollen in Ynysforgan and Wernfadog in Ynystawe. Both Estates were owned by industrialists, Captain Sidney Davies of Glyncollen and Mr W. J. Percy Player of Wernfadog – two men who had provided work for many of the local villagers of Ynysforgan and Ynystawe at their steel and tinplate works in Morriston and Clydach since the end of the 19th century. Both are now closed and the land and some of the buildings now form part of the modern industrial estates to be found in the valley.

Older residents recall childhood days at Wernfadog Farm playing in the woodland picking bluebells and violets in the spring, admiring the variety of trees and carving their initials on many of them, and with friends enjoying paper-chases on a Saturday afternoon. Fortunately the woods have not been destroyed. The children helped with the hay-making and corn harvests and sometimes led the horses and carts when necessary. The 1930s saw the arrival of the mechanical hay-loader and the tractor, but they still carried tea for the men to the fields located at the farthest end of the estate. Later in the year local village lads and some of the inmates of Swansea Prison would help to pick the potato harvest – very much a back-breaking task.

The Swansea Valley canal ran through both villages in picturesque settings and had been used to carry coal and other industrial products from the Valley to Swansea Docks for shipment to many parts of the world. Unfortunately the canal in this area was closed and filled in around 1970. It would have been ideal for boating these days when people are more leisure orientated.

In the 1920s and 1930s it was exciting to see the barges being towed by horses through Ynysforgan to the Park Road bridge at Ynystawe. Children, parents and helpers came from the Swansea Docks and Landore industrial areas for their Whitsun treats to the park, where the children had tea, played games and enjoyed the fresh air.

The river Tawe is also a feature of this area and is very popular nowadays with the younger generation who spend much of their free time fishing.

The Swansea tram service gave way for buses in the 1930s and eventually the village was divided in two to make way for the M4 motorway, as did Glyncollen House and much of the land. The Swansea

187

to Brecon LMS railway also ran alongside the villages, but after closure, together with the canal, it provided the necessary land for the bypasses which now exist.

Ystradowen ✑

Ystradowen is a rural village situated in the Vale of Glamorgan about three miles north of Cowbridge. The B4270 road from Cowbridge to Llantrisant passes through the village. Houses have been built on either side of it. The White Lion, the only public house, is a popular venue for meals. There is also an old church, a garage and a timber mill but no shops or a school. On one side of the road the first small housing development built in the village was of Council owned houses. Two more small housing developments of attractive executive type houses have sprung up since. Surrounding the village are a few farms.

The church is dedicated to St Owain. The present church was built in 1868 on the site of the old one. An older church was mentioned in records and was standing in 1291. It was demolished and the present one built on the same site in the same design.

The tenor bell was first cast in 1686 and was given by Sir Leoline Jenkins of Cowbridge. He was a lawyer and statesman and was the second founder of Cowbridge Grammar School. He purchased the school from Sir Edward Stradling and bequeathed it to Jesus College, Oxford and left a sum of money to maintain it. His brother in 1699 gave some land in Ystradowen to the church so that the bell could be maintained. This bell developed a crack in the 1980s so this land was sold and the money used for the bell which was recast in 1986 and the new bell was hung in the church.

Children from the village either attend the Church School (Primary) at Llansannor a few miles away or Maendy primary school about three quarters of a mile distant.

According to old records the village was at one time spelt Ystradowain (the Welsh way). In the earlier part of this century Ystradowen had its own cattle market, a thriving saw mill, two inns and a village store. It was quite a bustling little place. There was also a village blacksmith named Tom Griffiths, and his smithy was the rendezvous for all the young children in the 1930s. He used to make them iron hoops to play with, hence the attraction to the smithy.

In 1850, as a result of opposition from local property owners in Cowbridge, the South Wales Railway was routed in a seemingly illogical

188

curve well to the north of the town with a station near Llantrisant at the village of Pontyclun. Later, realizing the commercial folly of this decision, promoters of the Cowbridge Railway planned to link the town with Llantrisant and the South Wales Railway. Incorporated on 29th July 1862, it opened for goods traffic in February 1865 and for passengers in September of the same year. The line was not at first a commercial success. In 1867 the Cowbridge Railway was taken over by the Taff Vale Railway Company and the line was linked with Pontypridd and the Ely valley. Between Llantrisant and Cowbridge were two stations – Llanharry and Ystradowen. The commencement of a passenger service from Llantrisant to Pontypridd in January 1875 increased the popularity of the Cowbridge Railway, especially on market days. The Ystradowen porter, 'John John' was famed for his great strength, not only in man-handling the crates of vegetables, poultry, eggs, and rabbits onto the walking train, but even (so local legend has it) in his willingness to give the train a little extra help up the Ystradowen incline.

Sadly with the decline in freight and passenger traffic after the First World War, the engine sheds at Cowbridge were closed in 1924, the passenger service south of Cowbridge in 1930 and goods traffic in 1932. The Cowbridge to Llantrisant line, however, survived for almost twenty years more and on 26th November 1951 the last train from Cowbridge to Llantrisant passed through Ystradowen. The station, once known for the beauty of its trim and well-kept gardens soon became derelict and overgrown. The marshy ground reclaimed the once ordered footpaths and the lines were taken up. Now little is left to mark the Cowbridge Railway, though its path through Ystradowen is perhaps the clearest indication of a once busy and useful line.

After the closure of the railway in 1951, the village went into a decline. Then in the late 1960s Ystradowen's Friendly Society was formed to inject more life into the community. The ladies and gentlemen of the society used to meet in the White Lion Hotel and organise social events e.g. carnivals, sports, historical events and raise funds, which eventually led to the fund raising for the building of the Village Hall.

The village is proud of its Village Hall, which was built entirely by the villagers. They also raised the funds to cover the cost. It was a community effort. Work started on it in 1985 and it was opened in September 1987. As soon as the hall was available the Ystradowen and District WI was formed in October 1987. The Village Hall is also used for other social activities including whist drives and dinners. The Brownies meet there each week and a playgroup meets there each day.

Today on the land sold by the Church for money to re-cast the bell, a few attractive new houses have been built.

Index